Roses

The TIME LIFE
Complete Gardener

Roses

By the Editors of Time-Life Books
ALEXANDRIA, VIRGINIA

The Consultants

Peter Haring is president of the American Rose Society. A member of the ARS for more than 35 years, he is a Life Accredited Rose Judge, evaluating roses at local, district, and national shows throughout the United States. He is also a Consulting Rosarian, an expert appointed by the ARS to advise rose gardeners in the region that includes Shreveport, Louisiana, where the society is headquartered and where Haring resides. He shows, photographs, and speaks and writes about roses extensively, and has grown over 400 varieties annually for many years in Shreveport and Stony Brook, New York, his previous home. Haring is a graduate of the U.S. Naval Academy and a retired submarine officer.

Michael G. Shoup is the founder and owner of the Antique Rose Emporium in Brenham, Texas, which specializes in the reintroduction and distribution of old garden roses. He also serves on the board of directors of the Heritage Rose Foundation, an organization dedicated to the preservation of these varieties. An expert in propagation and cultivation, Shoup has opened display gardens in Texas and Georgia to show the versatility of old roses. He has written numerous articles and supplied photos for trade and national periodicals, and with Liz Druitt is coauthor of *Landscaping with Antique Roses* (1992). He earned a master's degree in horticulture from Texas A&M University in 1975.

Time-Life Books is a division of **TIME LIFE INC.**

PRESIDENT and CEO: John M. Fahey Jr.

TIME-LIFE BOOKS

Managing Editor: Roberta Conlan

Director of Design: Michael Hentges
Editorial Production Manager: Ellen Robling
Director of Operations: Eileen Bradley
Director of Photography and Research: John Conrad Weiser
Senior Editors: Russell B. Adams Jr., Janet Cave, Lee Hassig, Robert Somerville, Henry Woodhead
Library: Louise D. Forstall

PRESIDENT: John D. Hall

Vice President, Director of New Product Development: Neil Kagan
Associate Director, New Product Development: Quentin S. McAndrew
Marketing Director: James Gillespie
Vice President, Book Production: Marjann Caldwell
Production Manager: Marlene Zack
Quality Assurance Manager: Miriam Newton

THE TIME-LIFE COMPLETE GARDENER

Editorial Staff for *Roses*

SERIES EDITOR: Janet Cave
Deputy Editors: Sarah Brash, Jane Jordan
Administrative Editor: Roxie France-Nuriddin
Art Director: Kathleen D. Mallow
Picture Editor: Jane A. Martin
Text Editor: Darcie Conner Johnston
Associate Editors/Research-Writing: Sharon Kurtz, Robert Speziale
Technical Art Assistant: Sue Pratt
Senior Copyeditor: Anne Farr
Picture Coordinator: David A. Herod
Editorial Assistant: Donna Fountain
Special Contributors: Jennifer Clark (research); Dena Crosson, Carole Ottesen, Mariana Tait-Durbin (research-writing); Marfé Ferguson-Delano, Rita Pelczar (writing); Lynn Yorke (editing); John Drummond (art); Lina B. Burton (index).

Correspondents: Christine Hinze (London), Christina Lieberman (New York).

Library of Congress Cataloging in Publication Data
Roses / by the editors of Time-Life Books.
p. cm.—(The Time-Life complete gardener)
Includes bibliographical references (p.) and index.
ISBN 0-7835-4109-0
1. Rose culture. 2. Roses. I. Time-Life Books. II. Series
SB411.R659915 1996 635.9'33372—dc20 95-40912 CIP

This volume is one of a series of comprehensive gardening books that cover garden design, choosing plants for the garden, planting and propagating, and planting diagrams.

Cover: Cascading brilliant pink 'Tausendschön' and mounds of 'White Meidiland' roses bloom with purple clematis and other roses, including antique gallicas and damasks, in a lush Maryland garden. End papers: At the entry gate of a New Mexico home, a single bush of the species Rosa foetida bicolor, also called 'Austrian Copper', adds a natural, inviting accent. Title page: Trained as a tree rose, or standard, shocking red 'Showbiz' drapes over the deep-colored contrasting foliage of Heuchera americana in a sunny North Carolina border backed with American boxwood.

CONTENTS

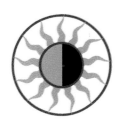

CHAPTER ONE

The Genus Rosa

The rose is, without question, the world's favorite flower. Lauded by ancient Greek poets, buried with the pharaohs in Egypt, glorified in Roman festivals, and praised in every way by other cultures of antiquity from the Persians to the Chinese, roses have captivated hearts and imaginations for thousands of years. And over the millennia this most beloved of blooms has been cultivated and crossbred so extensively that the number of varieties is now beyond counting.

With such an abundance, there is a rose for every gardener, for any garden. Many gardeners avoid roses, believing they require too much time and nurturing, but in fact there are hundreds that perform beautifully with little fuss—including the 'Baronne Prévost', 'Blush Noisette', and 'Madame Isaac Pereire' gracing a stone wall in the South Carolina garden at right. The truth is nearly any rose will flourish as long as the climate and other basic conditions are to its liking. By choosing wisely from the many types of roses profiled in this chapter, you'll be rewarded with a show of magnificence that befits the flower's near immortal status.

A. *Nepeta x faassenii 'Six Hills Giant' (3)*
B. *Paeonia 'Duchesse de Nemours' (3)*
C. *'Baronne Prévost', hybrid perpetual (1)*
D. *Penstemon 'Hyacinth-Flowered Mixed' (5)*
E. *Erigeron karvinskianus 'Profusion' (2)*
F. *'Blush Noisette', noisette (1)*
G. *Artemisia x 'Powis Castle' (1)*
H. *'Madame Isaac Pereire', bourbon (1)*

The key lists each plant type and the number of plants needed to replicate the garden shown. The letters and numbers above refer to the type of plant and the number sited in an area.

The Features of a Rose

A rose is *not* just a rose. Rather, roses are a huge clan whose members vary widely in flower color, fragrance, size, and form; plant height and habit; and foliage texture and hue. Most have thorns or prickles, but a few don't. Many flower for months, while others produce one spectacular burst of blooms each year. Some put on a winter show with colorful ripe fruits, and a few grow a mossy coat on their buds—indeed, the list of individual quirks is nearly endless. How the *Rosa* population came to be so diverse is a story that begins in antiquity and will likely continue for as long as gardeners grow what one poet called the queen of flowers.

A Cast of Thousands

In the beginning—tens of millions of years ago—there were what are now called species roses. These wild roses are the ancestors of all the varieties available today, which number into the thousands. Wind and insects transferred the pollen of one type of rose to another, creating entirely new varieties through natural crossing. Other new roses have come into being through spontaneous mutation; these roses, called sports, are different in some way—usually flower color, number of petals, or plant habit—from their parent.

However, the vast majority of today's roses are not the work of nature but of human hands. For centuries, in painstaking efforts to combine the best traits of various roses, botanists, horticulturists, and passionate gardeners have been crossing—or hybridizing—different varieties in a ceaseless quest for ever greater beauty.

All hybrids and their sports can be grouped into two general categories—old garden roses and modern roses—according to when they first appeared. The dividing line is the year 1867, the official date of introduction of the first modern rose. Called the hybrid tea, it set a new standard of beauty for roses and is the one most people envi-

FOUR FLOWER FORMS
As illustrated below, single blooms produce one open layer of 5 to 8 petals; semidoubles also open wide, framing the flower's center with two layers of overlapping petals ranging in number from 8 or 9 petals to as many as 25; double blooms have 21 to 50 petals that unfold from a pointed bud; and very double blooms seem to burst with anywhere from 50 to 200 petals.

Single　　　*Semidouble*　　　*Double*　　　*Very Double*

SPREADING
These roses have long, leafy canes that grow horizontally over the ground; the plant is much wider than its typical height of 1 to 3 feet.

UPRIGHT
Sometimes called bushes, roses with upright habits have canes that sprout few leaves but produce large blooms at the tips. Taller than they are wide, they usually reach a height of between 3 and 6 feet.

sion when they think of a rose. Unfortunately, some rose varieties—including most hybrid teas—are too tender for very cold climates, are vulnerable to an array of pests and diseases, or need substantial amounts of pruning and other care. Lovely as they are, these plants have given all of rosedom a reputation for difficulty. And yet there are many healthy, hardy, and even low-maintenance beauties as well, including species roses, several old garden types, and a number of modern ones that defy trouble while representing the rose family in all its gorgeous variety.

The Blooms

Anyone venturing outdoors in spring is witness to the fact that roses bloom in a rainbow of colors—all shades of pink, red, white, yellow, orange, and exotic hues of apricot and mauve. What you may not know is that the bloom can also take a number of forms. Depending on how many petals they have, how the petals open, and how much they reveal of the pistils and stamens at the center of the flower, rose blossoms are categorized as single, semidouble, double, or very double *(opposite)*.

The season when the flowers start blooming and how long the bloom season lasts also vary from rose to rose. Some produce one flush in spring or summer that lasts for a few weeks, then rest until the following year. Others, called repeating or remontant roses, can put out flowers continually from spring or summer through fall, or in a succession of waves with respites in between.

Growth Habits in Roses

Although the bloom is what the word *rose* usually calls to mind, roses are, of course, complete plants—woody shrubs that, like their flowers, also come in many shapes and sizes. They can restrict themselves to several inches in height or grow stems, called canes, as long as 50 feet. Their habits, as illustrated below, include spreading ground covers, upright and full bushes and shrubs, treelike "standards," and vertical climbing roses. Miniatures, a group of modern roses, don't have a distinct habit; rather, they can be round or upright or even climbing—habits found in their larger relatives, but on a smaller scale.

CLIMBING
Most very long caned roses, classified as either stiff-caned "climbers" or more pliable "ramblers," grow from 8 to 25 feet or more and should be secured to a fence, trellis, wall, or other support.

FULL
Graceful with leafy, arching canes, these shrubby roses are handsome even when they are not in bloom. They can be as wide as they are tall, although larger plants—reaching up to 10 feet or so—don't achieve a girth equal to their height.

STANDARD
Not the work of nature, standards are roses whose buds are grafted by plant growers onto a separate, leafless trunk to imitate the habit of a tree. The leafy, blooming rose has either a lollipop shape or a loose, cascading one, depending on the variety.

9

The Wild Species Roses

Long before there were gardens and gardeners, there were roses. These wild roses—about 200 distinct species of the genus *Rosa*—evolved throughout the Northern Hemisphere, and over thousands of years each has become as unique as its place of origin. Many grow rampantly, while others stay small and neat; some are at home in extreme cold, and others thrive in hot climates, sandy soil, or swamps. Even their fragrances are individually sweet, spicy, or earthy. What defines species roses is their ability to reproduce true versions of themselves from self-pollinated seed that ripens in fruits known as hips. Hybrids, by contrast, don't breed true from self-pollinated seed.

Besides their reproductive ability, perhaps the only other feature shared by most wild roses is flowers that are single in form. These cheerfully open-faced blooms usually range from pale pink to deep purplish red. *R. rugosa,* which is exceptionally hardy and nearly impervious to most diseases, and *R. eglanteria,* known as the sweetbrier or eglantine rose, are two of the most popular. Some wild roses differ from the majority by being white or yellow, and a handful have sported to semidouble or double-bloomed forms. *R. banksiae banksiae* and *R. banksiae lutea,* for example, are beautiful white and yellow double-bloom forms of *R. banksiae.* Rugosa roses include the original dark pink species and its sports *R. rugosa alba,* whose blooms are white, and *R. rugosa rubra,* whose mauve flowers are larger than its relatives'.

Rugosas begin blooming in spring and produce

A BEAUTIFUL BOUNDARY
Rosa rugosa, grown as a hedge, separates a trim lawn from the wooded area behind it on this Washington State property. Deep pink petals surrounding a creamy center bloom repeatedly throughout the season, offering months of pleasing contrast with the bright green foliage.

their blossoms continually into fall. But most species roses, like most other flowering shrubs, bloom just once during the season, putting on a display that can last up to several weeks. Species from warmer climates tend to bloom earlier than those native to regions where frequent spring frosts can damage a plant in flower. *R. banksiae,* from the temperate regions of China, blooms in early spring, for example; the eglantine rose, from Europe, flowers before midsummer; and North American *R. carolina* generally blooms anywhere between early summer and late summer.

Although wild roses typically don't produce blossoms through the entire growing season, they often make up for the lack of blooms with interesting foliage. *R. rugosa*'s rounded foliage is a lustrous medium green with the appearance of textured leather, while the soft green leaves of *R. spinosissima*—a small, hardy bush known as the Scotch rose—are daintily edged, giving the leaves a lacelike quality. The foliage of many species also turns attractive colors in the fall. *R. virginiana* takes on shades of scarlet, orange, and yellow, whereas the mountain rose, *R. woodsii,* and *R. gymnocarpa* from the American West turn red-orange and bright yellow. European *R. glauca* doesn't wait until fall to produce colorful foliage; the red tint of its leaves deepens during the growing season, becoming a smoky purple by autumn.

Stamina and Vigor

Despite their differences, all species roses share an indefinable air of wildness: They simply look as though they can take care of themselves—and they can. In the process of adapting over millennia to their environments, these roses became completely self-reliant, needing no chemicals to ward off disease and pests, no protection from winter cold, no fertilizer or watering or soil amendments—in short, no gardener's help.

PRETTY IN PINK
Known as the eglantine or sweetbrier rose, R. eglanteria produces charming five-petaled blooms amid glossy apple-scented foliage (below). An ideal hedge rose, it is 8 or more feet tall, has a bushy habit, and has thorny canes to discourage intruders.

The Troubled Legacy of Rosa foetida

Species roses are generally the most resilient plants in the genus, and the wild Iranian rose *R. foetida* is no exception. Having had to fend for itself in the hot, dry climate of its native land, this rose is unfazed by the challenges such conditions create. However, because *R. foetida* was never forced to defend itself against the commonest of rose diseases—the fungus black spot, which thrives in moist conditions—it is gravely susceptible to it.

The solution is not as simple as banning *R. foetida* from your garden, though. Its blooms are a rich golden color—a trait that was rare and highly coveted during the 19th century, when rose breeders were crossing species and hybrids at a frenzied pace in a quest for new colors as well as other qualities in the offspring. In 1893 a French breeder named Joseph Pernet-Ducher produced a brilliant yellow rose using *R. foetida persiana,* a double-flowered form of the species. He named his prize 'Soleil d'Or'—sun of gold. 'Soleil d'Or' was then used to breed 'Rayon d'Or', the first yellow hybrid tea.

As might be expected, other hybridizers seized upon Pernet-Ducher's creations. The result was a revolution in the spectrum of modern roses: Most of today's yellow, orange, salmon, apricot, and flaming red-orange roses owe their brilliance to *R. foetida.* Unfortunately, along with their beautiful color, most of them—especially hybrid teas—inherited *R. foetida*'s vulnerability to black spot. If you live anywhere but the driest climate and you want healthy roses without the help of chemical fungicides, your best bet is to choose a rose without *R. foetida* in its ancestry. But if your heart is set on a yellow rose, experts suggest an unusually resistant hybrid tea called 'Elina', the miniature 'Rise 'n' Shine', a medium yellow climber named 'Golden Showers', or the shrubby 'Sunsprite'.

Rosa foetida persiana

With such independence, wild roses make gloriously easy-care additions to your landscape, doing the yeoman's work of hiding the chain-link fence or standing sentinel at the far reaches of the yard where a hose won't reach. Most grow so large that they require more room than a bed or border has to offer. *R. rugosa,* which reaches a height of at least 8 feet and tolerates temperatures as low as -40°F, can serve as a thick hedge where space allows, spreading quickly into wide colonies by putting out new shoots from its roots. The superlong canes of *R. banksiae,* extending more than 25 feet, can be used to drape a shed or other structure you want to dress up with little fuss. And dense, 8-foot-high thickets of pink *R. palustris* do especially well in wet areas, where other roses fail—a trait that earned it the nickname swamp rose.

Native Roses

A number of species grow freely in North America because they originated here. If you'd like to grow roses in a wildflower garden, large natives such as *R. palustris* and the Virginia rose, *R. virginiana,* are perfectly suited. And although most species are amply sized, there are a few natives that are so compact and refined you can put them in a formal border. One of the loveliest of these, dark pink *R. carolina* (the pasture rose) usually grows to a height of only 3 feet. *R. carolina* looks fragile and sounds as if it might be a tender plant from the South, but its native range—the area it spans in the wild—stretches all the way from Nova Scotia west to Minnesota and south to Texas and Florida.

At home as far north as southern Ontario, pink-flowered *R. setigera* is the only North American native climber, with canes growing more than 16 feet. You can train it up a support or let it grow horizontally as a low-maintenance ground cover. Another native that has spread widely throughout the United States and Canada is *R. nitida,* a short, dainty shrub that produces deep pink blooms and, in the fall, crimson foliage. The state flower of Georgia, *R. laevigata*—also called the Cherokee rose—is actually from China but has established itself so thoroughly in the southern United States that most people think of its charming, floppy white spring flowers as native wildflowers.

New Roses from Wild Blood

Nonnative species like the Cherokee rose that thrive and spread without assistance have "naturalized," in horticultural parlance. Species roses

sometimes come from environments so trying that when they take root in more hospitable conditions they don't simply naturalize but run rampant. Notorious among these is *R. multiflora,* from the poor mountain soils of Japan and Korea. This species can take over your landscape and should be avoided, but its boundless vigor has been put to good use by rose hybridizers, who have used it in the breeding of most ramblers and a number of other modern varieties.

R. multiflora is also used as a rootstock. Rose growers often graft the buds of one rose onto the roots of another, combining the beauty of the former with the vigor or stamina of the latter. Multiflora is one of the most popular rootstocks, supporting plants that are less aggressive than it is but that are quick to grow and reach maturity.

This species is not the only one with qualities that appeal to hybridizers. In the early 20th century, Dr. William Van Fleet produced climbers using the vigorous, disease-resistant Asian *R.*

wichuraiana; the most famous of his cultivated varieties bears his own name: 'Dr. W. Van Fleet'. And in 1952, German hybridizer Wilhelm Kordes created a new species by crossing *R. wichuraiana* with resilient *R. rugosa.* The resulting *R. kordesii* has been used by a number of breeders to parent a group of exceptionally healthy and hardy modern hybrids called kordesii shrubs. The cold-hardy Explorer series from Canada, for example, includes some indomitable kordesiis bearing the names of famous explorers, such as 'Champlain' and 'John Cabot'.

At Iowa State University, plant scientist Griffith Buck has used diminutive, bristly *R. arkansana* and a Siberian species to breed a series of Dr. Buck roses, which can take extreme temperature changes. The Arkansas rose, whose range stretches from Texas to Canada, has also been used by horticulturists in Canada to breed Parkland (Morden) roses, which are prized for their hardiness, resistance to disease, and long bloom periods.

A NORTH AMERICAN NATIVE
The 2-inch-wide pink blooms of native R. carolina—the pasture rose—can be seen in clusters as well as one to a stem on this bush in New York. The hardy plant waits until late spring or early summer, long after the danger of frost is past, to put on its floral show. In fall, the foliage glows a warm orange and yellow.

Old Garden Roses

In the 17th century, Dutch and Flemish artists painted roses with what appear to be impossibly opulent, heavy-headed blooms. Such flowers were not figments of the imagination but realistic re-creations of the most popular rose varieties cultivated at the time. These are the European old garden roses, early hybrids whose luxuriant blossoms differ noticeably from both free-spirited species roses and the elegantly tight-budded modern varieties that would begin to emerge in the 1860s.

The old garden types, also known as antique, are among the most fragrant of all roses; some of the most redolent are listed below. Exceptionally large bloomed, many old garden roses have their petals arranged in whorls—a pattern known as quartering—and their full, sometimes cupped shape lends them an old-fashioned look that sits well on the graceful shrubs. If nostalgia, beauty, and perfume are not reason enough to grow them, old garden roses are also less demanding and less fragile than many of the modern varieties.

Old garden roses are divided into several groups, or classifications, on the basis of their ancestry. In the family of European old garden roses, the most ancient is the gallica, which was cultivated by the Greeks and Romans for its beauty, perfume, and medicinal qualities. Noted for their exceptional cold and heat tolerance, disease resistance, and lack of prickles, gallica shrubs typically grow 3 to 5 feet tall and sprout dark green foliage. The flowers, in shades of palest pink to mauve, range from single to very double. Most are semidouble, however, including the first known gallica, dark pink 'Apothecary's Rose', and its striped sport 'Rosa Mundi'.

Gallicas figure in the ancestry of the exotically scented damasks, which are also hardy and fuss free. Unlike gallicas, though, damasks have thorny canes, and the shrubs are taller—usually 5 to 6 feet, with gray-green, sometimes downy foliage. Their semidouble to very double flowers bloom in clusters, mostly in shades of clear pink, and erupt only once each summer—except for 'Autumn Damask', a renegade whose blossoms repeat in the fall.

Fairer still are the albas; this class of antique roses blooms in shades of pale pink and pink-tinged white. Usually 4 to 6 feet tall, upright in habit, tough, and hardy, albas are among the easiest roses to grow because they are supremely tolerant of less than ideal conditions, including shade.

A fourth class, the centifolias, were once believed by rose fanciers to have a heritage as old as the gallicas, but 20th-century plant scientists have determined that most were developed by Dutch hybridizers in the 1600s. Centifolias are open, thorny shrubs that need a sunny site in the garden to keep their foliage free of fungal disease. This drawback is mitigated, though, by their production of some of the roundest and largest very double flowers in all of rosedom, earning them the nickname cabbage roses. The flower color spectrum of these roses is broad, ranging from white to crimson to mauve. As the fragrant blooms open,

Highly Scented Old Garden Roses

'Alba Semi-plena'	'Nastarana'
'Baronne Prévost'	'Paul Neyron'
'Boule de Neige'	'Petite de Hollande'
'Camaieux'	'Reine des Violettes'
'Cardinal de Richelieu'	'Rêve d'Or'
'Catherine Mermet'	'Rosa Mundi'
'Celestial'	'Rose de Rescht'
'Celsiana'	'Sombreuil'
'Communis'	'Souvenir
'Complicata'	de la Malmaison'
'Duchesse de Brabant'	'Tuscany'
'Fantin-Latour'	'Variegata di Bologna'
'Félicité Parmentier'	'Zéphirine Drouhin'
'Ispahan'	
'Königin	
von Dänemark'	
'Lamarque'	
'La Reine Victoria'	
'Louise Odier'	
'Madame Alfred	
Carrière'	
'Madame Hardy'	
'Madame Isaac	
Pereire'	
'Madame Plantier'	
'Maman Cochet'	
'Marchesa Boccella'	
'Mrs. B. R. Cant'	

'Fantin-Latour'

A TOUCH OF THE ANTIQUE
Deep pink very double blossoms of the bourbon 'Louise Odier' add an old-world flair to this Colorado garden in early summer. Pale yellow 'Windrush', a hardy modern rose; the leggy magenta herb Hesperis matronalis; and petite white blooms of Campanula latifolia 'Alba' surround the old rose centerpiece.

Hips: The Fruit of the Rose

If the blooms of certain roses are allowed to fade on the plant and lose their petals, fleshy fruits called hips will form. As they ripen and color, the hips produce a vivid show in fall and winter that's almost as delightful as the flowers in summer. Generally, the roses that set hips are most likely to have single or semidouble blooms. This is because flowers with fewer petals have an easier time self-pollinating—the first step in hip formation. Species roses and the single and semidouble gallicas, albas, and damasks have some of the most beautiful hips, whereas most centifolias, which are dense with petals, don't set them at all.

Hips are as varied as the roses that produce them. Some are round like the red globes of 'Apothecary's Rose', some are pear shaped, such as those of 'Alba Semi-plena', and some—like those of *R. moschata*—appear in sprays of tiny fruits. Their colors range from the bright orange of the gallica 'Complicata' to the glorious crimson of *R. rugosa (above)* to deep wine and black. This lovely late-season treat also occurs on some modern roses, including many hybrid rugosa shrubs. A number of moss roses set hips as well, and when they do the fruits are usually covered with the same moss that cloaks the buds. The large red hips of *R. laevigata* are bristly, and the oval fruits of the eglantine rose are abundant and especially long-lasting, asserting their bright red color throughout the winter.

Rose hips are edible as well as beautiful—and a rich source of nutrition. During World War II, for example, when citrus fruits were scarce in Britain, rose hips were found to have a vitamin C content 400 percent greater than that of oranges. In 1941 over 200 tons of the bitter red fruit of the country's ubiquitous *Rosa canina* were collected and made into syrup for civilian and military consumption.

they change from cup shaped to flat, finally revealing a button eye.

In the late 1600s, a centifolia sport was discovered with a curious feature that gave rise to a new class: the mosses. This sport had a unique coating on its buds and stems that looked like moss but was actually a layer of soft, enlarged glands that released a sticky, fragrant substance when touched. 'Communis', as the rose is known, has mossy buds that open to intensely sweet, rich pink quartered blossoms. Damask roses produced moss sports as well, and in the 1800s other varieties were bred.

Repeat-Blooming Varieties

In the Orient, where the tradition of gardens is far older than in the West, roses have probably been cultivated for longer than 5,000 years. As trade between Europe and Asia grew in the 18th century, it was not long before roses from the East reached the gardens of the West. This happened in the final years of the 1700s, when a few hybrids of *R. chinensis* were smuggled into England from China.

Shorter than other shrub roses and bearing single or, at most, double blossoms, the China roses weren't as hardy as their European counterparts. However, they possessed a trait that most European roses lacked: the ability to bloom not once but continuously throughout the season. As might be expected, rose enthusiasts immediately began mating the new arrivals, including 'Old Blush', with the European roses and spawning thousands of new varieties—and several new classifications.

Around 1800, repeat-blooming portland roses, named for England's Duchess of Portland, emerged in France. Though small in stature for an old garden rose—only 3 to 4 feet tall—portland shrubs are neat and round, bearing semidouble to very double flowers in a range of colors. The original 'Duchess of Portland' has a semidouble red bloom, while the later 'Rose du Roi' has double blooms that are a bright red-shaded violet.

The French also introduced the bourbons, a class of everbloomers that combine the China imports with damasks. Taller than portlands and laxer in habit, most bourbon shrubs reach a height of 5 to 6 feet. Some have sported climbers, such as the 12-foot 'Queen of Bourbons'. All bear large, cupped flowers that bloom into the fall, perfuming the air. Deep pink 'Madame Isaac Pereire' is perhaps the most powerfully fragrant of all roses.

Tea roses, so named for their scent of fresh tea leaves, also trace their roots to China. Probably a cross between small, neat *R. chinensis* and a large evergreen species, *R. gigantea*, the original tea was shipped to Europe in the early 19th century and used to breed repeat bloomers endowed with its refined foliage and long canes. 'Sombreuil', a very double white climbing tea, reaches 8 feet or more. Although 'Sombreuil' is a little hardier than others of its class, tea roses are generally tender plants that fare best in the gardens of the South.

On the other side of the Atlantic, John Champneys, a plantation owner in South Carolina, created a new rose in the early 1800s by crossing a China variety with a form of the musk-scented species *R. moschata*. Noisettes, as the class came to be called, produce clusters of roses on canes that stretch to 15 feet or so, making them ideal for training on arbors and walls. 'Madame Alfred Carrière', a very double pale pink rose, climbs to 20 feet. Not particularly hardy, noisettes decrease in vigor the farther north they are grown, but they thrive in southern gardens and require little pruning.

Between 1840 and 1900, hybridizers engaged in a riot of pollen exchange using all of the European and new classes, creating thousands of old garden roses whose genealogy was more complicated and confused than ever before. Most of the results were repeat bloomers called hybrid perpetuals. These roses were bred for huge, fragrant, upward-facing blooms that would win prizes in floral competitions. Myopically, breeders tended to neglect the habit and appearance of the shrub in favor of its flower, and as a result many hybrid perpetuals failed to catch on commercially. Most of these roses are no longer available. However, some hybrid perpetuals managed to inherit a long list of attributes, including a pleasing habit, and have survived in cultivation. 'Paul Neyron' shrubs, for example, are neat, sturdy, and disease resistant, producing intensely fragrant, rich pink, very double flowers that can measure an astounding 7 inches across.

Found Roses

Remnants of the old rose revolution are continually being discovered, growing unattended in fields, gardens, parks, cemeteries, and other public and private places on both sides of the Atlantic. Orphaned, without records or memory of their lineage, these plants are called found or mystery roses and given unofficial names while horticulturists attempt to identify them. As beautiful as their pedigreed counterparts, these nameless, persevering old roses come in all possible colors and habits. Many are propagated by specialty growers for sale through mail-order catalogs and are exceptionally reliable, having survived for what may be a century with no one's loving care.

Modern Roses

Eighteen sixty-seven was a watershed year in rose-dom. It was then that a French hybridizer named Jean-Baptiste Guillot discovered growing in his experimental beds a rose that was a cross between an old garden tea and a hybrid perpetual. This flower was so different from antique varieties that it not only established a new classification but also ushered in the modern era of rose breeding. That rose, 'La France', is officially recognized as the first hybrid tea.

Since that time, as plant science has grown increasingly sophisticated, other classes have made their debuts, and each of these modern types exemplifies some combination of the finest qualities of habit, hardiness, health, and beauty from all members of the genus *Rosa*. And yet, the first of the modern age still remains America's most popular rose.

A COTTAGE GARDEN
Pink cups of 'Simplicity'—a vigorous floribunda with a full, relaxed habit—bloom freely among yellow and lilac irises, white Hesperis matronalis, indigo spikes of annual larkspur, pink phlox, and cheerful purple-eyed pansies in this informal garden on the Connecticut seashore.

Hybrid Teas

Unlike the plump buds of antique roses that open wide in maturity, the hybrid tea is at its peak in lean youth, the pointed bud of its semidouble or double bloom only partly unfurled. The rose blends the best features of its ancestors: From the bred-to-show hybrid perpetual it inherited superb large flowers, and from the tea parent came refined form and foliage and long, straight stems for cutting. China blood from both parents endowed the new arrival with flowers that were everblooming.

With the introduction in the 1890s of vivid yellow blooms *(page 12),* the color spectrum—once mainly pink, white, and rosy red—burst its bonds. The tantalizing possibilities of vibrant color coupled with elegant flower form kept breeders'

heads turned toward fashioning the ultimate display flower: a single large, perfect bloom borne at the top of a long, straight stem. Indeed, hybrid teas—many of which are listed on page 20—are ideal for cutting and showing off in arrangements.

In striving for the perfect bloom, however, breeders continued to pay little mind to how the overall plant looked or fared in the garden. Many varieties of these long-stemmed beauties—which number in the thousands—grow on bushes that lack the grace of the European old garden roses, a minor quibble if your desire is to display the showy blooms indoors. They also tend to be short on the admirable sturdiness of species roses and require more of the care and maintenance tasks outlined in chapter 3 of this book.

Hybrid teas aren't as renowned for fragrance as the intoxicating old gallicas and damasks, but there are several that exude wonderful perfumes. A number in the class have even received the very selective James Alexander Gambel Award for Fragrant Roses, named for an English rose lover who donated funds in 1961 to encourage and reward

Musk Roses, Old and New

Like cousins many times removed, *Rosa moschata*—the original musk rose—and a group of modern shrub roses known as hybrid musks, which got their name primarily because of a rich, musky dimension to their scent, are only distantly related. *R. moschata*, a species that probably originated in southern Europe, appears in plant texts from 16th- and 17th-century England. These old sources describe the rose as a climber growing to 10 or 12 feet, with small, neat leaves, and either single or double flowers with the scent of musk. The texts also state that the rose flowers in late summer to autumn. The hybrid musks, for their part, are the progeny of teas, Chinas, hybrid teas, noisettes, and a couple of ramblers, all of which were crossed by an English priest at the beginning of the 20th century. Only the noisette part of their legacy contains *R. moschata* blood.

Hybrid musks are versatile garden shrubs that come in a variety of habits. Some, such as the upright and mannerly pink-flowered 'Erfurt' *(below)*, are dense and useful as hedging, while others are weeping shrubs or climbers. Apricot-colored 'Clytemnestra', for example, has long canes that can be trained on a support. Prolific bloomers in other shades of white to pink to scarlet, hybrid musks put out voluminous clusters of single or semidouble flowers in spring and fall, with scattered flowers in between. Best of all, they are somewhat shade tolerant and highly resistant to fungus diseases.

Sometime, probably in the late 18th century, a rampant summer-flowering rose was misidentified as the musk rose, and the error was perpetuated for over a century. But the true species has since been identified with the help of the old sources, and today both the old musk rose and a number of the misleadingly named hybrid musks are available for the garden. Although they have little in common, what they do share is an uncommon earthy-sweet perfume.

the introduction of scented roses. These hybrid tea winners include 'Crimson Glory', deep red 'Chrysler Imperial', rich yellow 'Sutter's Gold', two-toned red-and-white 'Double Delight', scarlet-orange 'Fragrant Cloud', multicolored 'Granada', and satiny pink 'Tiffany'.

The Next Generations

Following close on the heels of the hybrid tea was another of Guillot's creations, the polyanthas. Meaning "many-flowered," polyanthas are the offspring of a dwarf China rose and *R. multiflora,* a genetic commingling that produced clusters of small, everblooming double flowers on low, compact bushes. 'Cécile Brunner', for example, erupts in clusters of small, beautifully shaped pink blooms from spring to fall on billowing 4-foot shrubs.

Polyanthas are quite hardy, but their flowers are tiny compared with those of the hybrid teas. In an effort to combine the best qualities of the two classes, breeders in Denmark began crossing polyanthas with large-flowered hybrid teas, which are generally too tender to be grown successfully in the stern Scandinavian climate. The result of the Danes'

efforts, and the efforts of hybridizers who followed them, was the floribundas.

Floribundas have fuller habits, enabling them to serve gracefully in landscaping, and they continually produce clusters of medium-sized flowers over a long season. The blooms can be single, semidouble, or double. 'Escapade', for instance, has a mauve-and-white semidouble blossom; ruffly dark pink 'Betty Prior' is a single; and the white blooms of 'Iceberg' are double and open flat.

Inevitably, hybrid teas and floribundas were crossed, thereby spawning, in 1954, the grandiflora class. Like the floribundas, grandifloras bear flowers in clusters rather than one to a stem, but they have the size and formal shape of hybrid tea blooms and grow on longer canes. Grandiflora shrubs, most of which are about as hardy as hybrid teas, can grow over 6 feet tall. The first grandiflora, 'Queen Elizabeth', sets an almost impossible standard in beauty: It produces copious sprays of long-stemmed cotton-candy pink blooms on a vigorous shrub that can grow 10 feet tall. Prune it to 6 feet, however, to show it to best advantage.

Miniature and Climbing Varieties

If your bed or border isn't large enough to accommodate 6-foot bushes, or if you garden in containers on a patio or balcony, you can take advantage of the many beautiful roses that come in small sizes. Most of these plants, classified as miniatures, range from a few inches in height to just over 2 feet. All boast handsome small-scale foliage and flowers that come in a wide variety of shapes and colors.

In short, miniatures do all the things that other roses do. 'Popcorn', for example, has semidouble 1-inch white blooms centered on golden "kernels"; these profuse blossoms are borne on upright 15-inch bushes. The 24-inch 'Paper Doll' covers itself with high-centered hybrid-tea-like blossoms in pale salmon; 'Mossy Gem', with magenta pompoms, is a diminutive version of a moss rose; and 'Jeanne Lajoie', with pretty pink double blooms, is a miniature climber that exceeds 4 feet in height.

Climbing roses, both large and miniature, are simply those that have the long canes needed to

'Chrysler Imperial'

'William Baffin'

make a vertical statement on a wall or freestanding support. It's not unusual for a bush or shrub rose in any of several classes to have a climbing sport, often identified by the abbreviation "Cl." The polyanthas 'Pinkie', 'Cécile Brunner', and 'The Fairy' all have long-caned forms, as do the China rose 'Old Blush' and the hybrid teas 'Peace' and 'Crimson Glory'. Such roses are like their parents in hardiness and disease resistance as well as in flower color and form.

Many long-caned varieties are not sported versions of their bushy parents but individuals in their own right. Those in the class officially termed climbers, or large-flowered climbers, are usually everblooming, producing an array of flowers ranging from the blood red singles of 'Altissimo' to the lemony double blooms of 'Golden Showers'. Classed separately from large-flowered climbers are ramblers, which, like pink 'Tausendschön', usually have R. wichuraiana and R. multiflora in their blood. Rambling roses bloom in clusters once per season, and their canes grow faster and are thinner and more supple than those of their climber cousins.

The Catchall Class: Modern Shrubs

Many of the most recent modern roses, which often have elaborately mixed parentage, can't easily be grouped into one class or another and are simply termed modern shrubs. Their flowers come in all forms and in all colors of the rose rainbow, and the plants can be low growing, upright, full, or even short climbers. What many have in common is foliage and habits so attractive that they warrant a place in the garden even when the shrub is not in bloom.

Cutting Roses for Indoor Arrangements

If you grow roses for beauty indoors as well as out, the best time to cut them, according to experts, is early morning, when the blooms have been out of the sun overnight and have replenished their moisture. For maximum fragrance, allow them an hour of morning sun—just enough warmth to release the scented oils. Choose blossoms that have already begun to unfurl, since buds cut when they are tightly closed may never open.

Using sharp shears, make a cut at a 45° angle a quarter inch above a healthy outward-facing bud that is just beginning to swell. Also, make sure to leave at least two sets of leaves on the stem. These techniques ensure that the cane will regenerate and grow slightly outward to keep the plant's habit open. After bringing the flowers inside, you must recut the stems underwater to prevent air from blocking the movement of water up the stem, which would cause the flower to droop.

Remove any leaves and thorns that will be underwater in the vase so they won't rot, and stand the roses in very warm (110° F) water. This encourages them to draw in the water and become firm. After the water cools, place the container of roses in the refrigerator for several hours.

To preserve your flowers as long as possible, add 1 teaspoon of sugar and a few drops of chlorine bleach to each quart of water, or simply pour in a few ounces of flat lemon-lime soda. By recutting the stems, changing the water, and replenishing the preservative daily, you should be able to enjoy your roses for up to a week. The cooler your home is, the longer the flowers will last.

A number of modern shrubs mingle *R. rugosa* with polyanthas, teas, and other classes, even other rose species. These roses, collectively termed hybrid rugosas, are more refined than their namesake species, and yet many retain its iron constitution. 'Frau Dagmar Hartopp', for example, is a handsome, compact 3-foot shrub with clove-scented pink flowers that enjoys exceptional disease resistance. 'Agnes' bears yellow very double blooms on upright 4- to 6-foot bushes that are extremely winter hardy. Like other modern shrubs, including hybrid musks *(page 19)*, hybrid rugosas need minimal pruning.

In Great Britain, the hybridizer David Austin has bred dozens of modern shrub varieties—known unofficially as English roses—specifically to capture the fragrant, lush, delicately colored blooms of old European garden roses in a repeat-blooming bush. Among the best known are 'Graham Thomas', a large bush with yellow double flowers, and 'Heritage', whose cupped blooms are the palest of pinks with a citrus scent. Both have proven themselves reliable bloomers and healthy in cooler regions on the American side of the Atlantic.

Where the emphasis in breeding the English roses has been on combining old garden charm with modern hybrid vigor and bloom, Meidiland roses from the House of Meilland in France have been bred for low maintenance above all else. Their blossoms are relatively small, but they repeat bloom, and the shrubs are exceptionally hardy and require little or no pruning.

The foliage on the Meidiland roses is also extremely disease resistant, which is one of the qualities that hybridizers rank high on their list of desired qualities in the newest roses. In Germany, hybridizer Werner Noack spent many years developing 'Flower Carpet', which is nearly disease-proof, before its North American introduction in 1995. A low, bushy shrub, 'Flower Carpet' also puts on a very long floral show, blooming for 5 to 10 months, depending upon climate.

For gardeners in cold climates, species and old European varieties have always been excellent choices because of their hardiness. Joining the list in the modern era are the Dr. Buck roses, the Canadian Explorers and Parklands, and the kordesiis—all of them bred specifically to cope with extremes in temperature.

Choosing the Best Roses for Your Garden

When selecting roses for your garden, a little research at the outset may prevent many pounds of chemical cure and a great deal of frustration later on. Informing yourself about which plants will do best in your particular climate and conditions makes all the difference between a garden full of beautiful, healthy roses and one in which they have to struggle to survive.

First, hone your list of options by eliminating the obviously unsuitable. If you live in a region where winter temperatures dip below -10° F, you're limited to species, old garden, and modern shrubs bred specifically for cold climates. If you garden in the hot South, the Chinas, teas, and noisettes will perform beautifully. Although they produce flowers most abundantly when the daytime temperature is between 70° and 80° F, these roses continue to bloom in midsummer heat.

In the Midwest, where cold winters alternate with hot summers, you'll need a rose that tolerates both extremes. Consider a once-blooming rose, such as a European antique, which will give you a magnificent show in early summer before the heat arrives—soaring temperatures tend to stifle the flowering of most everbloomers. But if a repeat bloomer is your desire, choose a hardy modern shrub; some floribundas, grandifloras, and hybrid teas will also do well as long as they are protected through the winter *(page 77)*.

In cold regions you may want to purchase roses that are growing on their own roots instead of on grafted ones, because own-root roses survive harsh winters better. When canes of grafted roses die back during extreme cold, you may get new growth only from the rootstock and not from the rose variety you purchased the plant for. In Florida and other areas where plants never go dormant, roses grown on the roots of *R. fortuniana* do especially well.

In the Pacific Northwest, where the rust fungus is a particular problem, avoid rugosas and their hybrids. Elsewhere, though, rugosas are practically immune to diseases, and they perform especially well in the sandy soil and salt spray of the northeastern Atlantic region. Hybrid musks are also noteworthy for their disease resistance. The chart on page 24, which lists general characteristics for each rose classification, can help you see at a glance which types may work best for you.

Function and Maintenance

After you've crossed the obviously wrong off your list, consider how you plan to use your roses. If you're growing them for cut flowers, try hybrid teas, floribundas, and grandifloras. Many of the old garden varieties and David Austin's modern shrubs also produce blooms that are stunning in arrangements. If you're choosing roses to serve specific landscaping functions, such as lining a driveway or blanketing a slope, look for those whose heights and habits are most likely to do the job before you factor in flower color, form, and fragrance.

Next, consider your own habits. If you find puttering around plants relaxing, and you have the time to prune, fertilize, and perform other needed tasks, then you can confidently choose hybrid teas, floribundas, and grandifloras, or a climber or standard—all of which need more pruning than other types. If, on the other hand, your time is limited, you'll be happier with species and old garden varieties or low-maintenance modern shrubs.

National and Local Resources

Roses are notorious for performance that varies—perversely—from one region to another. Nothing beats local experience and information, and with roses there is a wealth of such information available. Public gardens that feature the rose can be found just about anywhere in the country. By visiting them you'll get a good idea of the varieties that are likely to thrive in your own landscape.

More than 100 of the United States' largest public gardens show new roses that have been judged exceptional by the All-America Rose Selections (AARS), a nonprofit association of professional rose producers and hybridizers. AARS judges at many U.S. locations evaluate new hybrids from around the world for 2 years, testing their vigor, growth habit, disease resistance, foliage, flower production and form, and fragrance. A small percentage are officially designated "AARS winners"—look for them when you're buying your plants.

Another invaluable resource is the American Rose Society (ARS), composed of 360 local rose

Species

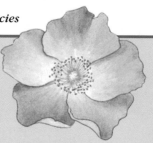

Rose Classifications

SPECIES Fragrant, once-flowering, usually single blooms are often pink but may be white, red, or yellow. Plants are vigorous; many are hardy and disease resistant. Height and habit vary widely.

Gallica

China

Old Garden Roses

GALLICAS Scented blush, pink, or mauve single, semidouble, or double flowers bloom once per season on 3- to 5-foot shrubs. Upright plants are disease resistant and extremely hardy.

DAMASKS Extremely fragrant blooms are semidouble or double, pink or white; all but 'Autumn Damask' are once-blooming. Very hardy, shrubby plants are 5 to 6 feet tall and generally disease resistant.

ALBAS White or pink, fragrant, single to double flowers bloom once per season in clusters on vigorous, upright 5- to 8-foot shrubs with bluish foliage. Plants are very hardy and moderately disease resistant.

CENTIFOLIAS Clusters of intensely fragrant, very double flowers bloom once per season, in white to deep pink. Most plants are 4 to 6 feet tall and hardy, but may be susceptible to fungal disease.

MOSSES A mosslike growth covers parts of the plant. Fragrant, double or very double flowers are white to deep mauve or red; most bloom once per season. Plants can be susceptible to disease and vary in height, habit, and hardiness.

CHINAS Small single or double flowers repeat bloom in a wide range of colors that darken with age. These mostly 3- to 4-foot plants need little pruning and are fairly disease resistant; some are tender.

PORTLANDS Compact, round shrubs up to 4 feet tall produce waves of fragrant, very double flowers in pinks or reds. Plants are not particularly hardy or vigorous; disease resistance varies.

BOURBONS Fragrant semidouble to very double flowers are white, pink, red, or purplish, and repeat on vigorous and somewhat hardy shrubs. Some are climbers. Plants are more susceptible than other old garden roses to black spot.

TEAS Foliage and flowers are tea scented; elegantly shaped semidouble or double repeating blooms come in many delicate colors. Plants can be climbers or shrubs; vigor and disease resistance varies; most are tender.

NOISETTES Repeating large flowers come in many colors and forms. Plants are vigorous climbers—in warm climates only—and resistant to diseases.

HYBRID PERPETUALS Large, fragrant, double or very double white, pink, or maroon flowers usually repeat. Vigorous bushes can grow to 7 feet. Hardiness varies; disease resistance depends on climate.

Damask

Tea

Noisette

Centifolia

Hybrid Perpetual

Shrub

Modern Roses

HYBRID TEAS Mostly semidouble or double elegantly shaped flowers repeat bloom in a wide range of colors on upright, formal bushes. Fragrance varies. Most plants are susceptible to disease; hardiness varies.

POLYANTHAS Small, clustering flowers are usually double, come in many colors, and repeat; fragrance is slight. Plants are hardy, compact, and disease resistant.

FLORIBUNDAS Repeating blooms grow in clusters, are single to double, and come in all colors. Plants are generally shrubby and vigorous, but some are susceptible to disease. Hardiness varies.

GRANDIFLORAS Large, generously repeating blooms cluster on upright canes that grow more than 6 feet tall; they have the elegant form and wide range of colors of hybrid teas. Hardiness varies; some plants have good disease resistance.

MINIATURES First bred for containers, this class includes small-scale versions of other classes. Plants usually grow to about 2 feet, although climbers can reach 8 feet. Hardiness and disease resistance vary.

CLIMBERS Flowers in all colors, forms, and fragrances are mostly repeat blooming; canes are stiff and grow up to 50 feet. This broad class includes large-flowered hybrids and climbing sports of other classes. Vigor, hardiness, and disease resistance vary.

RAMBLERS Long canes on vigorous plants are more pliable than climbers' and have many lateral shoots. Flowers usually bloom once per season in clusters and come in many colors. Hardiness and disease resistance vary.

SHRUBS Flowers bloom in all colors and forms on attractive leafy plants in a range of habits and heights. Most are everblooming, disease resistant, hardy, and easy to care for. Hybrid musks, hybrid rugosas, and kordesii roses are all groups of modern shrubs.

Hybrid Tea

Floribunda

Miniature

Top-Rated Roses

The roses in this list have received ARS ratings in the "outstanding" range, 9 and above. Those with an asterisk are AARS winners as well.

'Altissimo'	'Minnie Pearl'
'Ausburn'	'Monsieur Tillier'
'Ballerina'	'Olympiad' *
'Bonica' *	'Pierrine'
'Dainty Bess'	'Plum Dandy'
'Dortmund'	'Pristine'
'Europeana' *	'Queen Elizabeth' *
'Henry Hudson'	'Rainbow's End'
'Immensee'	'Rise 'n' Shine'
'Jean Kenneally'	R. rugosa alba
'Jeanne Lajoie'	'Sexy Rexy'
'Kingig'	'Snow Bride'
'Koricole'	'Starina'
'Madame Hardy'	'Touch of Class' *
'Magic Carrousel'	'William Baffin'

'Queen Elizabeth' with clematis

societies around the United States, with tens of thousands of members. Besides providing assistance and encouragement to its membership, the ARS has a Consulting Rosarians program available to anyone who wants to grow roses. Even if you aren't a member, one of these consultants, an expert rose grower in your region, will try to answer your questions and help troubleshoot problems.

In addition, ARS members conduct ongoing evaluations of all roses in commerce—not only modern varieties but also species and old garden roses. The results are used to establish quality ratings on a scale of 1 to 10: Roses rated 9 and above are considered "outstanding," an 8 rating is "excellent," and any rose rated below 6 is deemed "of questionable value." The ratings, which factor in the same qualities judged by the AARS, are published each year in the society's *Handbook for Selecting Roses,* available for a small fee from the society. The ratings also appear in many other rose and gardening publications and are included in the encyclopedia entries at the back of this book.

Keep in mind, though, that the best strategy for choosing your roses is the simplest: Talk to your local rose society and to neighbors who grow them. Ratings and awards are only a guide; a high-rated rose might do poorly for you, while one with a mediocre rating might be a showstopper where you live. Another good source of information is your local Cooperative Extension Service. Don't hesitate to talk to any of the experts, both amateur and professional, who know the roses that do best in your area—and which ones to avoid.

Roses for Every Garden

Roses have a place in every garden. Their ravishing blooms and seductive fragrance captivate any gardener, and the versatility of their many shapes and sizes makes them indispensable. Finding the right place in your garden for the queen of flowers involves understanding all her regal virtues. Whether you decide on the gemlike radiance of a modern hybrid tea, the pastel refinement of an old garden rose, or the elegant froth of an ancient species, roses make a garden picture perfect.

Their wonderful landscape potential is evident in this rose-brightened Charlottesville, Virginia, garden. 'First Kiss', a bushy pink floribunda, and 'Mary Rose', a compact, rich pink shrub, arch over an urn of lavender pansies at the edge of a brick terrace. In the background, airy sprays of 'Cl. Cécile Brunner' glide across a gateway arch flanked by terra-cotta pots containing the dainty blush pink China 'Hermosa' and hedges of three easy-care roses: white 'Madame Hardy', 'Pink Meidiland', and bright pink 'Königin von Dänemark'.

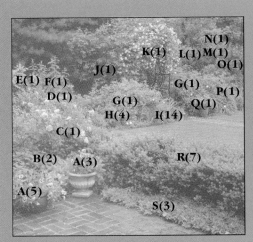

The key lists each plant type and the number of plants needed to replicate the garden shown. The letters and numbers above refer to the type of plant and the number sited in an area.

A. *Viola x wittrockiana* (8)
B. *Lysimachia clethroides* (2)
C. 'Mary Rose' (shrub) (1)
D. 'First Kiss' (floribunda) (1)
E. *Magnolia grandiflora* (1)
F. *Buddleia davidii* (1)
G. 'Madame Hardy' (damask) (2)
H. *Paeonia sp.* (4)
I. *Hemerocallis sp.* (14)
J. *Malus* 'Snowdrift' (1)
K. 'Cl. Cécile Brunner' (climbing polyantha) (1)
L. *Clethra alnifolia* (1)
M. *Syringa sp.* (1)
N. *Cercis canadensis* (1)
O. 'Pink Meidiland' (shrub) (1)
P. 'Königin von Dänemark' (alba) (1)
Q. 'Hermosa' (China) (1)
R. *Ilex helleri* (7)
S. *Hedera helix* (3)

A Versatile Beauty

**A FORMAL
ENCLOSURE**
*An arbor blanketed
with 'Cl. First Prize' and
'Abraham Darby' serves
as a threshold between
rose beds with such
beauties as deep red
'Chrysler Imperial' and
a cutting garden be-
yond. The strict geome-
try of the Long Island
garden is delineated by
a trim yew hedge, low
edgings of boxwood,
and a wide brick walk.*

With their multitude of colors, shapes, and sizes, roses exist for almost any garden situation. In choosing the plants that bring the most beauty into your garden, you'll be considering the hues of both flower and foliage, the texture of the leaves, and even the winter charm of hips. But it is the form of the plant that will help you decide how best to use it. Plump shrubs make sumptuous hedges, stiffly elegant bushes are for formal beds, tall climbers enliven a trellis or fence, and low growers blanket the ground—and these are only some of the ways to introduce roses into your landscape.

For many gardeners, the thought of a rose garden conjures up an image of upright bushes neatly arranged inside a formal, geometric frame of dense, clipped greenery. This stately, even spare, look can be magnificent, showcasing the beautiful long-stemmed blooms of hybrid teas such as the deep red 'Mister Lincoln' or the pale yellow 'Elina' and grandifloras such as the elegant pink 'Queen Elizabeth'. If growing roses for cutting and exhibiting in competitions is your goal, devote space solely to these showy types, and—because hybrid teas and grandifloras are typically scant on leaves—enclose the bed with a low hedge of yew, holly, or boxwood to contribute foliage to the overall picture. A protective barrier of greenery also creates a pleasant microclimate for roses, shielding them from strong winds and shading the soil to slow the rate of evaporation. Partial afternoon shade will help keep the blossoms looking their best longer and preserve their fragrance.

If you're planning a large traditional garden, plant a network of several rose beds, divided by paths of brick, stone, or turf grass. The straighter the paths and the more symmetrical their arrangement, the more formal your rose garden will look. And any number of special touches can be added. For variety in height, try planting climbers and ramblers, trained along arches and tripods *(page 35)*. Ornaments such as urns, a sundial, or statuary will give the garden a sense of whimsy, dignity— or whatever personality you wish to convey.

Hedges: Double-Duty Roses

Roses can also play a substantial role outside of the formal setting. Define the perimeter of your property with species roses; separate one area from another with teas and shrubs; edge a walkway with miniatures or clustering floribundas. The floribunda 'Betty Prior', for example, makes a lush yet tidy hedge to guide visitors to your front door. Plant a single row of 'Betty Prior' 3 feet apart and keep the bushes trimmed to shorter than 5 feet. Unlike 'Betty Prior', modern shrub roses such as pink 'Bonica' and the snow white hybrid rugosa 'Blanc Double de Coubert' spread out and form a loosely cascading hedge. Use these shrubbier roses as a transition between the patio and the lawn or as a low screen to block the view of your neighbor's yard. Planted in staggered rows about 2½ feet apart, the shrubs create an impenetrable barrier of thorny canes and foliage. Roses suitable for both formal and informal hedges are listed on page 31. For information on planting rose hedges, see page 66.

Woody Shrubs and Roses

If you have room for only one hedge, try combining evergreen shrubs with roses. In moist, well-drained soil in the hot southeastern United States,

A RADIANT WELCOME
Upright and vase shaped in habit, the floribunda 'Iceberg' rises to 5 or 6 feet and spreads only slightly, making it an ideal rose for use as an open hedge. Its plush, pure white 3-inch flowers offer a textural contrast to this driveway of concrete pavers in southern California.

Roses and Herbs: Sharing a Gardening Heritage

Roses and herbs have made ideal garden companions for centuries. The oldest known gallica and the first rose known to be cultivated for medicine and perfume, *Rosa gallica officinalis*—'Apothecary's Rose'—shared pride of place with fragrant herbs and, in time, with other roses in the enclosed walls of medieval monastery gardens. For hundreds of years, essences were distilled from the plants and combined into conserves, syrups, balms, and ointments that were used for treating ailments ranging from lung and liver disorders to headaches and hangovers. These rosy admixtures contained the petals of gallicas and their citrus- and clove-scented damask descendants such as 'York and Lancaster' and 'Celsiana', vitamin-rich hips of rugosas, and such pungent herbs as lavender, chamomile, and fennel.

Today, a garden of herbs and roses is still an enticing blend of function and beauty. Herbs may be grown for their culinary and possible medicinal value, and their powerful aromas help ward off insects and pests from prized roses. In addition, the striking foliage of such plants as gray-green santolina, silvery artemisia, and lacy-textured tansy offers an ideal foil for roses' showy blooms. Bushy herbs like germander also have a place, forming short, dense hedges of tiny, glossy green leaves, which add a sober note to the heady tumble of color and fragrance. In commingling roses and herbs in your own garden, you can devise anything from a casual cottage version, with roses spotted here and there, to a near theatrical setting that echoes its historical antecedents, like the Atlanta garden shown at right.

Traditionally, roses were awarded the prime sites within a walled garden, surrounded by low, trimmed hedges outlining island beds in ornamental shapes. In the garden pictured here, the narrow, walled space is divided into three main diamond-shaped beds, each defined by a clipped hedge of true dwarf box and ground-hugging, yellow-green marjoram. A weeping standard of the polyantha 'The Fairy' adds a vertical dimension to the center of each bed, and underplantings of herbs and vegetables such as basil, chives, lettuce, and chard fill the areas inside the hedges. At left center, a potted standard lemon verbena and a rosemary topiary echo the upright form of the roses and relieve the austere symmetry of the surface patterns. The net result is a bountiful feast for the senses.

plant *Photinia* x *fraseri* (Fraser photinia), whose new foliage is tipped with red, and *Raphiolepis indica* 'Springtime' (Indian hawthorn), which forms stiff mounds of dark green foliage, behind 'Buff Beauty' and 'Mrs. Dudley Cross' to get a gorgeous living fence. 'Buff Beauty' is a fragrant hybrid musk with 2-inch pale apricot blooms that grows to 6 feet, and 'Mrs. Dudley Cross'—a 4-foot tea rose that does especially well in warm climates—has smaller, pink-tinged yellow flowers. The photinia grows quite straggly if left untamed and should be pruned to 6 feet, while the Indian hawthorn tops out at 6 feet and needs only occasional shaping.

Farther north, alternate cool-climate needled and broad-leaved evergreens with the hardy silvery pink rugosa 'Frau Dagmar Hartopp', pruned to 4

'Bonica'

PEACEFUL PASTELS
Beside a trickling fountain in this garden in Vancouver, British Columbia, apricot 'Leander' blooms mingle gently with the off-white peony 'Coral Sunset'. The blue foliage of common rue, the pure green leaves of a pink shrub rose, and the glossy evergreen foliage of a cherry-laurel hedge bring the soft tints into sharper focus.

feet in height and width. *Picea pungens* 'Montgomery', a spruce with a bluish cast that forms a dwarf pyramid, and *Ilex glabra* 'Compacta' (dwarf inkberry), with dark green foliage and black berries in fall, will complement the rugosa's flashy passage to winter as its foliage turns deep maroon, then golden yellow, and its large hips ripen to red.

Color Schemes for Beds and Borders

Get the most out of your roses' vibrant color display by placing them in beds and borders with other flowering shrubs, perennials, and annuals. The opportunities to compose a stunning picture

of color and form are infinite; just make certain that the companions you choose share the same cultural conditions required by most roses—fairly acid, well-drained, loamy soil, and plenty of sunlight and water.

Tall or spiky plants such as lilies, hollyhocks, and foxgloves complement the arching or rounded shapes of rosebushes. Low-growing plants, including annual 'Carpet of Snow' sweet alyssum and candytuft, conceal the bare, twiggy ankles of hybrid teas—and they produce white flowers that go with roses of any color. Combining roses with other, rich-hued flowering plants calls into play the principles of harmony and contrast at work in any visually satisfying garden. *Geranium psilostemon*, whose vivid magenta flowers are difficult to com-

Recommended Roses for a Hedge

FORMAL HEDGES

UNDER 3 FEET
'Cécile Brunner'
'La Marne'
'Marie Pavié'
'Nearly Wild'
'White Pet'

3 TO 5 FEET
'Archduke Charles'
'Autumn Damask'
'Betty Prior'
'Carefree Beauty'
'Elina'
'French Lace'
'Iceberg'
'Old Blush'
'Olympiad'

TALLER THAN 5 FEET
'John Cabot'
'Penelope'
'Queen Elizabeth'

INFORMAL HEDGES

3 TO 5 FEET
'Ballerina'
'Belle Poitevine'
'Blanc Double de Coubert'
'Bonica'
'Erfurt'
'Hansa'
'Sea Foam'

TALLER THAN 5 FEET
'Belinda'
'Cl. Pinkie'
R. glauca
R. palustris
R. rugosa alba
'Simplicity'
'Will Scarlet'

31

bine in a garden, works well with the perfumed deep pink bourbon 'Madame Isaac Pereire'. The two colors harmonize, and the rose acts as a brace for the tall-growing geranium.

Since roses come in virtually every color except blue, try pairing them with perennials and annuals that supply tints and shades of this missing piece of the spectrum. The yellow-pink blooms of the hybrid tea 'Peace' or the bright pink trusses of the bourbon 'Louise Odier' rising above the pale blue, cloudlike flowers of *Nigella damascena* (love-in-a-mist)—a self-sowing annual—paints a portrait of soothing pastels. For more drama, plant the clear yellow shrub 'Graham Thomas' with deep violet 'Black Knight' delphiniums. If you want truly eye-popping color, pair 'Playboy'—whose blooms are splashed with orange, yellow, and scarlet—with blue-violet flower stalks of *Nepeta* x *faassenii* (catmint) and *Salvia* x *superba* 'May Night' (sage). If the combination seems too garish for your taste, add bright yellow 'Moonshine' achillea to temper the mix.

BRIGHT COLOR CONTRAST
Saucer-shaped semi-double pink blooms of the floribunda 'Simplicity' contrast merrily with sunny yellow bearded iris. At upper right, the deep blue spikes of rocket larkspur and white and lilac dame's rocket add a sedate note to the cheery scene.

The Whitest Roses

'Alba Semi-plena'	R. rugosa alba
'Blanc Double	'Sally Holmes'
de Coubert'	'Sea Foam'
'Boule de Neige'	'Silver Moon'
'Fair Bianca'	'Snow Bride'
'Frau Karl Druschki'	'Sombreuil'
'Iceberg'	'White Meidiland'
'Irresistible'	'White Pet'
'Lamarque'	
'Linville'	
'Madame Alfred	
Carrière'	
'Madame Hardy'	
'Madame Legras	
de St. Germain'	
'Madame Plantier'	
'Marie Pavié'	
'Nastarana'	
R. banksiae banksiae	

'Frau Karl Druschki'

The Many Tones of White

White roses come in creamy tones tinged with yellow—the climbing tea 'Sombreuil' is one example—and blush tones flushed with the lightest tints of pink, such as 'Celestial', an alba. When placed amid delicate pastel flowers of pink and apricot, these near white roses seem to deepen the tints of their neighbors. And in a garden of hot colors—orange, scarlet, fiery red—a mass of pure white roses is a refreshing respite.

For a cool midsummer display, plant white 'Frau Karl Druschki', using a technique called pegging to create a low habit and encourage prolific blooms *(page 38)*. Back the rose with the sculpted foliage of sea kale and its lacy mounds of dainty white flowers, then let tall, steel blue spherical flower heads of *Eryngium* x *tripartitum* (three-lobed eryngium) lean on the sea kale for support.

The large floribunda 'Iceberg' helps make a gleaming white statement when it is combined with the almost translucent white cups of *Campanula persicifolia alba* (white bellflower) and a pure white cultivar of fireweed, *Epilobium angustifolium* 'Album'. In back of this trio—which will bloom from early summer through fall—plant a tall stand of the big-leaved foliage of *Macleaya cordata* (plume poppy), which should reach at least 7 feet by July, lending an otherworldly quality to the luminous landscape.

Bicolored/Multicolored Roses

Not all rose blooms are one solid color. Apricot-and-salmon 'Party Girl' and yellow-and-red 'Rainbow's End', for instance, are blends, which means that varying degrees of each color merge in the blooms. A bloom can also be striped, blotched, or mottled with separate colors, or there may be an "eye" of a second color at its center. The oldest striped rose of record, 'Rosa Mundi', a sport of the gallica 'Apothecary's Rose', has pale pink blooms blotched with the vivid pink of its parent. Alternate plants of 'Rosa Mundi' and 'Apothecary's Rose' for an enchanting hedge or border.

'Camaieux', with crimson, purple, and lilac stripes on a creamy background, is at home with solid-colored flowers such as the wine red and pink hybrids *Penstemon campanulatus* 'Garnet' and 'Evelyn'. The colors of the two penstemons match the rose's stripes, but the shape of their blooms is tubular, making for a pleasing contrast in form against the roundness of the rose. Add white foxglove to complement the red and pink.

Companions Worth Cultivating

Pair roses and ornamental grasses for a sensational-looking garden, says Mike Shoup, founder of the Antique Rose Emporium in Brenham, Texas. Ornamental grasses come in many colors, to be combined with roses of all hues, and their graceful, linear growth habit—tufted, mounded, arching, and upright—offers a refreshing counterpoint to the more rounded shapes of rosebushes and their blooms. To delight the eye with a planting composed of varying forms, textures, and colors, try the following combinations:

- Tufted, fine-textured, icy blue *Festuca ovina* var. *glauca* 'Blaufuchs' with soft pastels such as light pink 'Old Blush' and 'Cécile Brunner', rose pink 'Duchesse de Brabant', and pink-apricot 'Perle d'Or'.

- Arching, burgundy-leaved *Pennisetum setaceum* 'Rubrum' (purple fountain grass) with yellow-pink 'Lafter', 'Dr. Eckener', and yellow 'Graham Thomas' for dramatic contrast.
- Metallic blue *Panicum virgatum* 'Heavy Metal' (switch grass) and *Elymus arenarius* 'Glaucus' (blue Lyme grass) with mauve 'Reine des Violettes' and 'Cardinal de Richelieu', bright pink 'Betty Prior', and rose pink 'Nearly Wild'.
- Tall *Miscanthus sinensis* 'Morning Light' (Japanese silver grass), whose slender green leaves have a narrow margin of clear white, with red shrub rose 'John Franklin' and in front of climbers such as bright pink 'Zéphirine Drouhin' and dark red, tiny-leaved 'Red Cascade'.

'Gruss an Aachen' and Helictotrichon sempervirens (blue oat grass)

Climbers and Ramblers: The Rising Stars of Rosedom

Climbers and ramblers are perhaps the most versatile of roses for landscape use, transforming a garden into a ballet of form and color by adding movement up high, at eye level, and along the ground. Scaling a trellised wall, stiff-caned climbers can cloak an expanse of gritty masonry with lush foliage and velvety petals from late spring until frost. Blanketing a fence or sprawling down a slope, long-limbed ramblers erupt into a cascade of early-summer blooms that soften the rough edges of wood, warm up the cold glare of cast iron, and cushion rocky ground with mounds of color and texture. Trained up and over a tall arch, they invite a stroll beneath them to other parts of the garden, and viewed from beneath the open crossbeams of a pergola, a plush awning of blooming climbers and ramblers expands a garden heavenward. The following pages will show you how to exploit the particular attributes of these roses to enhance the landscape.

LOFTY LANDMARKS
The robust rambler 'Albéric Barbier', whose creamy white double blooms emit the scent of apple blossoms, scales a wrought-iron four-legged support, while nearby fiery red 'Dortmund' festoons an identical quadropod. The contrasting towers of red and white emphatically divide the rose bed in this Portland, Oregon, garden from the flat green lawn.

Growing Roses Upward

Most climbing and rambling roses combine the best qualities of their bushier cousins—abundant flowers, fragrance, and ruggedness—with the long, foliage-covered shoots and bloom clusters that characterize vines. But unlike true vines—such as Japanese wisteria, cup-and-saucer vine *(Cobaea scandens),* and climbing hydrangea, to name only a treasured few—these roses are shrubs that need a gardener's assistance to grow to great heights. Because roses do not possess the ability to coil around or cling tenaciously to vertical structures, their canes must be tied or fastened to a support *(pages 78-80).*

Few vines, however, can match the spectacular floral display of climbing and rambling roses. 'Madame Alfred Carrière', whose pink buds open to white cups, 'Cl. Crimson Glory', with shocking

Supports for Roses That Climb

CONTAINER ROSE SUPPORTS

A dome of interwoven loops of seasoned willow shoots, grapevines, and other pliable sapling branches adds an attractive rustic element to a utilitarian container.

TRIPODS AND QUADROPODS

Three-legged tripods and four-legged quadropods —designed of metal or rot-resistant hardwoods, or homemade of poles lashed together—are effective when wrapped or braided with roses.

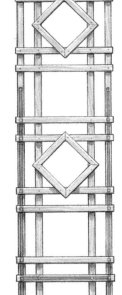

TRELLISES

Freestanding as a screen or attached to a wall, a trellis made of geometrically patterned latticework or fashioned in a more casual freehand design is a versatile support for roses.

WIRE GRIDS

Climbers can be tied to wire grids installed in stone or masonry. Fanning over the wall, the foliage and blooms of the rose hide the network of wire.

FENCES

Sturdy fences of natural or painted wood, wrought iron, and wire mesh ensure privacy, enclose spaces, and define boundaries while offering support for climbers and ramblers.

PERGOLAS

Wood, stone, or brick posts supporting an open-beam or latticework roof transform robust climbers and ramblers into a tunnel of blooms. These handsome architectural features garner immediate attention and should be sited with care to lead to another part of the garden or to frame a sitting area furnishing a shaded haven for relaxation.

ARCHES

As an eye-pleasing gateway into or out of a garden, or outlining a view or defining a path, arches of treated wood or nylon-coated steel support vigorous climbers and ramblers.

A GOOD SPORT
The glossy dark green leaves and blush pink blooms of the climber 'New Dawn' tumble over a gray picket fence in southern California. 'New Dawn', a sport of the lusty climber 'Dr. W. Van Fleet', was awarded the first-ever U.S. plant patent in 1930. Unlike its parent, which blooms just once, 'New Dawn' flowers continuously throughout the growing season.

deep red blooms, and 'New Dawn', with a multitude of delicate apple-blossom pink flowers, are just a few examples of robust climbers that bloom over and over throughout the growing season. The prickly rambler 'Albertine' has so many large salmon pink blooms in early summer that its foliage is virtually hidden, while the robust and nearly thornless 'Veilchenblau' sports a profusion of semidouble violet-blue flowers that fade to a lovely gray-tinged mauve during a burst of glory that lasts up to 4 weeks.

Choosing between Climbers and Ramblers

When selecting a climber or rambler to cover a support, consider the differences between the two types of long-caned roses. Ramblers bloom only once per season, with smallish flowers borne in large clusters. Although some climbers also bloom just once, many others flower repeatedly

during the growing season, and their blooms can be quite large. Climbers also have larger leaves than do ramblers, but their canes are slower growing and generally stiffer and less pliable, making them more difficult to train.

Two traits make ramblers more labor-intensive than climbers. Because ramblers bloom only on new wood produced the previous growing season, they need extensive pruning after flowering. Climbers, on the other hand, need less pruning because even older canes produce the lateral shoots that bear flowers.

Second, although many climbers and ramblers are rugged specimens—winter-hardy to temperatures as low as -5°F—ramblers are prone to mildew, which is exacerbated by poor air movement. For this reason, ramblers are better suited for clambering up and over open, airy structures rather than walls. Their inherent vigor quickly covers arches, pergolas, fences, and freestanding lattices as well as sparsely foliated, deciduous trees with foliage and flowers. Climbers, too, work well

Easy-Care Roses for Training

'Altissimo'	'Madame Alfred
'America'	Carrière'
'Ballerina'	'Marchioness
'Belinda'	of Londonderry'
'Blaze'	'New Dawn'
'Buff Beauty'	'Cl. Pinkie'
'Cl. Cécile Brunner'	'Prosperity'
'Céline Forestier'	'Rêve d'Or'
'Cl. Crimson	'Silver Moon'
Glory'	'Sombreuil'
'Dortmund'	'Cl. Souvenir
'Dublin Bay'	de la Malmaison'
'Handel'	'Cl. The Fairy'
'Joseph's Coat'	'William Baffin'
'Lamarque'	'Will Scarlet'
'Lavender Lassie'	'Zéphirine Droubin'

on these supports, and they tolerate more con-fined situations where there is less air circulation, such as a trellis or wire grid attached to a wall.

Selecting Structural Supports

Covered with roses, an architectural framework adds a great deal of decorative interest to the gar-den. Fences, tripods, trellises, arches, and pergolas are just some of the many supports that can serve as major design features in your garden *(page 35),* shaping and defining space in much the same way that paths, walls, trees, and tall hedges do.

Drape a rose over a fence or train it up a free-standing lattice. Any way you use them, ramblers and climbers soften the hard edges of wood, tim-ber, brick, stone, or metal fencing with their gen-tle curves. Even an ordinary chain-link or steel mesh fence at the perimeter of your property can be a breathtaking sight when it supports a mantle of rose foliage and flowers. Be sure, though, that whatever you choose to cover with roses is con-structed of sturdy materials and solidly anchored. A vigorous rambler or climber will quickly engulf a fence or lattice with weighty canes, causing a weak one to buckle and eventually collapse.

When you choose a rose to cover your fence or lattice, pick one that matches the support's tex-ture and color. Yellow roses, for example, com-plement natural wood, whereas white blooms stand out against paints and stains of forest green. For pink and red roses, a whitewashed picket fence makes an especially cheerful background.

If you want quick coverage, keep in mind that ramblers generally grow faster than climbers. Try 'Tausendschön', whose 3-inch deep pink flowers

Weaving Roses and Vines Together

While slower-growing but more enduring roses wend their way aloft, annual and tender perennial vines sprint up a wall or support, offering nearly instant foliage and color. Once the sturdy rose canes are established, they supply even more support for vines of all sorts. *Lonicera heckrottii* (goldflame honeysuckle), for example, has gracefully coiled itself around a found rose on the leafy, bloom-laden Texas fence shown here.

A classic trio to mantle a trellis or arbor consists of roses, honey-suckle, and clematis, all of which come in a wide assortment of col-ors. White *Clematis* 'Alba Luxuri-ans', the single vivid red flowers of *Rosa* 'Dortmund', and dusky yel-low *Lonicera sempervirens* 'Sul-phurea' create an arresting con-trast of color and flower shape. Or combine orangy *Lonicera sem-pervirens* (trumpet honeysuckle) with the white climber 'Silver Moon' and the huge purple flow-ers of *Clematis* 'Gipsy Queen'. This combination of plants needs sun to bloom profusely, but make sure the roots of the clematis are in shaded, thickly mulched soil.

How to Peg a Rose

Roses that aren't tall enough for trellises or arches but at the same time don't have a pretty, compact shape can achieve full glory in the garden by pegging. To peg a rose, simply arch the canes downward and anchor their tips close to the ground to form low mounds of flowers and foliage that radiate from a central point in half-moon, spiral, and spoke-shaped patterns. Plants with canes between 5 and 7 feet long—such as bourbons and hybrid perpetuals as well as some damasks and centifolias—are ideal candidates. Besides giving the plants an attractive shape, horizontally training their canes alters the distribution of nutrients so that roses bloom at every bud joint rather than just the top one—transforming a thicket of near bare canes into a dazzling sprawl of color.

Choose vigorous canes *that bend easily, and remove any leaf buds at the tips. Arcing it downward, secure one cane to the ground with a 20-inch rustproof, U-shaped pegging staple or long metal hook positioned at a point a few inches from the cane's tip (inset). Keep the cane at least 2 inches above the soil to prevent it from taking root and to allow for air circulation. Peg the other canes in the same way, arranging them in the desired pattern. Prune back unpegged canes to the base of the shrub.*

'John Hopper'

flecked with white grow on thornless canes that extend as far as 10 feet by early summer. There are some vigorous climbers, though, such as 'Altissimo'; this rose has dark gold stamens surrounded by a blood red collar of seven to 10 petals instead of the five petals typical of most single blooms. Another reliable climber for covering a fence or lattice is the popular hybrid tea 'Cl. Etoile de Hollande', whose deep crimson blooms are not only jumbo-sized but are also narcotically fragrant.

Simple Supports

The simplest freestanding support is a tripod or quadropod. These three- and four-legged structures add a strong vertical dimension when situated at the rear of a bed or border. More than one tripod placed side by side or in various geometric configurations anchors a garden design and adds a sense of permanence to the planting. Sited in isolation—at the edge of a lawn, for instance—these roughly conical structures command immediate attention.

For an altogether spectacular effect, plant a different climber at the foot of each tripod leg. In a warm climate—or in a protected setting colder than Zone 6—grow the 4-inch daffodil yellow blooms of 'Golden Showers' up one leg; 'America', whose salmon buds open to coral pink, on the second; and multicolored 'Joseph's Coat' up the third. The latter's yellow blooms diffused with orange and pink will bring together the colors of all three roses in a medley of tints and contrasts.

Grand Supports

More elaborate structures such as arches and pergolas require thoughtful placement in your garden if they are to be used to best advantage. Arches can be used to mark an entranceway or crown a gate; a series of them creates a living, leafy, flowering tunnel called an arbor. Pergolas—open structures with flat, peaked, or curved roofs—can create a shaded walkway or a sanctuary where one sits enveloped in color and scent.

Both arches and pergolas should be at least 8 feet tall and 5 feet wide so that two people can walk side by side through them without brushing against dangling blooms or wayward thorns.

Position these dramatic structures purposively—to form an inviting threshold at a garden entrance, to span a seating area beneath lavish blooms, or to embellish the intersection of paths in your garden.

'American Pillar', a robust rambler with single bright pink white-centered blooms, and *Rosa banksiae lutea* (yellow Lady Banks' Rose), which grows rapidly to 25 feet and bears a wealth of 1-inch lemon yellow double flowers, will swiftly cover an arch or a pergola. If you decide to plant once-blooming ramblers on a pergola, you may want to alternate them with everblooming climbers to prolong the color display. Fast-growing climbers to ascend an arch or the columns of a pergola include the buff yellow 'Rêve d'Or', the sweetly perfumed, pale pink 'Cl. Cécile Brunner', and the buttery white 'Sombreuil', with puffy, cakelike petals arranged in near perfect symmetry.

Attached Supports

You can also send roses to lofty heights by blanketing the walls of your home or other buildings with climbers, using trelliswork and wire grids. Choose walls that face south or west and that bask in direct sunlight most of the day, and when you position the support *(page 80)*, maintain as much as a foot of space between it and the wall to allow adequate air circulation.

Boldly wreathe the window or doorway of a white or gray clapboard house with the crimson-streaked white globular flowers of 'Variegata di Bologna' or the giant smoky red blooms of 'Don Juan'. Bedeck a brick wall with the clear yellow of 'Lawrence Johnston', the lemon-tinted white flowers of 'Lamarque', or the pale pink blooms of disease-resistant 'Dr. W. Van Fleet', which blooms once but grows far more robustly than its silver-pink sport, the everblooming 'New Dawn'.

For a wall of big, voluptuous, ruffled blooms, the old-fashioned bourbon 'Zéphirine Drouhin' is hard to beat. Partner its blowzy pink flowers with rich purple *Clematis* x *jackmanii* (Jackman clematis) for a soothing color harmony *(page 37)*. And peg a few of its thornless plum red canes to the ground in front of the wall to simulate a churning waterfall of pink and purple.

Roses to Carpet the Ground

Besides providing vertical interest, long-caned roses can do horizontal service in your landscape: Certain roses with long, trailing canes become graceful low mounds of flowers and foliage if allowed to sprawl over uneven ground and bare slopes. The single pink, yellow-eyed 'Max Graf', the single white, gold-centered 'Paulii Rosea', and the creamy white 'Sea Foam' form thorny mats with glossy foliage ideal for covering old tree stumps, hiding unsightly humps, and concealing drainage covers and utility lines. Their dense growth smothers weeds and helps control erosion because their canes frequently take root, producing new plants that can later be separated from the parent. Climbing miniatures can also lend their beauty to the landscape in less utilitarian ways. 'Red Cascade', for example, which hugs the ground with glossy foliage and 1-inch brilliant red flower clusters, or two-toned 'Jeanne Lajoie'—pink with a dark pink reverse—makes an ornate edging for a garden path.

SNOW WHITE DRIFTS
The canes of 'White Meidiland' grow to 5 feet, spreading on the ground and forming mounds of large white blooms that sparkle in the sunlight at the edge of this Virginia lawn. Disease resistant and virtually maintenance free, the rose has thick canes that need little pruning and just the occasional deadheading of spent blooms to prolong its pristine beauty.

Roses for Town and Country

Whether your home is an apartment in the city, a sprawling country oasis, or anything in between, opportunities abound for growing the most diminutive members of the rose family. A walled townhouse garden or any backyard deck can host the flawless buds and exquisite colors of miniatures and small polyanthas in containers, where they convey an impression of neat refinement. At the other extreme, roses that reach the grandest proportions—species, large shrubs, hardy rugosas, and the newer landscape varieties with broad, spreading outlines—belong at the wilder fringes of your property.

Portable Roses

Roses in containers impart a spot of color and a waft of sweet perfume in the most unlikely places. And they need not stay put. Even heavy tubs of roses can be moved if they are placed on dollies or have casters. Move outdoor container-bound roses to follow sunlight, bring them inside for decora-

tion, and rearrange groups of them to spotlight the ones in luxuriant bloom and create different color combinations. When working with groups, you'll find they look best when arranged in odd numbers of containers in an assortment of sizes.

A surprising number of roses can be grown in containers, provided the pot is large enough to give the bush sufficient soil to spread its roots. Miniatures, of course—such as the scarlet-tipped lemon yellow 'Rainbow's End' or the creamy apricot 'Loving Touch'—are excellent candidates for window boxes, small terra-cotta pots, or just about any container at least 8 inches deep and wide. Diminutive salmon pink 'Margo Koster' and pure pink 'China Doll', both polyanthas, need larger containers for their mature dimensions, which are slightly greater than 12 inches by 12 inches. Compact damasks and floribundas up to 3 feet tall and wide—such as the fuchsia-red 'Rose de Rescht' and the fleshy pink 'Gruss an Aachen'—need at least a 5-gallon tub, or try planting three of them in a half-barrel to spruce up a corner of your garden.

Let potted roses share their confined space

Roses for Containers

'Cécile Brunner'
'Dreamglo'
'Gabrielle Privat'
'Gruss an Aachen'
'Irresistible'
'Jean Kenneally'
'Kristin'
'La Marne'
'Linville'
'Loving Touch'
'Magic Carrousel'
'Marie Pavié'
'Margo Koster'
'Minnie Pearl'
'Nearly Wild'
'Nozomi'
'Old Blush'
'Paper Doll'
'Perle d'Or'
'Pierrine'
'Rainbow's End'
'Red Cascade'
'Rise 'n' Shine'
'Starina'
'The Fairy'
'White Pet'

'Paper Doll'

with annuals that enhance their appearance. Red and pink *Dianthus deltoides* (maiden pink) flows with quiet elegance over the rim of a white urn planted with the single rosy pink floribunda 'Nearly Wild' or the dainty pink-apricot noisette 'Perle d'Or'. Or use *Lysimachia nummularia* 'Aurea' (golden moneywort), a shallow-rooted annual with 2-inch-high yellow foliage, to add lowlights to the deep orange-red miniature 'Starina', which grows to a compact 12 inches all around.

To illuminate a corner of your patio or deck at night, pair the white flowers of 'Marie Pavié' with tiny *Campanula cochleariifolia* 'Alba'—and place them in front of a wall of deep green ivy to spotlight the planting even more. A basket of 'Red Cascade' suspended above eye level from a beam of your side porch needs no further adornment; the acrobatic dangle of scented deep red blooms will swing in the breeze. In general, contained roses shine brightest when the design is kept simple.

Petite Plantings

Any niche holding more than a half cubic foot of soil can support the smallest of rosebushes. The 2-foot-tall winter-hardy miniature 'Magic Carrousel', for instance, with white flowers edged in rose pink and shiny green leaves, makes a fine addition to an alpine rock garden, where it adds height and summer flowers to a planting typically composed of small spring bloomers. Disease-resistant 'Rise 'n' Shine', with yellow hybrid-tea-like blooms, provides show-stopping color at the edge of a sun deck or around the base of a rural mailbox. Also, the area alongside a brick or flagstone path or an asphalt driveway is ample for an edging of the compact double white flowers and dark green foliage of the polyantha 'White Pet'. When planting small roses in an open area like this, group them to avoid the toylike impression that a single bush can give.

Furnishing the Wild Garden

In contrast to the limited space occupied by miniatures and polyanthas, the far reaches of grassy yards, fields, and meadows, a sunny brink before a

ADDING HEIGHT TO A LOW BORDER
The bright red miniature ground-hugging shrub rose 'Ralph's Creeper' spills over a rocky border in Houston, Texas. 'Kronprinzessin Viktoria', a compact bourbon with satiny white blooms (center), rises above lavender phlox, and the white tea rose 'Puerto Rico' stands tallest at the back of the bed amid irises.

Bountiful blooms of the apricot-gold shrub rose 'Alchymist', single pink 'Complicata', soft pink damask 'Ispahan', a found pink rambler, and milky white 'Alba Semi-plena'—all robust growers—spill off a slatted fence at the fringe of an orchard-grass pasture in Glen Ellen, California.

shaded woodland, and a rolling expanse of seaside dunes are ideal spots for vigorous, self-reliant roses that provide fountainy bursts of color. Lax in habit and rangy of profile, species roses such as the single pink *Rosa eglanteria* and white *R. banksiae banksiae* and old garden roses such as albas, damasks, and centifolias can compete successfully with other shrubs and plantings in harsh conditions for space, light, water, and nutrients.

If you would like a wild garden of American natives, plant the 5-foot-tall but more widely sprawling *R. setigera serena* (nicknamed the prairie rose), which flowers pale pink in early summer after other wild roses have stopped blooming, and combine it with early-flowering *Fothergilla major*

and American beautyberry. The native shrubs may bloom before the prairie rose, but the yellow, orange, and red fall leaves of the fothergilla and the glossy purplish 2-inch bunches of tiny fruits on the beautyberry provide interest long after the roses have faded. Native perennials can bridge the gap between the summer blooms of the prairie rose and the fall foliage and berries of the shrubs.

Grace the edge of any large garden with a combination of 'Madame Hardy', a tough damask with regal swirls of satiny white petals blooming in profusion on graceful 5-foot canes, and 'Fantin-Latour', a centifolia with delicately cupped blooms of soft pink. Mass them in stands of three or more for a billowing, elegant effect.

In regions that are swept by salt air or situated as far north as Zone 4, hybrid rugosas—including mauve-red 'Hansa'; lilac-pink 'Delicata', a vigorous rugosa sporting beautiful hips the size of crab apples; and any of the 'Grootendorst' clan, with pink, red, or white flowers—offer both tenacity and beauty. If creamy white is the color you desire for a large rose, plant the rounded 6-foot-tall alba 'Madame Plantier', hardy to Zone 3. All of these blend into the wilder reaches of your garden.

Recent Introductions

Among the newest hybrids developed to be easy to care for, hardy, and disease resistant, French Meidiland shrub roses strew cushions and hillocks of blooms in white, pink, and scarlet over wide areas. Pink 'Bonica'—the only shrub rose to win the All-America Rose Selections award—makes a gorgeous 4-foot hedge that blooms spring through fall. 'Scarlet Meidiland', which tops out at 3 feet but stretches to 6 or more feet, will transform a slope or overhang a wall, and 2-foot high 'White Meidiland' makes a pretty ground cover of forest green leaves and sparkling white blooms in sunny areas.

Handsome, highly rated 'William Baffin', one of the Explorer Series hybrids from Canada, is the only everblooming climber that is hardy to -20° F. In cold climates festoon a trellis with its 10-foot canes that bear deep pink double blooms. Repeat bloomers 'Carefree Beauty', with sweetly scented 4-inch blossoms of rich pink, and highly perfumed blush pink 'Hawkeye Belle' are especially rugged roses developed by Dr. Griffith Buck at Iowa State University. Use them in abundance to form a disease-resistant 4- to 6-foot hedge around any cold and windy property.

Trouble Spots

Even where your garden seems altogether inhospitable to roses, there are solutions. If, for example, a spot receives morning sun but is partly shaded during the afternoon, or if you live where summer heat and humidity are intense, roses exist that will tolerate these conditions (list, right). If your soil is slightly alkaline, it is best to amend it with sulfur and compost to bring the pH down to 6.5 (page 66). But if these efforts prove futile, the list at right also names a handful of ungrafted roses that will tolerate slightly alkaline soil. When you purchase these roses, check to make sure that they have indeed been grown on their own roots rather than on some less tolerant rootstock.

Roses for Difficult Conditions

PARTIAL SHADE

'Ballerina'
'Belinda'
'Buff Beauty'
'Golden Showers'
'Lavender Lassie'
'Madame Alfred Carrière'
'Nastarana'
'Penelope'
'Cl. Pinkie'
'Prosperity'
R. palustris
'Will Scarlet'

SUMMER HEAT AND HUMIDITY

'Archduke Charles'
'Camaieux'
'Cardinal de Richelieu'
'Catherine Mermet'
'Céline Forestier'
'Complicata'
'Duchesse de Brabant'
'Lamarque'
'Louis Phillipe'
'Madame Alfred Carrière'
'Maman Cochet'
'Monsieur Tillier'
'Mrs. B. R. Cant'
'Mrs. Dudley Cross'
'Mutabilis'
'Nastarana'
'Old Blush'
'Rêve d'Or'
'Rosa Mundi'
R. palustris
'Sombreuil'
'The Fairy'
'Tuscany'

SLIGHTLY ALKALINE SOIL

'Archduke Charles'
'Carefree Beauty'
'Duchesse de Brabant'
'Monsieur Tillier'
'Mutabilis'
'Mrs. B. R. Cant'
'Mrs. Dudley Cross'
'Nearly Wild'
'Old Blush'

Captivating Medleys

Roses are often most enchanting when bolstered by a supporting cast of other plants. Indeed, a garden devoted solely to roses—despite their singular beauty—may strike some gardeners as fussy or even dull. Setting the graceful bloomers among one or more attractive companions, however, can elevate their appeal from merely charming to captivating. A simple evergreen hedge, for example, provides a backdrop that enhances the form and color of any rose in bloom. Likewise, an artistic array of flowering perennials seems to spotlight the presence of roses.

In the gardens featured here and on the following pages, roses share the stage with other plants. But there is no question about which performer receives top billing.

A LAKESIDE SHOWSTOPPER
Set against a misty Virginia lake, the repeat-blooming floribunda 'Betty Prior' shares space in a long perennial border with a stand of bluish Amsonia tabernaemontana, puffs of white Valeriana, and purple Siberian iris.

A BLOSSOMING BARRIER
In this Long Island garden, a mass planting of 32 varieties of roses—including the apricot-colored 'Sweet Juliet', deep yellow 'Graham Thomas', light pink 'La Reine Victoria', and deep pink 'Madame Isaac Pereire'—creates an inviting yet impenetrable hedge. The design is at once powerful and simple: A low row of English box hides the roses' bare legs and helps define the billowing wall of multicolored blooms. At the base of the planting, the small chartreuse flowers of Alchemilla mollis (lady's-mantle) echo the tint of the yellow roses in the hedge, while its large, lobed leaves provide a nice contrast to the foliage of the box and the roses.

TWO TIERS OF FLOWERS AND FOLIAGE
Sharing the spotlight in this Afton, Virginia, garden are five fragrant shrub roses: from left, 'Fair Bianca', 'Heritage', the crimson 'Othello', 'Mary Rose', and 'Gertrude Jekyll'. The mixed-perennial border includes golden Achillea 'Moonshine', the pink grandiflora 'Aquarius', the mauve-colored floribunda 'Angel Face', silvery gray foliage of Perovskia atriplicifolia (Russian sage), and purple Salvia nemorosa (sage). Not to be outshone is the bright red hybrid tea rose 'Mister Lincoln'. The garden, pictured here in May, was designed to have interest from March through November.

CASCADING CANES OF A NATIVE BEAUTY
*Arching gracefully over a quiet pool in this
Texas garden, Rosa palustris—the swamp rose—
provides a striking example of how roses can
enhance a naturalized setting. Unlike other
roses, the swamp rose doesn't mind wet feet;
indeed, it can thrive right at water's edge. Here,
the pool not only reflects the plant's graceful
shape but also serves to display its delicate fallen
petals. R. palustris blooms for 6 weeks or longer
in this garden, emitting a sweet scent when the
buds first open. The rose's pink color is intensi-
fied by juxtaposition with the yellow and green
foliage of the variegated canna. With its dark,
smooth bark, flowing lines, and oval hips that
appear after flowering, the swamp rose provides
four-season interest in the garden.*

FRAMING A FORMAL VIEW
*The glossy dark green leaves and large blush
pink flowers of the vigorous climber 'New Dawn'
adorn a pergola in this elegant Alabama garden. Leading the eye upward, the climber helps
frame the view of the bench beyond, beckoning
visitors to that part of the garden. A low hedge of
Camellia hiemalis sets off the walkway beneath
the pergola, while the bright green foliage of
'Nastarana' adds a lively note to the foreground. A tall Ternstroemia hedge describes the
garden's boundary and provides a handsome
background for the white bench.*

53

AN UNEXPECTED EDGING

Heavy with blooms, the canes of 'Constance Spry', a modern shrub rose, tumble onto a grassy walkway leading through this Sonoma, California, garden. Those strolling along the walkway are slowed by the presumptuous rose, pausing to take note of it and the other plants edging the petal-strewn passage. The stands of deep pink Erysimum 'Bowles' Mauve' and violet-hued Spanish lavender make harmonious color companions for the soft pink rose, and also provide a pleasing contrast in shape and size.

A Guide to the Gardens

A LAKESIDE SHOWSTOPPER

pages 44-45

A. *Sedum x alboroseum 'Medio-variegatus'* (3)
B. *Lathyrus sp.* (1)

C. *Iris sibirica* (14)
D. *Prunus x cistena* (1)
E. *'Betty Prior', floribunda* (1)

F. *Amsonia tabernaemontana* (3)
G. *Valeriana* (5)

A BLOSSOMING BARRIER

pages 46-47

A. *Alchemilla mollis* (10)
B. *Buxus sempervirens 'Suffruticosa'* (12)
C. White: *'Fair Bianca', shrub; 'Madame Hardy', damask; 'Maiden's Blush', hybrid alba.* Pink: *'La Reine Victoria', bourbon; 'Sombreuil', climbing tea; 'White Wings', hybrid tea.* Light pink: *'Alfred de Dalmas', moss; 'Constance Spry', shrub; 'Fantin-Latour', China; 'Félicité Parmentier', alba; 'Heritage',*

shrub; 'Marchesa Boccella', hybrid perpetual; 'Souvenir de la Malmaison', bourbon. Medium pink: *'Cottage Rose', shrub; 'Général Kléber', moss; 'Gertrude Jekyll', shrub; 'Ispahan', damask; 'Madame Louis Lévêque', moss; 'Mary Rose', shrub; 'Paul Neyron', hybrid perpetual.* Mauve: *'Charles de Mills', grandiflora; 'Lilac Rose', shrub; 'William Lobb', moss.* Deep pink: *'Madame Isaac*

Pereire', bourbon. Pink blend: *'English Elegance', shrub; 'Honorine de Brabant', bourbon.* Orange-pink: *'Abraham Darby', shrub.* Apricot: *'Sweet Juliet', shrub.* Yellow: *'The Pilgrim', shrub.* Deep yellow: *'Graham Thomas', shrub.* Medium red: *'Othello', shrub* (31)
D. *'Pierre de Ronsard', large-flowered climber* (1)
E. *Wisteria floribunda 'Rosea'; wisteria floribunda* (2)

**TWO TIERS
OF FLOWERS
AND FOLIAGE**

pages 48-49

A. *Coreopsis verticillata
'Moonbeam'* (3)
B. *Phlox subulata* (1)
C. *Geranium sanguineum
var. prostratum* (1)
D. *Lobelia x gerardii* (1)
E. *Perovskia atriplicifolia* (3)
F. *'Chrysler Imperial', hybrid tea* (1)
G. *Achillea 'Moonshine'* (3)
H. *'Angel Face', floribunda* (1)
I. *Hibiscus syriacus 'Aphrodite'* (1)
J. *'Aquarius', grandiflora* (1)
K. *Lilium Asiatic Hybrids,
mixed* (10)
L. *'Heritage', shrub* (1)

M. *'Fair Bianca', shrub* (1)
N. *'Othello', shrub* (1)
O. *Viburnum x juddii* (5)
P. *'Mary Rose', shrub* (1)
Q. *'Gertrude Jekyll', shrub* (1)
R. *Geranium 'Johnson's Blue'* (1)
S. *Salvia nemorosa* (3)
T. *'Lavender Lace', miniature* (1)
U. *Liriope muscari 'Variegata'* (3)
V. *Echinacea purpurea,
Echinacea 'Alba'* (5)
W. *'Mister Lincoln', hybrid tea* (1)
X. *Antirrhinum majus
'Rocket Red'* (2)

*NOTE: The key lists each plant type and the total quantity needed to replicate the garden shown.
The diagram's letters and numbers refer to the type of plant and the number sited in an area.*

CASCADING CANES OF A NATIVE BEAUTY

pages 50-51

A. *Pontederia cordata* (1)
B. *Canna sp.* (3)
C. *Iris Louisiana Hybrids* (6)
D. *Salvia farinacea* (12)

E. *Rosa palustris* (1)
F. *Lonicera sempervirens* (1)
G. *Myriophyllum aquaticum* (1)

FRAMING A FORMAL VIEW

pages 52-53

A. *'Nastarana', noisette* (2)
B. *Camellia biemalis* (4)
C. *Ophiopogon japonicus* (12)
D. *Vinca rosea* (9)
E. *'White Pet', polyantha* (1)

F. *'New Dawn', large-flowered climber* (8)
G. *Salvia 'Victoria Blue'* (6)
H. *Cycas revoluta* (2)
I. *Ternstroemia sp.* (6)

J. *'American Beauty', hybrid perpetual* (1); *'Reine des Violettes', hybrid perpetual* (1); *'Rosa Mundi', gallica* (1); *'Gruss an Teplitz', bourbon* (1)

NOTE: *The key lists each plant type and the total quantity needed to replicate the garden shown. The diagram's letters and numbers refer to the type of plant and the number sited in an area.*

F(1)

C(2)

B(1)

E(2)

D(1)

A(1)

AN UNEXPECTED EDGING

pages 54-55

A. *Lavandula stoechas* (1)
B. *Cynoglossum amabile* (1)
C. *Erysimum 'Bowles' Mauve'* (2)
D. *Cistus 'Sunset'* (1)
E. *Geranium incanum* (2)
F. *'Constance Spry',*
shrub(1)

CHAPTER THREE

Planting and Culture

Some of the most enduring myths in gardening revolve around growing roses—that it takes a special talent to grow roses, that they attract every pest and disease under the sun, that they need constant feeding and pruning, and on and on. They're enough to scare off the most stalwart gardener. And they're not true.

What it takes to grow robust roses—like the light pink hybrid tea 'Antoine Rivoire' and the cabbagelike medium pink tea 'Mrs. B. R. Cant' filling the front yard of this Independence, Texas, home—is a savvy gardener who knows that preparation is the key. There is no substitute for starting out with healthy, disease-resistant plants that are suitable for your climate and preparing an appropriate planting site for them. From there, if you keep your roses fed and watered, are vigilant about inspecting them for pests and diseases, and prune them when they need it, they will reward your efforts in their own lavish, delightful way.

A. *Verbena sp.* (6)
B. *'Mrs. B. R. Cant' (tea)* (2)
C. *'Antoine Rivoire' (hybrid tea)* (1)
D. *'Duchesse de Brabant' (tea)* (1)
E. *Juniperus scopulorum 'Skyrocket'* (1)
F. *'Bon Silène' (tea)* (1)
G. *'Maréchal Niel' (noisette)* (1)
H. *Phlox divaricata* (6)
I. *Lupinus texensis* (1)

The key lists each plant type and the number of plants needed to replicate the garden shown. The letters and numbers above refer to the type of plant and the number sited in an area.

Selecting the Proper Site and Plants

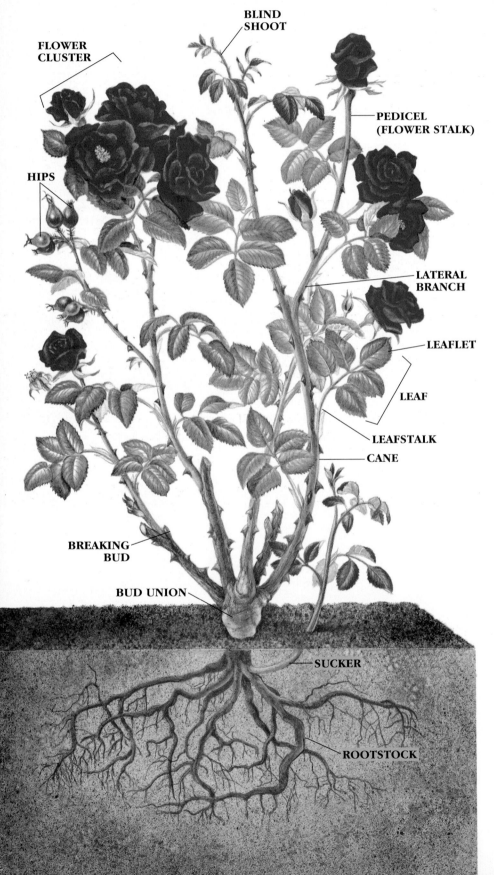

FLOWER CLUSTER

BLIND SHOOT

HIPS

PEDICEL (FLOWER STALK)

LATERAL BRANCH

LEAFLET

LEAF

LEAFSTALK

CANE

BREAKING BUD

BUD UNION

SUCKER

ROOTSTOCK

For all their varied forms, most roses require essentially the same kind of treatment. They need plenty of sun, rich, well-drained soil, and room to breathe. A gardener who understands these basic needs—and who starts off on the right foot with top-quality plants—is well on the way to a successful rose garden.

Roses need at least 5 to 6 hours of sun a day to sustain vigorous, healthy growth. A south-facing site provides the best light, but an eastern exposure also has advantages: The morning sun dries the dew quickly, which is a plus since moisture promotes disease.

Good soil drainage is another must—roses will drown if their roots stand in water. To test how efficiently your soil drains, dig a hole 18 inches deep (the depth of the roots of most rosebushes), fill it with water, and record the time it takes for the hole to drain completely. If water remains after more than an hour, you will need to amend the soil before you plant *(pages 65-68).* Test the soil again once you've enriched it. If drainage is still sluggish, consider building a raised bed for your roses. Not only will a raised bed let you customize the soil, it can also enhance the appearance of your garden.

The third requirement for healthy roses is good air circulation, since plants growing too close together are prone to mildew and other diseases. To encourage a good flow of air, allow adequate space between your rosebushes *(chart, page 66),* as well as between your roses and other plants in the garden. Proper spacing will also help alleviate root competition with existing trees or shrubs and with some deep-rooted perennials, which can rob roses of much-needed water and nutrients.

As you consider spacing and air circulation, also think about exposure to harsh elements like wind.

ANATOMY OF A ROSE

Most roses share the same basic anatomy: Flowers appear singly or in a cluster at the end of a main cane or a lateral branch. A blind shoot is a mature stem that produces leaves—composed of five leaflets—but no flowers. On some roses, spent flowers produce hips. A breaking bud signifies a growth point on a stem from which a branch emerges; pruning cuts are made just above a bud. On most modern roses, a cultivar is budded onto the rootstock of another, more vigorous rose at what is called the bud union. Suckers, which do not share the desirable characteristics of the top growth, often arise from the rootstock.

Roses love a breeze, but hot summer winds and cold winter gusts can dry them out. So avoid planting on high, exposed ground. Likewise, try to stay away from low-lying areas where air can become stagnant; still, moist air can lead to fungal diseases. Such spots also become frost pockets in winter, which can kill even the hardiest roses.

Obviously, you can change neither the climate nor the fundamental lay of the land in your garden. But if you plant your roses along the south wall of your house, for example, they'll have the sunlight they need, some protection from hot afternoon sun, and a barrier against cold north winds. A hedge or fence can also be the perfect windbreak. With forethought and a little ingenuity, you can find or create microclimates in your yard where roses will flourish.

A Guide to Buying Roses

Once you've found the best home for your roses, the next step is to buy them. First, you must decide which ones you wish to grow—the information in this book will help you choose, as will a visit to a nearby public garden, a call to your local rose society, and a conversation with your rose-growing neighbors. Also compare the ratings, described on page 25, for the various roses that arouse your interest. Then you must decide whether you want to purchase bare-root plants by mail order or pick out container-grown plants at a garden center or nursery.

Experts often recommend buying bare-root plants because they are less expensive, the choic-

A STRIKING BALANCE
The exuberance of this California garden belies its careful planning. Planted against a wood fence that offers protection from wind and sets off the plants' varied hues, 'White Delight' and orange-red 'Fragrant Cloud' roses harmonize with a profusion of deep pink phlox (left), white Shasta daisies, purple clematis, and the variegated foliage of geranium (foreground).

A Grading System for Roses

Both bare-root and container-grown roses are evaluated according to strict quality standards and then assigned a rating, or grade, based on the number and diameter of their canes, as well as on the general vitality of the plant. The grading system, established by the American Association of Nurserymen, a nonprofit trade organization, applies only to roses budded onto rootstock. Roses are graded from highest quality to lowest: 1, 1½, or 2. The grade is usually indicated on the plant's label or container; if you order by mail, you will generally find the grade in the nursery catalog.

Experts unanimously recommend buying Grade 1 plants. These roses will grow faster and produce more blooms in the first season than lower-grade roses. To be rated Grade 1, a bare-root plant like the one shown here must be 2 years old when taken from the field. Container-grown roses must have been growing in their container for at least 1 month during the growing season and have been in the container no more than two growing seasons. Both bare-root and container-grown roses must have at least three strong, healthy canes, pruned back to 6 inches or more above the bud union for bare-root plants and 4 inches or more for container-grown roses.

Grade 1 canes must measure at least ⁵⁄₁₆ inch in diameter; canes of polyantha, shrub, and low-growing floribunda roses must have a diameter of ¼ inch or more. The canes should branch no higher than 3 inches above the bud union. Grade 1½ plants will grow well but will take longer to develop. These plants must have two or more strong canes, at least ⁵⁄₁₆ inch in diameter and branched not higher than 3 inches from the bud union. The canes of polyantha, shrub, and low-growing floribunda roses must measure ¼ inch or more. Grade 2 plants must have at least two canes, one of which must be fully developed and at least ⁵⁄₁₆ inch in diameter. The second cane must measure at least ¼ inch. For polyantha, shrub, and low-growing floribunda roses, one cane must be at least ¼ inch in diameter. Use these roses only for mass plantings.

Container-grown roses must also meet a minimum container size. Grade 1 roses must be potted in a container at least 7½ inches high, with a diameter of 7½ inches at the top and 6½ inches at the bottom. For Grades 1½ and 2, the pots must measure at least 6 inches high, with a diameter of 6 inches at the top and 5 inches at the bottom.

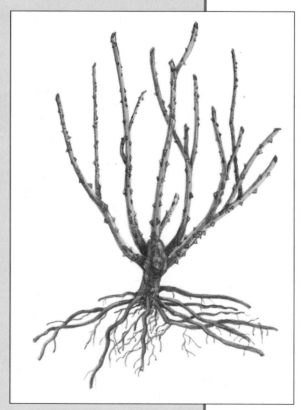

es are greater than with container-grown roses, and most important, they usually have longer roots than their potted cousins. Bare-root plants are taken from the field when they are nearly dormant, stripped of their leaves, and wrapped in moisture-preserving peat moss and plastic. Held in cold storage until they are shipped, bare-root roses must be put into the ground before warm weather starts them growing again or they will die.

When you buy a container-grown rose, on the other hand, the plant is actively growing rather than dormant. This gives you the advantage of being able to evaluate the quality and overall health of your plant before you take it home. Steer clear of a rose potted in a small container: The roots have likely been cut short or simply crammed into the pot. Always deal with a reputable nursery that pots its roses in containers large enough to accommodate long, healthy roots; these roses can happily remain in their pots for an entire growing season. At any time during that period, you can use them as additions or replacements in the garden.

Whether you choose bare-root or container-grown roses, try to make your purchases early in the season so you'll have the greatest possible variety to choose from. And to be sure you get the highest-quality plants, patronize reputable growers who specialize in roses or suppliers recommended to you by seasoned rose gardeners.

As soon as your bare-root plants arrive, unwrap them and look them over. A healthy, top-grade plant will have at least three strong canes and a sturdy root system proportionate to the top growth *(inset, left)*. The bark should be green and healthy, the pith white, and the canes smooth and plump, not dry or shriveled. The plant itself should be well shaped, with no obvious deformities or abnormal swelling, which would indicate disease. If your plant appears damaged, rotted, or diseased, return it for a refund.

If you decide to purchase container-grown roses, make sure that the nursery or garden center has kept its plants cool and moist. Inspect them for signs of damage or disease as you would with bare-root plants, and check the bottom of the container to be sure that the plant is not potbound; there should be no roots protruding from the drainage holes.

Soil Preparation and Planting

Roses grow best in rich, loamy, well-drained, slightly acidic soil that holds water and nutrients well and allows air to reach plant roots. To achieve such a combination, you'll probably need to amend your soil with both organic and inorganic materials. If the overall quality and texture of your soil is generally inferior for growing roses, you'll want to work on the entire bed. If the soil is in good shape, you can focus your attention on the roses' planting holes. Either way, soil preparation takes time, but it can mean the difference between roses that limp along from year to year and those that are long-lived, with lush growth and opulent blossoms.

Using Soil Amendments

There is an array of organic and mineral amendments to help bring your soil to peak condition. To improve drainage in tightly compacted clay soil or help sandy soil retain moisture, incorporate organic materials such as peat moss, leaf mold, ground-bark mulch, well-rotted manure, or compost. As an added bonus, these amendments also provide plant roots with some of the nutrients they need and help keep soil pH in the slightly acid range preferred by roses. Just be sure that any organic mat-

A GAILY BLOOMING BARRIER
With their clusters of pink blossoms dancing at the tips of gently arching stems, 'Ballerina' hybrid musk roses create a lovely informal hedge in this Houston, Texas, garden. The plants are closely spaced to create a continuous line of color but allow enough room for maintenance.

ter you dig into the soil is well decomposed—it should be dark, crumbly, and earthy smelling.

Mineral amendments include gypsum, which helps to loosen heavy clay soils and lower the pH of alkaline soil. Coarse sand, perlite, vermiculite, and pumice are other mineral amendments that improve soil by adding bulk and changing texture. Do not use vermiculite in heavy clay, however, since it tends to absorb and retain water. The amount of mineral amendments you use will depend on your particular soil. Organic material, however, should make up about one-quarter of your total soil volume.

Roses prefer a pH level of around 6.5. To determine the pH level of your soil, you can pick up an inexpensive testing kit at any garden center. Or, for a more detailed analysis, take a soil sample to your local Cooperative Extension Service or to a private laboratory. Either way, aim to test and amend the soil a few months before putting your roses into the ground—in the late fall before spring planting, for example—so that the pH balance has a chance to adjust properly.

If your soil is too acidic, you can raise the pH by adding dolomitic limestone. Work it into the top 6 inches of soil and then water. Your soil type will dictate how much lime to apply—sandy soils generally require the least amount of lime to raise the pH level by one point; clayey soils need more. Since too much lime can burn tender roots, start out cautiously, digging in no more than 5 pounds of lime per 100 square feet of area. Then wait a month or so before retesting your soil and adding more lime, if needed.

To lower the pH of alkaline soil, dig in iron sulfate, ground sulfur, or gypsum, following package directions. Use a maximum of 2 pounds per 100 square feet per application, then wait a month and retest. Experts recommend lowering or raising your soil's pH level no more than one point per year. Since extremely alkaline soil can be difficult to alter, you may want to consider growing your roses in raised beds or containers as an alternative.

SPACING BETWEEN ROSES

Type of Rose	Planting Distance
Miniatures	1–1½ ft.
Hybrid Tea, Grandiflora, & Floribunda Bushes *Compact and average varieties*	2–2½ ft.
Hybrid Tea, Grandiflora, & Floribunda Bushes *Tall varieties*	2½–3 ft.
Low-Growing Shrubs	3–4 ft.
Standards	4 ft.
Shrubs	4–6 ft. or half of expected height
Climbers & Ramblers *Trained horizontally*	8–10 ft.

Spacing for a Lush Hedge

To achieve the lushest possible effect with medium-sized hedges (3 to 5 feet tall), *plant your roses in staggered rows. Although the size and growth habits of your particular variety should determine the distance to be kept between plants, if you aim for 1½ to 2 feet of space, you will create a dense feel and still have enough room between the plants to perform maintenance chores.*

Preparing the Rose Bed

Gardeners once believed that planting new roses in a bed where other roses had grown would result in "rose sickness"—reduced vigor caused by the depletion of trace elements in the soil or vestiges of root diseases left in the soil by the old plants. Experts now agree that as long as the soil is amended to replenish nutrients or replaced if there has been disease in a particular spot, there's no reason to avoid repeated plantings in the same bed.

To ready a bed for planting, begin by removing any existing sod. Then, with a hoe, dig about 16 inches down into the soil, removing any large rocks. If you're willing to spend extra time with the soil, consider double digging. This involves digging up and removing to a wheelbarrow or garden cart a layer of topsoil about 12 inches deep, then breaking up and amending to an equal depth the layer of subsoil beneath it. The topsoil is then amended and replaced in the bed. For a large area, work in adjacent trenches about a foot wide.

Whether or not you double dig, mix and add all of your amendments during the digging phase. This is also the best time to add bone meal or another source of phosphorus—at 3 to 4 pounds per 100 square feet—to promote healthy root growth. Unlike the other major nutrients, phosphorus is

Planting a Bare-Root Rose

Before planting your bare-root rose, do the following: Rinse the plant under a hard stream of water from a garden hose to clean off any bacteria or fungal spores. Then immerse the rose in a bucket of water for at least 1 hour and no more than 24 hours to replenish the plant's moisture. Never leave the rose soaking more than a day, or the plant may die. Using a pair of sharp shears, prune off any broken or injured roots just above the point of the injury, and cut back any canes that are damaged or are the diameter of a pencil or less. Set the plant aside, keeping it in water until you are ready to transfer it to the planting hole.

1. Dig a planting hole at least as wide and as deep as the spread of the plant's roots. *If you haven't already prepared the soil, add the necessary amendments to the soil removed from the hole. Next, return enough of the improved soil to the hole to form a cone-shaped mound; this will serve as a support for the plant.*

2. Lay a spade across the hole to mark ground level, *then set the plant on top of the mound, spreading its roots out evenly all around. Allowing for changes as the soil settles, adjust the height of the mound so that the plant's bud union will be just above ground level in climates where temperatures do not drop below 20°F, or 1 to 2 inches below ground level in colder climates.*

3. Fill the hole about halfway with soil *and tamp it down gently with your hands; this removes air pockets around the roots. Fill the hole with water and allow it to drain. Then fill the hole to the top with soil and water once more. Check to see that the bud union remains at the proper level; if not, add or remove soil as necessary.*

4. Mound additional soil around the bottom of the plant *and up to within 3 inches of the tops of the canes; this will keep them from drying out while the plant is getting established. Check every 2 to 3 days for new growth. When buds sprout, usually after about 2 weeks, gradually and gently remove the soil mound with water from a garden hose or with your fingers. Loosen the plant's nametag so that it does not constrict the cane as it grows.*

Planting a Container-Grown Rose

A container-grown rose can be planted any time from early spring to midfall, as long as the ground is not frozen or waterlogged and the plant has enough time to establish itself before frost occurs. Choose a day that is overcast, with no wind or direct sun to dry canes and roots. If you must plant on a sunny day, wait until late afternoon to spare the plant the midday sun. If the rose has been sitting in a sunny location while waiting its turn for planting, this precaution is unnecessary.

1. Dig a hole slightly wider than the container and, *if your soil has been prepared, of equal depth. If the soil is unprepared, dig 6 inches deeper and add amendments to the removed soil; return about 6 inches of soil to the hole. Then loosen the plant from the sides of its container by gently inserting a trowel in a few places around the pot. Take care not to disturb the roots.*

2. Support the plant at its base and invert the container to slide it out; *if the plant won't slide out on its own, press on the bottom of the container, or carefully cut away the pot from around the plant. Keeping the soil intact and without disturbing the roots, position the plant in the hole.*

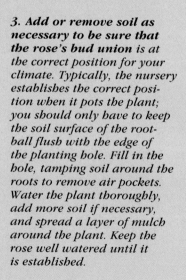

3. Add or remove soil as necessary to be sure that the rose's bud union *is at the correct position for your climate. Typically, the nursery establishes the correct position when it pots the plant; you should only have to keep the soil surface of the rootball flush with the edge of the planting hole. Fill in the hole, tamping soil around the roots to remove air pockets. Water the plant thoroughly, add more soil if necessary, and spread a layer of mulch around the plant. Keep the rose well watered until it is established.*

difficult to supply to roots once plants are established. You can also include a granular fertilizer if you are preparing the bed about a month before planting; the idle weeks before you plant will give the fertilizer time to blend with the soil *(page 71).*

Spacing Your Plants

Spacing between rose plants is determined by climate, growth habits, and the visual effect you want to achieve *(chart, page 66).* However, a few rules always apply. Most important, never crowd your plants. Crowding hampers air circulation and makes it more difficult for you to get between your plants to tend them. Second, arrange plants so you can avoid as much as possible having to step into the bed; walking on the bed compacts the soil.

When to Plant

The climate in your area and whether your rose is bare-root or container grown will determine the best time for planting. Ideally, bare-root roses should be planted as soon as you receive them—in late winter in areas where temperatures remain above freezing year round; in early spring or late fall where winter temperatures remain above 0° F; and in midspring where winters are extremely cold. Before you plant, make sure all danger of hard frost has passed and that the ground is neither hard or frozen nor soggy and waterlogged. Container-grown roses may be planted anytime from early spring to midfall. If you plant during hot weather, however, be sure to keep the rose well watered for the first 6 weeks.

If you intend to plant your bare-root roses within a few days of receiving them, keep them in their shipping materials and place them in an unheated but frostproof location, such as a garage or shed. But if it will be 2 weeks or more before you plant, you must heel the roses in. Dig a shallow V-shaped trench, lay the plants side by side in the trench, and add just enough moist soil to cover the roots. This will insulate the plants and keep them from becoming dehydrated. If you must wait awhile before planting container-grown roses, keep them in a warm, sunny spot out of the wind, and keep the soil moist.

The Care and Maintenance of Roses

There are certain maintenance tasks that all plants require, and roses present no exception. Watering, mulching, weeding, and feeding will help keep your roses productive, as will trimming off faded flowers. And by keeping up proper maintenance throughout the year, the need for chemical intervention will be minimal (below, right).

Watering

Roses are thirsty plants. They need at least an inch of water each week during the growing season, and at the height of summer—when roses are in full flower and the days are at their hottest—your plants may need an inch of water every other day. If you live in an area of ample regular rainfall, you may not have to supplement it. In most regions, however, intervention with a hose is necessary.

Check the moisture level of your soil every few days, and more often during spells of high heat; check frequently, too, if your soil is on the sandy side and drains quickly. When the soil is completely dry an inch or two below the surface, it's time to water. When you do, water to a depth of 15 to 18 inches. The deeper you water, the deeper the roots will grow, which makes for healthy, strong, drought-resistant roses. A soaker hose is ideal for supplying a slow, steady flow of water just where you want it. You can also use a hand-held hose or a sprinkler, as long as you keep it on long enough for the water to reach the correct depth. Morning is the best time to water. In the midday sun, you'll lose water to evaporation, and if you leave the task for the afternoon or evening, foliage may stay wet overnight, which invites fungus to grow.

Roses growing in containers dry out more quickly than those in the ground and will need to be watered more often. Check the soil daily when the weather is particularly hot or windy.

Mulching and Weeding

During the growing season, a protective layer of mulch keeps roses cool and moist. It insulates the soil against summer's soaring temperatures and reduces the evaporation of moisture. Mulch also keeps mud—and any soil-borne disease organisms—from splashing up on your plants during watering and helps control the growth of weeds.

When choosing a mulch, it pays to go organic. As natural materials such as shredded bark, leaf mold, compost, well-rotted manure, and pine needles break down, they release nutrients into the soil, improving its structure and drainage. If you use fresh woodchips or sawdust, however, you'll need to add extra nitrogen to the soil since these materials consume it as they decompose. Avoid using sphagnum peat moss altogether, as it forms a thick, impenetrable crust over the soil.

Spread 2 to 4 inches of mulch around the plants, keeping it a couple of inches away from the canes themselves to avoid rot. In areas where summer temperatures reach 90° F or higher, apply the mulch in early spring to keep the soil temperature

---

TIPS FROM THE PROS

Using Chemicals to Control Disease and Pests

"Selecting the proper rose and keeping it culturally happy will all but eliminate the need for chemicals," says the Antique Rose Emporium's Mike Shoup. However, high humidity, steady rainfall, or drought—conditions beyond your control—can sometimes take their toll on even ideally situated plants, opening the door for black spot, mildew, rust, or a host of insects. When this happens, you may be tempted to spray an arsenal of fungicides and pesticides on your plants.

Use great care. Toxic chemicals are hard on the environment and on you. In fact, even the few remaining legal fungicides are currently under review by the Environmental Protection Agency and may soon be banned because of their harmful ecological effects. "First try organic materials like Safer's soap and light oils as sprays, rather than the stronger chemicals," counsels Peter Har-

ing of the American Rose Society. "And some rosarians use ladybugs and other insect predators to control pests." Shoup agrees, recommending that at the first sign of black spot or mildew gardeners spray their roses once a week for 3 weeks with a solution of 1 tablespoon baking soda and 1 teaspoon vegetable oil (or ¼ teaspoon horticultural oil) to 1 gallon of water (pages 86-91).

If you absolutely must use chemicals, identify the problem accurately—with help from your local Cooperative Extension Service—and treat it specifically. Follow all directions on the label to the letter. Familiarize yourself with the dangers of the product, and wear protective clothing, eye protection, and a face mask. Spray on a windless day, early in the morning after the dew (which can dilute the product) has evaporated and before the sun is at its hottest.

moderate. Also, you'll have fewer fungus problems as the season progresses, because the mulch blankets organisms in the soil before they become active. Where the growing season is short and cool—Zone 5 and colder—you'll also need to spread a layer of light mulch, such as straw, hay, or leaves, as protection during the winter *(page 77)*. Remove it in late spring and give the soil a chance to warm up before you apply your growing-season mulch.

As your plants begin to grow in spring, so too may the weeds. If a stubborn few happen to poke through your protective blanket of mulch, eliminate them the old-fashioned way: Pull them by hand or use a hand cultivator as soon as you see them emerge—while they are still easy to remove and before they have time to set seed.

Fertilizing

Although an organic mulch will deliver essential nutrients to your rose plants as it decomposes, it won't do the whole job. The simplest way to boost a rose's diet—and possibly the most reliable in terms of delivering a complete range of nutrients—is to use a commercial fertilizer sold as a "rose food." These dry, granular products contain a combination of natural organic materials, which break down over time and have the long-term benefit of nourishing the soil, and inorganic chemicals, which make nutrients immediately available to the plant.

Dry fertilizers are worked into the soil as shown opposite. Follow the package directions precisely when measuring the product. In general, you'll want to feed your roses before they come out of dormancy in the early spring and again about 2 months before the first expected frost date. In warm climates where frost isn't a threat, though, you can feed your plants late in the season for a burst of autumn bloom.

Give roses that bloom repeatedly an additional dose of fertilizer after their first bloom cycle. If you want to grow the largest blooms possible on repeat-blooming modern roses, you may fertilize every month during the growing season, up to the

frost cutoff date. Check the fertilizer label, however, for instructions on when and how often to apply a specific product. Some fertilizers are slow-release formulas that work for longer periods in the soil and should be applied less often.

Roses growing in containers will need more frequent feeding than plants in the ground because the near daily watering they require tends to leach nutrients away from the soil. Your best bet with these plants is to cut the recommended dosage of rose food in half and apply it twice as often. You may also use an appropriate liquid fertilizer—a complete chemical formula mixed with water and typically applied every 2 weeks.

Disbudding and Deadheading

You can further enhance your display of roses if you regularly perform two minor pruning tasks—disbudding and deadheading—on certain types of roses throughout the bloom period.

Disbudding is simply removing certain buds as they sprout so that other buds will produce bigger blooms. For exhibition-size blooms on hybrid teas and grandifloras, pinch off any buds that sprout below the top, or terminal, bud *(above, right)*. Do this when the buds are tiny, because later disbudding will leave black scars on the stem.

On floribundas and miniatures, which produce clusters of blossoms, pinch off the terminal, or central, bud in a cluster. Ordinarily, the terminal bud blooms first, then fades and leaves a hole in the cluster just as the adjacent buds are opening up. For prettier sprays that bloom together, remove the terminal bud as early as possible. The other blooms will fill in the space and be more uniform in size. Disbudding is not necessary for old garden roses, shrub roses, species roses, climbers, and polyanthas.

While disbudding encourages buds to open into the prettiest blooms, deadheading—cutting away spent flowers—stimulates hybrid teas, grandifloras, floribundas, and repeat-blooming climbers to produce another round of flowers. It also keeps the plants looking their most attractive. Cut away the old blooms throughout the growing season *(above, right)*, stopping several weeks before the first frost—you don't want to promote any new growth that would be vulnerable to the cold. Species, old garden, and shrub roses, as well as climbers that bloom once per season, don't need this treatment.

Encouraging the Most Beautiful Blooms

By disbudding, deadheading, and fertilizing your roses, you can spur them to produce abundant blooms that are even more gorgeous than usual. Removing certain buds affects the size or proportion of remaining buds and the flowers that follow; deadheading stimulates the plant to bloom again sooner than it otherwise would. A good diet ensures that the plant has the nutrients it needs to put on a spectacular show.

DISBUDDING *Grasp the cane securely and with your fingers gently pinch off all buds that sprout on the sides of the cane (right). Do this as soon as these lateral buds appear. If the rose is a type that produces clusters of blooms, pinch off the terminal, or center, bud to get blooms of equal size in the spray.*

DEADHEADING *After a bloom has passed its peak, use a clean pair of pruning shears to cut the stem and remove the flower. Make the cut at a 45° angle on the cane, ¼ inch above the highest outward-facing leaf bearing five leaflets (left). The dormant bud seated on the cane at the base of the leaf will grow into a new shoot and produce a bloom within 6 weeks.*

FEEDING *Water the soil thoroughly around the plant. The next day, measure an appropriate fertilizer according to the package directions, pull the mulch away from the plant to expose the soil, and sprinkle the fertilizer around the drip line—the area beneath the outermost leaves. Use a trowel to dig the food into the top 2 inches of soil (right). Last, sprinkle the soil with water to dissolve the nutrients and start them seeping into the soil.*

Pruning Your Roses

Pruning is a necessary chore for many plants, roses above all others. Sooner or later, any unpruned rose—even a species or low-maintenance shrub rose—will grow lanky, and flower production will gradually diminish as older canes become exhausted. Neglected, unpruned roses are also more vulnerable to pests and diseases, and can eventually die if left untended. Pruning not only protects the plant's health, it also encourages strong root development and stimulates growth. Well-trimmed plants are attractively shaped, their flowers are bigger and more abundant, and their canes are stronger and more vigorous.

What to Prune Away

How and when roses are pruned varies according to the type of rose in your garden, the growth habits you hope to encourage, and where you live. But there are some general approaches to pruning you'll need to know before tackling your particular plants. First, you should examine the base of the rose for suckers—canes growing up from the rootstock, below the bud union. If left unchecked, these can overwhelm and eventually kill the grafted cultivar. Clipping them off at ground level is an exercise in frustration, however; they will only grow back. You must remove them as close to the bud union as possible.

Next, look for dead, diseased, and damaged canes; they will appear blackened and withered. Cut the canes back to healthy white or pale green pith, or back to the bud union if no healthy tissue is visible. It is also a good rule of thumb to remove any cane thinner than a pencil, including small, twiggy shoots with fewer than five leaves; if they appear too weak to support blossoms, remove them. Canes growing in awkward directions—into the center of the plant or into tangles where they will rub against each other and become damaged—are also candidates for pruning. Cutting

Roses That Need Little Pruning

'Ballerina'
'Belle Poitevine'
'Blanc Double
    de Coubert'
'Bonica'
'Boule de Neige'
''Erfurt'
'Frau Dagmar
    Hartopp'
'Gabrielle Privat'
'Hansa'
'Henry Hudson'
'Jens Munk'
'La Marne'
'Linda Campbell'
'Max Graf'
'Mrs. B. R. Cant'
'Nearly Wild'
'Nozomi'
'Pinkie'
'Red Cascade'
R. banksiae
    banksiae
R. palustris
'Roseraie de l'Hay'
'Sea Foam'
'The Fairy'
'Thérèse Bugnet'
'White Meidiland'

'Hansa'

Pruning a Hardy Rose

Hardy roses include such old garden varieties as damasks, gallicas, centifolias, albas, and mosses, as well as shrub roses and some species roses. These tend to be robust plants that require less pruning and care in general. Nevertheless, all hardy roses benefit from a spring cleanup that includes trimming away dead, diseased, or damaged canes; canes too thin and weak to support flowers; and any crossing canes or canes growing into the center of the plant. Hardy roses benefit as well from an overall shaping to improve the appearance of the plant. Pruning all the longer canes back by one-third will give the bush a well-tended, healthy look; it will also promote outward growth and abundant blossoms. Make the cuts in late spring, after the rose has flowered.

A. *Cut off dead canes and those more than 4 years old* at the bud union (left). Cut back diseased or damaged canes to healthy wood ¼ inch above an outward-facing bud, or, if there is no healthy tissue, to the bud union. Use loppers for canes over ½ inch in diameter and make clean, angled cuts.

B. *When two canes are entangled* or rubbing against each other, cut away the smaller of the two. Prune below the point of contact and about ¼ inch above an outward-facing bud; this will direct new growth away from the center of the plant.

C. *Cut spindly stems that are too weak* to support blossoms—generally those thinner than a pencil—back to a junction with a larger, healthier cane.

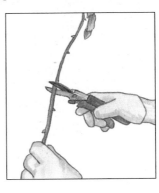

D. *To give the plant an overall full, rounded shape,* cut off one-third of the overall length of the longer canes. Cut off the tips of all other canes to stimulate growth.

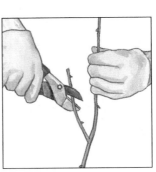

E. *To increase plant fullness* and encourage the production of more blossoms, cut lateral growth down to an outward-facing bud, pruning as much as one-third of the length of the cane.

How to Remove Suckers

Suckers—those canes that sprout from the rootstock below the bud union—are aptly named since they drain energy from the rootstock and can overcome and kill the cultivar if they are not removed. You can easily identify suckers: They are thinner and paler than the cultivar and display a different leaflet pattern. Do not cut suckers off at ground level, as this stimulates growth just as pruning does. Instead, dig gently down to where the sucker attaches to the rootstock and pull it away, taking care not to disturb the plant.

them away will not only improve the appearance of the rose and avoid further injury to canes, it will also open up the center of the plant to air and light, which will help prevent disease.

How Much to Prune

Once the initial pruning of unwanted wood is complete, further cuts are usually made to stimulate growth, or to give your rose an overall shaping. Shaping typically takes the form of light, moderate, or hard pruning.

Light pruning, usually performed on old garden, species, and shrub roses, involves cutting back the ends of most canes by no more than one-third. In fact, some gardeners cut away just the tips of canes on species roses and low-maintenance shrubs. Grandifloras and floribundas should also receive this type of light pruning if abundant blooms are desired. But if your species

Pruning a Modern Rose

1. Cut off dead canes and those more than 4 years old at the bud union. *Cut back diseased or damaged canes to healthy white or pale green pith (inset), or, if no healthy tissue can be found, to the bud union. Next, remove canes that are crossed and those smaller than a pencil in diameter. Thin out any canes growing toward the center of the plant. Make all cuts at a 45° angle ¼ inch above an outward-facing bud.*

2. Decide whether you wish to do moderate or hard pruning. *If hard pruning is your goal, remove all but three or four healthy canes, leaving them no more than a foot long (below). This will yield large, show-type blooms. For moderate pruning, leave six to 12 canes at about one-third of their original height, or 1 to 2 feet. This will produce abundant, slightly smaller blooms and a fuller rosebush. In deciding how to prune, remember that modern roses with an upright habit look best if pruned to an urn shape, with canes growing evenly outward and upward.*

and shrub roses begin to grow leggy under this regimen, prune some of the main canes back by one-third and the rest back by about two-thirds to bring them back to a healthier, fuller shape.

Moderate pruning is generally practiced on modern roses with an upright habit and where a larger, fuller plant is desired. Remove all but six to 12 canes, and cut back the remaining canes to a length of 1 to 2 feet. Practice moderate pruning if you are inexperienced or unsure about the growth habits of your roses. Severe, or hard, pruning is practiced on hybrid teas and grandifloras when show-quality blooms are desired. In this case, all but two to four canes are removed; those left should be cut to a length of between 6 and 12 inches, or up to 18 inches with grandifloras. In northern climates, where roses can be badly damaged during the winter, plants may need hard pruning in spring. In milder climates, hard pruning may restore a weakened, neglected plant to health.

Making a Cut

Before making a cut, look for a healthy bud that is just beginning to swell and that faces in the direction in which you want the new shoot to grow. Generally this will be facing outward on the cane, but in some cases you may wish to encourage growth toward the center of a leggy, spreading plant. Make a clean, sharp cut at a 45° angle ¼ inch above, and in the same direction as, the bud. The angled cut ensures that rainwater will run off the stem rather than collect as it would in a flat cut. And some experts believe that such a cut, by exposing more of the cane to the air, will help it heal more quickly.

Tools for Pruning

You will need three cutting tools for pruning roses: pruning shears, long-handled loppers, and a pruning saw. Bypass pruning shears, which have curved, scissor-action blades, are the best for all-purpose work such as removing canes, flowers, and leaves. Avoid anvil shears, which have a straight blade that strikes against a blunt surface: They can crush delicate rose canes and leave them vulnerable to pests and diseases. Anvil shears should be used only on wood that is completely dead.

Long-handled loppers have short, heavy-duty blades useful for cutting canes that are too thick for pruning shears, or that are difficult to reach. For woody canes that are too thick even for lop-

Pruning Climbers and Ramblers

To prune ramblers and once-blooming climbers, *wait till after they flower so as not to remove potential flowering buds. Cut off old, woody canes at the bud union (above), and remove all weak, diseased, or overlong canes. Cut flowering shoots back to four or five sets of leaves.*

Prune repeat-blooming climbers while they are dormant, *in late winter or early spring. Remove suckers; dead, diseased, or damaged canes; and weak new growth. Prune out the oldest canes, keeping three or four vigorous young canes; trim these back to promote even distribution of buds. If you tie long young canes horizontally to a support, pointing their ends downward, you will encourage lateral growth and more blooms.*

pers, use a pruning saw with large teeth and a long, thin, curved blade.

Keep all of your pruning tools sharp and clean. Dull blades make jagged cuts and can even tear the canes, creating entry points for infestation. Disinfect pruning tools after each use with rubbing alcohol or a solution made from 1 part household bleach to 9 parts water.

As important as the right tools for the job are the right clothes. Be sure to wear gloves—thick leather ones are best—so that you can grasp thorny stems properly to make the cleanest cuts. And when you need to reach into the spiky interior of a plant, you'll appreciate having on long sleeves and pants.

The Right Time of Year to Prune

In general, the best time to prune is just as the plant's dormancy period ends—when you see buds beginning to swell on the plant but before active growth has begun. In mild climates, dormancy may end in late winter—as early as January—or in early spring; in locations with severely cold winters you may have to wait until April. In any event, you must be sure the threat of a late freeze has passed. Some gardeners wait to prune their roses until forsythia is in bloom.

The timing and extent of pruning is also determined by the type of roses in your garden. Hybrid tea roses, grandifloras, floribundas, miniatures, and standard roses should all receive a hard pruning in early spring before the onset of new growth. Since these roses bloom on new wood, pruning is necessary to stimulate the growth of new canes and ensure an abundance of blooms. Old garden roses and shrub and species roses may require no more than a hygienic pruning in spring to remove dead, diseased, or damaged canes. If the plants have become unshapely, however, wait until after their flowers have faded to prune them back within bounds. There are exceptions to this rule: Hybrid perpetuals, hybrid musks, noisettes, Chinas, repeat-blooming damasks and portlands, old garden tea roses, and moss roses bloom on new wood, so if they require shaping up, it should be done in early spring.

Ramblers and once-flowering climbers bloom on year-old growth, so early-spring pruning should involve nothing more than the removal of dead wood. Wait until the plants have finished blooming to perform any shaping that needs to be done. Prune repeat-blooming climbers while they are dormant—in late winter or early spring.

After spring pruning is finished, keep your plants well watered. Pruning induces new growth, and water is crucial to maintaining it.

In summer, deadheading is all that's necessary. But if you are cutting roses for flower arrangements, make the same type of cut you use when pruning—angled, and ¼ inch above a bud. Stop deadheading and cutting blooms a month before the first expected frost to avoid winterkill of new growth.

Fall pruning is undesirable in most climates, except to cut back excessively long canes. But where winter temperatures drop to between 10° and 15°F for as long as 2 weeks at a time, hybrid roses will need pruning after the first frost. Cut the plant down to three to six canes, and shorten each to 1 to 2 feet. You should also take extra precautions to protect the rosebushes from extreme cold *(page 77)*.

Pruning a Standard Rose

Begin pruning a standard, or tree, rose by removing suckers, which in this case grow not only from the rootstock but along the trunk. Pull them from the rootstock, and cut them as close as possible from the trunk. Remove undesirable canes, twiggy stems, and canes that rub or grow into the plant center (right). Next, depending on the cultivar, trim to produce either a round, symmetrical shape or a loose, cascading one. Aim for even spacing and uniform cane length, leaving four to six canes pruned to about 12 inches (far right). Prune only to outward-facing buds.

Winter Protection

In late summer to midfall, reduce watering and stop deadheading and applying nitrogen fertilizers, both of which spur new growth. Where temperatures drop to between 10° and 15°F for 2 weeks at a time, you can protect most roses by heaping material around the plant's base *(far right)*. Where temperatures drop below zero, bury the entire plant *(below);* this is especially important for tree roses. To insulate climbers, remove them from their support and tie the canes loosely with twine. Dig a trench, lay the canes in it, and cover with soil and organic mulch. Add more mulch after the ground freezes. Do not start winter protection too soon; the increased warmth may produce new growth that will be hurt by a sudden chill.

1. After the first frost, cut back all canes to 1 to 2 feet. This helps the plant conserve energy and eliminates the parts that are the weakest and likeliest to suffer damage in a freeze. It also eliminates the possibility of injury caused by canes whipping against each other in the wind.

2. In climates where winter temperatures drop periodically into the teens or go as low as 10° to 15°F for 2 weeks at a stretch, surround rosebushes with imported soil, mulch, or leaves. Pile the insulating material up around the plant and between the canes to a height of 6 to 12 inches above the bud union. Then spread a layer of straw, loose leaves, peat moss, or ground bark over the mound.

4. Next, fill the cage to the top with leaves, straw, or ground bark. Make sure not to pack the insulating material too tightly; wet, matted leaves can harbor disease. Avoid removing the cages too early at winter's end—a late-spring freeze can be fatal to a newly exposed rose. After the last freeze, gently remove the leaves or straw and carefully scrape away the earth mound covering the canes. Rinse the canes with a light spray of water.

3. If winter temperatures regularly drop below 0°F, or if extended frigid weather is predicted, mound soil around the base of the plant to a height of 6 to 12 inches above the bud union. Then form a cage from chicken wire or tar paper stapled together, and place it around your rose. To secure the cage, pack another few inches of earth around its base.

Training Climbers and Ramblers

Climbers and ramblers add a delightful vertical dimension to any garden. They must be trained to accomplish this effect, however, since roses will not naturally twist around a support or send out tendrils as do vines. The task can be as uncomplicated as coaxing the plants to drape over an existing fence or wall in your garden. Or you may choose to build a freestanding support, such as an arch, pergola, trellis, pillar, or tripod, and train your roses to adorn it.

Be sure to select a rose that will not only bloom when you want it to but will also be able to adapt to the kind of support you have in mind. Climbers have thick, sturdy canes; the canes of ramblers are more pliable and thus may be easier to train to some supports. But ramblers bloom only once a season and are vulnerable to mildew, whereas many climbers bloom all summer and rarely have mildew problems.

No matter what rose variety and type of support you decide on, remember that most rose canes that are left to grow upward produce flowers only at their tips. Canes that are bent to grow horizontally, however, will produce flowers all along their length. So when you arrange your twining roses, you can trick nature into producing the fullest possible display of blooms by training a number of canes to grow laterally.

Materials for Supports

Choose support structures made of hardwoods such as cedar, black locust, redwood, cypress, and hickory. Avoid softwoods, which will rot after a few years. Metal is also appropriate for most supports; it is more durable than wood and never requires painting. Just be sure you use sturdy, galvanized metal, which won't rust. Anchor the supports deeply and securely in the ground. You can provide stability for the wood by setting the bottoms of the supports in concrete below ground level or by inserting the ends into hollow metal pipes driven into the earth.

Securing the Canes

Plant the rose about 16 to 18 inches from the support, and begin training the canes right away. Use materials that stretch, such as green plastic stretch ties, vinyl gardener's tape, or nylon hosiery, to secure the canes. You can use raffia or soft twine, but if you do, check the ties periodically to see if they

Training Climbers on a Vertical Support

Beginning about 2 feet from the ground, hammer U-shaped construction staples partway into the wood at about 4-foot intervals along the support. Next, wrap the canes around the support in an ascending spiral pattern, keeping them in a horizontal position as much as possible so that they will produce a greater display of blooms than they would if kept in their natural, or upright, position. Tie the canes loosely to the staples as you come to them, using either a figure-eight loop or a double loop (page 80). Once the main shoots reach the top of the support, you can either secure them there with more staples or allow them to drape over the top.

need loosening. Never use twist ties or any other form of wire—it will cut into the canes. Always secure canes loosely to their supports so that as they grow and thicken they won't be constricted.

To keep canes from rubbing and chafing against their supports in the wind, attach ties in a figure-eight or double-loop configuration *(below)* so that the tie, not the cane, is in contact with the support. Never weave canes in and out of narrow spaces in fences, lattices, or trellises; if you do, the canes will be nearly impossible to extricate for pruning or removal once they are fully grown.

Roses on Solid Surfaces

To train roses to grow on walls, you can either drive U-shaped construction staples into the mortar between bricks or stones and then tie the canes to them, or you can cover the wall with a wire grid made from strands of plastic-coated straining wire or 16-gauge utility wire. The wires fasten to brackets that hold them 4 to 12 inches away from the wall to allow for air circulation. Adjusting for the growth habit of your particular rose, space the brackets no more than 4 feet apart horizontally across the wall and about 1½ feet apart vertically to give adequate support to the grid and the roses. Attach the wire to the brackets and pull it taut.

Climbers and ramblers that grow 8 to 10 feet tall grow well on vertical wooden posts, tepees (three posts joined at the top), or tripods. When you plant the rose, tilt it toward the support to direct its growth, and wrap the canes in an upward spiral pattern *(page 78)*. For a fuller effect, you can wrap one plant clockwise and another counterclockwise on the same support. If you let the canes grow higher than the post, the roses will cascade from the top, creating an umbrella effect.

A WALL AWAKENED
Pink blossoms of 'Cl. Cécile Brunner' straddle a brick wall in this Charlottesville, Virginia, garden. These climbers were trained on a copper trellis and then allowed to spread freely along the wall.

Training Roses to a Trellis

Begin training the rose by working with an outside cane near the bottom of the plant. *Gently bend the cane into a horizontal position to encourage the best distribution of blossoms. Tie it loosely to the structure using either of the two loops shown at right. Continue positioning and tying the canes, working toward the center of the plant; then start on the other side and work inward to create a symmetrical design. Save the center canes for last.*

To create a figure-eight tie, loop vinyl gardener's tape or other material around the cane, *cross the strands, then bring them around the support and tie the ends together, making sure the crossed section of the eight lies between the cane and the support (above, left). To make a double loop, first knot the tie around the support and then knot it around the cane (above, right). The knot between the support and the cane will keep the two from rubbing together excessively.*

Answers to Common Questions

Why should I bother buying a rose that only blooms in the spring when I can have roses that bloom repeatedly for months?

If you only have one or two roses in your collection, repeat bloomers are probably the way to go, but when gardening with more, a few single-season bloomers can add dramatic interest to your garden. It is often said that these roses produce more flowers at one time than any of the repeat-blooming roses do during the whole year. Also, many roses that bloom only once per season—such as some species and old garden roses—happen to be among the hardiest and least fussy available.

I planted several climbers on my split-rail fence this spring. They are growing slowly and have few blooms. What can I do?

Try to be patient. Newly planted climbers often either bloom or put all their energy into just growing the first year. They rarely do both, and when they do, neither the growth nor the blooms are impressive. It usually takes 2 to 3 years for climbers to begin to perform well.

The Rosa banksiae banksiae that I planted 3 years ago refuses to bloom. What am I doing wrong?

You're probably pruning too early and too much. The Lady Banks' Rose needs to go dormant through the winter, protected from freezing, before it blooms in the spring. Don't prune live canes at the beginning of the season, because blooms will occur only on the canes that have overwintered, not on the new canes of spring. You might also check to make sure the rose is getting full sun exposure, since shade can significantly reduce the amount of bloom.

Why do some of my hybrid teas that put out large blooms of 3 inches or more in the spring and fall have blooms only half that size in the summer?

If you live in an area where summer temperatures regularly top 90° F during the day and don't go below the 70s at night, your roses will respond to the heat by producing smaller flowers or reducing the number of flower petals. They may even stop flowering altogether. Also, what blooms you get might appear bleached of color. When cooler weather returns, the roses should bounce back.

My 'Cl. First Prize' blooms up a storm in the spring but doesn't repeat well, even after I deadhead it. What can I do to get more repeat bloom?

Probably nothing will help this. By deadheading, you've done all you can, assuming you're feeding and watering it properly. 'Cl. First Prize' is a sport of the hybrid tea bush 'First Prize', and unfortunately, many climbing sports do produce good spring bloom but don't repeat well.

My 'Rosa Mundi' produces many beautiful pink-and-white striped flowers, but sometimes I see a pure deep pink rose, without any white. Why is this?

'Rosa Mundi' is a color sport of the ancient 'Apothecary's Rose', which is a solid deep pink. It isn't very unusual for color sports to revert to the coloration of their parent, but it's worth taking a picture of both flowers together when it does happen. Incidentally, the 'Rosa Mundi' bloodline has produced many of the modern striped roses.

This spring I noticed one of my hybrid teas, whose blooms are usually a soft apricot, blooming with a red flower. Is this a sport?

Probably not. Notice if the red flower is on a cane that emerges from below the bud union. If so, the cane is coming out of the rootstock and should be removed. The rootstock is probably the widely used 'Dr. Huey', whose own blooms are dark red and have the fine hybrid tea shape. ('Dr. Huey' is named 'Shafter' when it's used as a rootstock.) However, if the red flowers come from a cane above the bud union, then you do have a color sport.

DESIGN AND LANDSCAPE USE

Are roses compatible with other plants?

Most rosarians who grow exhibition roses like hybrid teas, grandifloras, and floribundas insist that roses should have little or no competition for space, water, and nutrients from other plants, such as annuals and perennials. Species roses, old garden varieties, polyanthas, hybrid musks, and modern shrubs and miniatures, on the other hand, lend beauty to the garden especially when planted with other plants. Generally, their diversity of form and their tolerance to pests and disease make these roses better garden plants.

How can I train my newly planted climber up the oak tree next to it?

There are two major considerations when training a rose into a tree: sun exposure and competition with the tree's root system. If your rose will grow 15 to 20 feet, it can be planted 4 to 6 feet away from the trunk of the tree and still be able to climb into it. The farther away, the less the root competition. Plant the rose on the south side of the tree, making sure any canopy of leaves does not shade it initially. Allow the rose to grow until its canes are long enough to tie along the trunk, using loose twine or stretchy ties. Once a few canes are established in the tree the rose will spread, eventually draping into the branches of the tree on its own.

How can I get my white roses to look good in my rose garden? The flowers that I pick and bring inside are beautiful, but outside they just don't show up.

The color white is one that needs a special garden stage on which to perform. Try backdropping the bed with thick green foliage plants like holly, privet, or yew. This will help set them off. Gardening with white flowers is most effective at dusk because the remaining light is reflected by the white flowers, creating a luminous scene with the onset of night.

GROWTH AND PLANT CONDITIONS

In my garden I have two bushes of the same modern rose, which I purchased from two different nurseries. One of the bushes grows very well, but the second is struggling. They are planted in the same rose bed and are treated the same way. What could be wrong?

There are a couple of possibilities. One is that the inferior bush resulted from a lesser-quality bud when it was grafted onto rootstock. When there aren't enough buds to meet the demand for a new rose, sometimes all available buds—including inferior ones—are used. You may have gotten a bad one. The other possibility is that the rootstock used for the struggling plant doesn't do well in your area. Find out what rootstock your roses are grown on and record their performance. Then stick with what does well.

My gallica 'Tuscany' produces new small plants all around it. Why is this?

When grown on their own roots, gallicas and rugosas sometimes do this. The plant is suckering from the roots, running outward near the surface from the mother plant and producing small new plants along the runner. When sufficient roots are established, these new small plants can be cut free from the main plant and given to friends or replanted somewhere else. If this becomes a nuisance to you, simply dig them out when you see them.

We have a summer place right on the ocean in Massachusetts. Are there any roses that will grow in this setting?

Any of the rugosa species and most hybrid rugosas, such as 'Blanc Double de Coubert' or 'Belle Poitevine', will grow and bloom in your situation. Rugosas tolerate salt spray and will grow in sand dunes unattended. The Japanese native species has even naturalized on beaches in the northeastern and northwestern United States.

My yard has a lot of shade. Are there any roses that will grow in it?

Roses need sun to perform well. The best ones to try under your conditions would be the modern hybrid musks, such as 'Ballerina', 'Belinda', 'Buff Beauty', or 'Prosperity'. If they don't grow and bloom there, no rose will.

Most books list rose size either by height or by height and spread, but my roses have grown well beyond the dimensions they were supposed to have. Do I have a green thumb or what?

Dimensions listed in catalogs and other literature usually indicate the size at which that rose looks best. All roses, even miniatures, will get oversized if they aren't pruned.

One of my antique roses has grown too big for its location. Can I move it?

Yes, but do so when the plant is dormant—in late February or March. First prepare the hole in the new location *(pages 65-68)*. Then cut the rose canes back to about 2 feet above the ground and carefully dig up the plant, keeping as much of the root structure as possible. Immediately place the rose in its new spot. Water, mulch, and watch for new growth in the spring.

My climbing tea 'Sombreuil' is 10 feet tall and has overgrown the spot where it is planted. Can I prune it back to make it a manageable shrub and not a climber?

Roses are individually predisposed to behave a certain way. The climbing rose 'Albéric Barbier', for example, is so vigorous that even severe pruning will not tame it into a shrub. 'Sombreuil' could be pruned three or four times a year to achieve a shrub look, but it would still be inclined toward climbing and would be better used gracing a pillar or trellis.

My rose plants sometimes produce two new stems at a leaf node after I dead-head. Why is that?

When you deadhead, you prune down to a five-leaflet leaf with a live dormant eye at the base. On either side of that bud eye is another bud eye. If the center bud eye is damaged in any way, both "guard" buds grow a new stem at the leaf node. If you let both grow and bloom, you will get two blooms. However, both stems and blooms will be smaller than usual. The best practice, when you notice such a situation, is to pinch off one of the new growths. That way you'll get one bigger flower.

PESTS AND DISEASES

I get black spot on my roses every year. I really don't want to use chemical fungicides, but I'm getting desperate. Isn't there anything I can do to keep the disease from ruining my plants without adding toxic chemicals to the garden?

Try this year-round preventive program that uses nonharmful products: Before the first frost, spray your roses with a commercial antidesiccant, according to label directions, to keep any fungus spores off the leaves during the winter. Then, while the plants are still dormant in the spring, spray them with wettable or liquid sulfur fungicide, followed by a thorough spray of dormant oil. Keep applying the sulfur periodically until frost—every week to 10 days at most. Don't spray sulfur, though, when the temperature is 85° F or higher because it may burn the foliage, and keep it away from rugosa roses and their hybrids altogether. Rugosas are damaged by sulfur—but they're immune to most fungi in the first place. This treatment will control not only black spot but also rust and powdery mildew, as well as infestations of aphids, thrips, and mites.

Are there any roses that deer do not eat?

Probably not. Try planting companions that deer dislike, such as rosemary or artemisia. Sometimes people put wire and fencing around their roses to keep deer from browsing, but this defeats the purpose of roses beautifying the garden. Instead, lay wire mesh on the ground near and in the rose bed, and plant ground covers such as ivy, phlox, or dianthus, making the mesh invisible. Deer will not step into these areas because of the disturbing footing.

SOIL, MULCH, AND MAINTENANCE

Can I spray around my roses to kill weeds?

There are many types of weed-killers, and most don't know the difference between roses and weeds. Systemic herbicides are absorbed through leaf and stem surfaces, not the ground; you have to be extremely careful that none of the chemical comes in contact with your rose plants. Soil sterilants and broadleaf weed-killers kill roses, period. Preemergent herbicides prevent weed seeds from germinating and are typically safe around roses but are not effective on existing weeds. The best weed-killer is the human hand.

The foliage on my roses is yellowish. My friend thinks that my woodchip mulch is to blame. Is this possible? What can I do to correct it?

The yellowish foliage is probably caused by a nitrogen deficiency. This often happens when you have used woodchips as a mulch, especially after they become worked into the soil, because their decomposition process takes nitrogen from the soil. To correct the condition, fertilize with high-nitrogen ammonium nitrate or urea. Then use a high-nitrogen fertilizer such as 30-10-10 whenever you feed your roses. Getting a soil analysis if the condition doesn't clear up would be a good idea.

Except for 'Old Blush', 'Mutabilis', and 'Duchesse de Brabant', my roses are all chlorotic, even though I've added iron and magnesium to the soil. What gives?

Chlorosis—a nutrient deficiency that turns foliage pale yellowish green—may result from improper soil pH. Try testing the pH of your soil. China and tea roses like those you mention can tolerate a slightly alkaline pH, but others cannot. Even though adequate micronutrients may be in your garden's soil, most roses can't make use of them unless the pH is in the slightly acid range, around 6.5.

Troubleshooting Guide

The old adage "An ounce of prevention is worth a pound of cure" is especially true of roses. Grown under the wrong conditions, virtually any variety is susceptible to pests and disease, although some roses—particularly those with tough foliage like the rugosa roses—are less vulnerable, and certain others—many hybrid teas, for example—are more so. Before you choose roses for your garden, check with your local Cooperative Extension Service or rose society to determine which roses are most resistant in your area. After planting, provide them with the appropriate care to keep them healthy, remove all debris and fallen leaves—which may harbor diseases and insect eggs—from the garden, and regularly inspect them for warning signs of trouble.

This guide is intended to help you identify and solve most of the pest and disease problems you may encounter. To curb pests, the many insects—such as ladybugs and lacewings—that prey on them should be encouraged. For all problems, natural solutions are preferred, but if you must use chemicals, treat only the affected plant. Try to use horticultural oils and fungicidal or insecticidal soaps; these products are the least disruptive to beneficial insects and will not destroy the soil balance that is at the foundation of a healthy garden.

P E S T S

PROBLEM: Insects appear on buds and other plant parts. Eventually, leaves curl, are distorted in shape, and may be sticky and have a black, sooty appearance. A clear, shiny substance often appears on stems and leaves. Buds and flowers are deformed; new growth is stunted.

CAUSE: Aphids are pear shaped, semi-transparent, wingless sucking insects, about ⅛ inch long and usually green in color, although sometimes pink or tan. Infestations are severest in spring and early summer when pests cluster on tender new shoots, on undersides of leaves, and around flower buds. Winged forms appear when colonies become overcrowded. Aphids secrete honeydew, a sticky substance that fosters the growth of a black fungus called sooty mold.

SOLUTION: Aphids are fairly easy to control. Pick them off by hand, or early in the morning knock them off by spraying plants with a strong, steady stream of water from a garden hose. Ladybugs or green lacewings, which eat aphids, may be introduced into the garden. In severe cases, prune off infested areas, and use an insecticidal soap or a recommended insecticide.

PROBLEM: Large round or oblong holes are eaten in leaves, leaf edges, and flowers, especially those that are light colored. Leaves may be reduced to skeletons with only veins remaining.

CAUSE: Japanese beetles, iridescent blue-green with bronze wing covers, are one of the most destructive of a large family of hard-shelled chewing insects ranging in size from ¼ to 1 inch long. Other genera include rose chafers, Fuller rose beetles, rose curculios, and goldsmith beetles. Adult beetles are voracious in the summer. Larvae, the white grubs, may feed on the roots and are present from midsummer through the following spring, when they emerge as adults.

SOLUTION: In early morning when beetles are sluggish, handpick small colonies, placing them in a can filled with soapy water. Don't use Japanese beetle traps; they only lure more beetles into your garden. The larval stage of most beetles can be controlled with milky spore disease. For heavy infestations call your local Cooperative Extension Service for information on registered pesticides and the best times to apply them in your region.

PROBLEM: Canes, new growth, and leaves droop and wilt. Canes turn brown and die. The centers of pruned canes are hollowed out, or swollen areas appear on the surface of canes.

CAUSE: Cane borers, the larvae of several insects, penetrate rose canes through pruned ends or by puncturing their sides, and then hollow them by consuming the pith. The commonest borer, the larvae of the small carpenter bee, develops from eggs laid on top of unprotected cut stems.

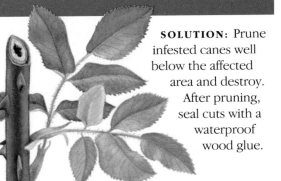

SOLUTION: Prune infested canes well below the affected area and destroy. After pruning, seal cuts with a waterproof wood glue.

PROBLEM: Holes appear in buds; large, ragged holes appear in leaves. Entire leaves are eaten or are rolled up.

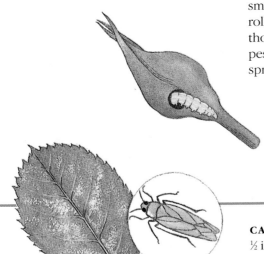

CAUSE: Caterpillars, the wormlike larvae of moths and butterflies, come in a variety of shapes and colors and can be smooth or hairy. Rose budworms, leaf rollers, and fall webworms are among those that attack roses. These voracious pests appear in gardens during the spring and late summer.

SOLUTION: Handpick to control small populations. *Bacillus thuringiensis* (Bt) kills many types of caterpillars when they are small without harming plants. Identify the caterpillar species to determine the control options and timing of spray applications. The botanical insecticide neem is also effective. Several species are susceptible to sprays of insecticidal soap, which must directly hit the caterpillar. Keep the garden clean, cultivate frequently, and destroy all visible cocoons and nests. Deep spading in early spring can destroy many species that pupate underground.

PROBLEM: Leaves curl upward and become stippled with white dots, then turn yellowish brown or have a burned look around the edges. Young leaves become distorted.

CAUSE: Leafhoppers are small (⅒ to ½ inch long), cricketlike, wedge-shaped sucking insects that jump quickly into flight when disturbed. They may be yellow-green, white, or brown. Most active in spring and summer, they feed on the undersides of leaves and on new stems. Some may secrete a sticky honeydew that fosters sooty mold.

SOLUTION: Spray with water to knock exposed leafhoppers off plants. Direct spraying with insecticidal soap will give short-term control, but leafhoppers migrate freely, so repeated applications may be necessary. A labeled systemic insecticide will provide the longest control.

PROBLEM: Leaves become stippled or flecked with yellow. Often the entire leaf becomes yellow or bronzed and curled. Flowers and buds discolor or dry up, and fine webbing may be seen on the undersides of leaves and on new growth. Leaves may drop. Growth is stunted.

CAUSE: Mites, about the size of a grain of salt, are spiderlike sucking pests that can be reddish, green, yellow, or brown. These insects can become a major problem, especially in hot, dry weather, when several generations of mites may occur in a single season. Adults of some species hibernate over the winter in sod, in bark, and on weeds and plants that retain foliage.

SOLUTION: Keep plants watered and mulched. In the early morning, regularly spray a strong stream of water at the undersides of leaves, where mites feed and lay eggs. Introduce predators such as ladybugs, green lacewing larvae, and predatory mites. Horticultural oil can also be applied to leaf undersides. Insecticides destroy the beneficial insects that control mites.

PROBLEM: Foliage at the tips of new growth appears burned around the edges. Flowers are deformed. Tender foliage and buds may suddenly turn brown or black.

CAUSE: Tiny (1/25 inch) white larvae of the rose midge, a kind of fly, emerge from eggs laid in the sepals of flower buds or in opening leaf buds; they slash plant tissue with sickle-shaped mouth parts and suck the sap. The larvae drop to the ground to pupate; adults emerge within days. Numerous life cycles may be repeated throughout the growing season. Damage is particularly severe in the summer.

SOLUTION: Prune off and destroy affected leaves and buds promptly to break the life cycle. For severe infestations spray a recommended insecticide.

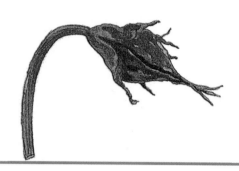

PROBLEM: Small holes are eaten out of leaves, or leaves are skeletonized.

CAUSE: Rose slugs, which are not actual slugs but the larvae of three different sawflies, feed on rose leaves. The half-inch-long, pale green common rose slug skeletonizes the upper leaf surface in early spring. The bristly rose slug is pale green and slightly longer, its wormlike body covered with stiff hairs when mature. It feeds on the undersides of leaves, first skeletonizing them and later chewing large holes. The curled rose sawfly larva, 3/4 inch long, consumes the leaves from a coiled position and burrows into pruned twigs to pupate, which opens twigs to fungal infection.

SOLUTION: Spray plants with a strong, steady stream of water to knock larvae off; most won't climb back up. Handpick to control small populations. Bristly rose slugs can irritate the skin, so wear gloves. In case of severe infestation, spray an insecticidal soap directly on the slugs.

PROBLEM: Leaves discolor, wilt, and drop. Growth is stunted. Stems, canes, and leaves are covered with small, white, cottony patches or with rounded or oval shells in various colors. The problem occurs most often on climbers that have not been pruned yearly.

CAUSE: Scale insects have hard or soft shells, 1/10 to 3/8 inch long, that may be white, yellow, green, gray, red, brown, or black. They usually appear in clusters. Hard-shelled adult males and females and soft-shelled females appear on stems or leaves as bumps. Adult soft-shelled males are minute flying insects with yellow wings. The insects suck plant juices.

SOLUTION: Remove scales with a cotton swab or soft toothbrush dipped in soapy water or an alcohol-and-water solution. Prune off and destroy any canes that are severely infested. Spray roses with horticultural oil in early spring to smother eggs before plant growth begins. Insecticidal soaps are effective when eggs have just hatched.

PROBLEM: Buds open only partway or not at all. Flower petals turn brown at the edges, darken, or have brownish yellow or white streaks and small dark spots or bumps. Young growth may be deformed or mottled. The problem is most evident on light-colored roses.

CAUSE: Thrips are quick-moving sucking insects that are barely visible to the naked eye. They look like tiny slivers of yellow, black, or brown wood. Emerging in early spring, thrips are especially active in late spring and early summer, attacking sepals of buds and sucking juices from the petals. Adults are weak fliers but are easily dispersed by wind and can therefore travel great distances.

SOLUTION: Control of thrips is difficult, especially during a migratory period in early summer. Lacewings, ladybugs, pirate bugs, and several predaceous mites feed on them; late in the growing season such predators often check thrips populations. Remove and destroy damaged buds and flowers. In severe cases, spray plants with an insecticidal soap or systemic insecticide.

PROBLEM: Circular black spots with fringed margins that are 1/16 to 1/2 inch in diameter appear on upper leaf surfaces. The spots enlarge and coalesce, and infected leaves turn yellow and drop. Raised dark reddish or black blotches appear on young canes.

CAUSE: Black spot, a fungus disease, is most often found under humid and rainy conditions because fungus spores germinate in water. Spores can be transmitted by splashing water, clothing, garden tools, or hands. A severe infection can defoliate a rosebush. The fungus overwinters on infected canes, on fallen leaves, and inside leaf buds.

SOLUTION: Plant roses that are less susceptible in your area. Water early in the day and avoid splashing leaves. Prune canes of infected plants farther back than normal to eliminate fungus that survives over the winter, and apply a commercial lime-sulfur spray before leaves open. If symptoms appear, remove and destroy all infected leaves, including those on the ground. For light infestations, spray a solution of 1 tablespoon of baking soda and 1/4 teaspoon of summer horticultural oil to 1 gallon of water every 5 to 7 days until symptoms disappear. For heavier infestation, remove the plant or spray with a fungicide to control fungus.

PROBLEM: A brownish gray, moldy growth appears on buds and flowers. Buds droop and fail to open. Discolored flecks or blotches appear on flowers, whose lower petals are wilted and brown. Dark lesions may extend down stems.

CAUSE: Botrytis blight, also known as gray mold, is a fungus that thrives in moist air and cool temperatures. The blight survives the winter as hard, black lumps in the soil or on dead plant parts, such as dead blossoms.

SOLUTION: Water early in the day. Avoid wetting plants. Remove and destroy fading blossoms and all infected plant parts, as well as any debris on the ground. To keep disease from spreading, spray with a fungicide.

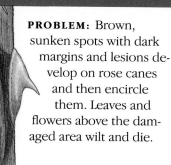

PROBLEM: Brown, sunken spots with dark margins and lesions develop on rose canes and then encircle them. Leaves and flowers above the damaged area wilt and die.

CAUSE: Canker, a fungal disease, spreads in water and enters canes through cuts or wounds, especially those caused by pruning, cutting flowers too far from a bud, or canes rubbing against each other. One type of canker develops during cold weather when roses have been covered by winter protection.

SOLUTION: Prune infected canes ¼ inch above the node below the canker, disinfecting tools with alcohol after each cut. Removing infected canes promptly will help prevent the spread of the disease. There are no chemical preventives or cures. Choose hardy roses that don't need winter protection.

PROBLEM: Corky growths, or galls, appear at the base of the plant, near the graft union, on roots, and occasionally on canes. Growths are white or light green at ground level when young and turn brown and woody as they age.

CAUSE: Crown gall is a disease caused by bacteria that live in the soil and enter a plant through wounds at the root area. The bacteria cause abnormal cell growth, which produces the galls, thus stunting the rose's normal growth.

SOLUTION: Inspect newly acquired plants for signs of gall and dispose of any diseased ones. Avoid wounding plants, especially near the soil line. Prune out and destroy galled canes, sterilizing the knife after each cut. Remove and destroy severely infected plants. Bacteria will remain in the soil for several years.

PROBLEM: Irregular purplish red to brown blotches appear on the upper surfaces of young leaves. Corresponding gray or tan fuzzy growths—most easily seen in early morning during humid weather—form on the undersides. Leaves may turn yellow and drop. Purplish brown blotches also appear on canes.

CAUSE: Downy mildew, caused by a fungus, is less prevalent than other diseases, but devastating. It spreads in cool, moist weather, often in late summer and early fall. It often starts at the top of a rosebush. The disease attacks internal rose tissue and can cause complete defoliation.

SOLUTION: Plant varieties that are less susceptible in your area. Water plants in the morning, and avoid wetting the leaves. Remove and destroy blighted plant parts. Use a fungicide to control the infection.

PROBLEM: Foliage is yellowed, plant looks wilted or stunted, and it may die. Root system is poorly developed and sometimes has knots or galls.

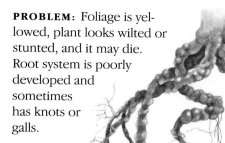

CAUSE: Soil nematodes—colorless, microscopic worms that live in the soil and feed on roots—inhibit a plant's intake of nitrogen. Damage is at its worst in warm, sunlit, sandy soils that are moist.

SOLUTION: Only a laboratory test can detect nematodes. In some areas, roses grafted onto certain rootstocks, such as *R. fortuniana* in the Deep South, are resistant. Enrich the soil with organic matter to encourage beneficial fungi that attack nematodes. In severe cases, dispose of infected roses and the surrounding soil, or sterilize the soil by fixing a sheet of clear plastic over the ground and leaving it in place for 1 to 2 months.

PROBLEM: Leaves are covered with spots or a thin layer of grayish white powdery matter. Infected parts may become distorted and curl, then turn yellow or purplish; leaves may finally drop off. Badly infected buds will not open properly.

CAUSE: The powdery mildew fungus thrives when nights are cool and humid and days are warm and dry. The disease is most noticeable in spring and in early and late summer, when plant growth is vigorous.

SOLUTION: Plant varieties that are mildew resistant in your area. Remove and destroy infected leaves from the rose, as well as any that have fallen to the ground. Spray a solution of 1 tablespoon baking soda and ¼ teaspoon summer horticultural oil to 1 gallon water every 5 to 7 days until symptoms disappear. In severer cases, fungicides or full-strength summer oil may be used to control spreading.

PROBLEM: Upper leaf surfaces have orange, brown, or yellow spots, and undersides and stems are covered with powdery orange raised pustules. Leaves may drop. Young growth may become distorted.

CAUSE: Rust, a fungus disease most active in the Southwest and along the Pacific Coast, is a problem especially in the late summer and early fall and is most prevalent when nights are cool and humid. The orange powder, consisting of fungus spores, spreads easily in wind.

SOLUTION: Plant locally resistant varieties. Water early in the day and avoid wetting leaves. Remove and destroy all infected leaves, including any on the ground. Spray with a fungicide to control infection.

PROBLEM: Red to brown or dark purple circular spots about ¼ inch in diameter appear on leaves. Spots develop white centers, which may fall out and leave holes. Leaves may turn yellow and drop. Stems have smaller raised brown or purple spots. Climbers with glossy foliage and ramblers are most vulnerable.

CAUSE: Spot anthracnose is a fungus that prefers moist conditions; spores are spread by splashing water. The fungus overwinters in lesions on infected canes.

SOLUTION: Prune out infected canes in early spring before new growth starts. A commercial lime-sulfur spray can be used on dormant plants. To keep a severe infection from spreading, spray plants with a fungicide.

PROBLEM: Leaves are mottled or striped with irregular patterns in abnormal colors ranging from light green to yellow. Growth may be stunted.

CAUSE: Rose mosaic is a disease caused by several different viruses and affects leaves but not flowers. The viruses are likely to have been contracted at the nursery from the grafting of infected buds onto rootstock. Symptoms are usually most obvious in spring.

SOLUTION: There are no chemical controls or cures for viruses infecting garden stock. Remove and destroy affected plants and inform the nursery where the plant was purchased.

Plant Selection Guide

Organized by predominant flower color, this chart provides information needed to select roses that will thrive in the particular conditions of your garden. For additional information on each plant, refer to the encyclopedia that begins on page 98.

WHITE	Zone 3	Zone 4	Zone 5	Zone 6	Zone 7	Zone 8	Zone 9	Zone 10	Partial Shade	Diseases	Heat	Seaside Conditions	Spring	Summer	Fall	Single	Semidouble	Double	Very Double	Miniature	Bush/Shrub <3'	Bush/Shrub 3-6'	Shrub >6'	Climber/Rambler	Fragrance	Cut Flowers	Hips
'ALBA SEMI-PLENA'		✓	✓	✓	✓	✓	✓	✓	✓	✓			✓				✓					✓	✓		✓		✓
'BLANC DOUBLE DE COUBERT'	✓	✓	✓	✓	✓	✓	✓	✓		✓		✓	✓	✓	✓		✓					✓			✓		✓
'BOULE DE NEIGE'			✓	✓	✓	✓	✓	✓		✓				✓	✓			✓				✓			✓		
'CANDEUR LYONNAISE'			✓	✓	✓	✓	✓						✓	✓	✓			✓				✓				✓	
'CITY OF YORK'			✓	✓	✓	✓	✓	✓			✓		✓				✓							✓	✓		
'FAIR BIANCA'		✓	✓	✓	✓	✓	✓						✓	✓					✓		✓				✓		
'FRENCH LACE'		✓	✓	✓	✓	✓	✓		✓				✓	✓				✓				✓				✓	
'GREAT MAIDEN'S BLUSH'		✓	✓	✓	✓	✓	✓						✓					✓				✓			✓		
'HANDEL'			✓	✓	✓	✓	✓		✓				✓	✓				✓						✓			
'HENRY HUDSON'	✓	✓	✓	✓	✓	✓	✓	✓		✓		✓	✓	✓	✓		✓				✓				✓		
'ICEBERG'		✓	✓	✓	✓	✓	✓		✓				✓	✓				✓				✓			✓	✓	
'IRRESISTIBLE'			✓	✓	✓	✓	✓						✓	✓				✓		✓						✓	✓
'KORICOLE'		✓	✓	✓	✓	✓	✓						✓	✓				✓		✓							
'LAMARQUE'			✓	✓	✓	✓	✓				✓		✓	✓					✓				✓	✓	✓	✓	
'MADAME ALFRED CARRIERE'			✓	✓	✓	✓	✓		✓		✓		✓	✓				✓					✓	✓	✓		
'MADAME HARDY'		✓	✓	✓	✓	✓	✓		✓				✓	✓				✓			✓				✓	✓	
'MADAME LEGRAS DE ST. GERMAIN'		✓	✓	✓	✓	✓	✓		✓	✓			✓						✓				✓	✓	✓	✓	
'MADAME PLANTIER'		✓	✓	✓	✓	✓	✓	✓					✓						✓			✓		✓	✓	✓	
'NASTARANA'			✓	✓	✓	✓	✓	✓			✓		✓	✓		✓						✓			✓		
'PRISTINE'			✓	✓	✓	✓	✓		✓				✓					✓				✓				✓	
'PROSPERITY'			✓	✓	✓	✓	✓	✓					✓	✓				✓				✓			✓		
ROSA BANKSIAE BANKSIAE					✓	✓	✓				✓		✓	✓				✓						✓	✓		
ROSA RUGOSA ALBA	✓	✓	✓	✓	✓	✓				✓		✓	✓		✓	✓						✓			✓		✓
'SALLY HOLMES'			✓	✓	✓	✓	✓		✓	✓	✓		✓	✓		✓							✓		✓	✓	
'SEA FOAM'		✓	✓	✓	✓	✓	✓	✓		✓			✓	✓				✓			✓			✓		✓	
'SILVER MOON'			✓	✓	✓	✓	✓						✓				✓						✓	✓	✓		
'SNOW BRIDE'			✓	✓	✓	✓	✓						✓	✓				✓		✓						✓	
'SOMBREUIL'			✓	✓	✓	✓	✓	✓	✓		✓		✓	✓					✓					✓	✓	✓	✓

Color	Rose	Zone 3	Zone 4	Zone 5	Zone 6	Zone 7	Zone 8	Zone 9	Zone 10	Partial Shade	Diseases	Heat	Seaside Conditions	Spring	Summer	Fall	Single	Semidouble	Double	Very Double	Miniature	Bush/Shrub <3'	Bush/Shrub 3-6'	Shrub >6'	Climber/Rambler	Fragrance	Cut Flowers	Hips
WHITE	'WHITE MEIDILAND'		✓	✓	✓	✓	✓			✓					✓	✓			✓			✓						
	'WHITE PET'			✓	✓	✓	✓	✓							✓	✓	✓			✓			✓					✓	
YELLOW	'ALBERIC BARBIER'			✓	✓	✓	✓	✓	✓	✓	✓	✓			✓			✓							✓	✓		
	'ALCHYMIST'			✓	✓	✓	✓	✓							✓					✓				✓	✓	✓		
	'CELINE FORESTIER'				✓	✓	✓	✓	✓			✓			✓	✓				✓					✓	✓		
	'ELINA'			✓	✓	✓	✓	✓							✓	✓			✓		✓			✓			✓	
	'GOLDEN SHOWERS'			✓	✓	✓	✓	✓		✓	✓				✓	✓			✓					✓	✓	✓	✓	
	'GOLDEN WINGS'	✓	✓	✓	✓	✓	✓	✓				✓	✓	✓	✓	✓	✓						✓			✓	✓	✓
	'GOLD MEDAL'			✓	✓	✓	✓	✓			✓				✓	✓			✓				✓			✓	✓	
	'GRAHAM THOMAS'	✓	✓	✓	✓	✓	✓	✓			✓				✓	✓			✓				✓	✓		✓		
	'GRANADA'		✓	✓	✓	✓	✓	✓							✓	✓			✓				✓			✓	✓	
	'LAFTER'			✓	✓	✓	✓	✓	✓		✓				✓	✓	✓						✓			✓		
	'MRS. DUDLEY CROSS'				✓	✓	✓	✓		✓	✓	✓		✓	✓	✓			✓				✓			✓	✓	
	'MUTABILIS'				✓	✓	✓	✓			✓			✓	✓	✓	✓						✓	✓		✓		
	'PARTY GIRL'			✓	✓	✓	✓	✓	✓		✓				✓	✓			✓	✓		✓				✓	✓	
	'PEACE'			✓	✓	✓	✓	✓			✓				✓	✓			✓			✓					✓	
	'RAINBOW'S END'			✓	✓	✓	✓	✓							✓	✓			✓	✓		✓						
	'REVE D'OR'				✓	✓	✓	✓	✓		✓			✓	✓	✓			✓						✓	✓		
	'RISE 'N' SHINE'			✓	✓	✓	✓	✓			✓				✓	✓			✓	✓		✓						
	'SUN FLARE'	✓	✓	✓	✓	✓	✓	✓		✓					✓	✓			✓			✓				✓	✓	
	'SUNSPRITE'			✓	✓	✓	✓	✓	✓		✓			✓	✓	✓			✓			✓				✓	✓	
ORANGE/APRICOT	'ALBERTINE'			✓	✓	✓	✓	✓							✓				✓					✓	✓	✓		
	'AMERICA'			✓	✓	✓	✓	✓			✓				✓	✓			✓					✓	✓	✓		
	'APRICOT NECTAR'	✓	✓	✓	✓	✓	✓	✓							✓	✓			✓		✓					✓		
	'BUFF BEAUTY'			✓	✓	✓	✓	✓	✓						✓	✓			✓				✓		✓	✓		
	'CHERISH'	✓	✓	✓	✓	✓	✓	✓			✓				✓	✓			✓		✓					✓		
	'FIRST EDITION'	✓	✓	✓	✓	✓	✓	✓	✓		✓				✓	✓			✓			✓				✓		
	'FOLKLORE'			✓	✓	✓	✓	✓	✓		✓				✓	✓			✓					✓		✓	✓	
	'JEAN KENNEALLY'			✓	✓	✓	✓	✓	✓		✓				✓	✓			✓		✓					✓		
	'JUST JOEY'			✓	✓	✓	✓	✓								✓			✓			✓				✓	✓	
	'LEANDER'	✓	✓	✓	✓	✓	✓	✓			✓				✓	✓				✓					✓	✓		
	'LOVING TOUCH'			✓	✓	✓	✓	✓	✓						✓	✓	✓			✓		✓					✓	✓

Roses reference chart — categories **ORANGE/APRICOT** and **PINK**.

Column groups: **ZONES** (Zone 3–Zone 10, Partial Shade) · **TOLERATES** (Diseases, Heat, Seaside Conditions) · **BLOOMING SEASON** (Spring, Summer, Fall) · **BLOOM TYPE** (Single, Semidouble, Double, Very Double, Miniature) · **PLANT HABIT** (Bush/Shrub <3′, Bush/Shrub 3–6′, Shrub >6′, Climber/Rambler) · **NOTED FOR** (Fragrance, Cut Flowers, Hips)

Category	Name	Z3	Z4	Z5	Z6	Z7	Z8	Z9	Z10	Part. Shade	Diseases	Heat	Seaside	Spring	Summer	Fall	Single	Semidouble	Double	Very Double	Miniature	Bush <3′	Bush 3–6′	Shrub >6′	Climber/Rambler	Fragrance	Cut Flowers	Hips
ORANGE/APRICOT	'MARGO KOSTER'			✓	✓	✓	✓	✓		✓					✓	✓			✓		✓							
	'PIERRINE'			✓	✓	✓	✓	✓	✓					✓	✓	✓			✓		✓					✓		✓
	'PLAYBOY'		✓	✓	✓	✓	✓	✓	✓	✓	✓			✓	✓	✓	✓						✓			✓	✓	✓
	ROSA FOETIDA BICOLOR			✓	✓	✓	✓							✓			✓						✓	✓				
	'STARINA'				✓	✓	✓	✓							✓	✓			✓		✓							
	'TOUCH OF CLASS'			✓	✓	✓	✓	✓							✓	✓			✓				✓				✓	
	'TROPICANA'			✓	✓	✓	✓	✓	✓				✓		✓	✓			✓				✓			✓	✓	
PINK	'AQUARIUS'			✓	✓	✓	✓	✓	✓			✓		✓	✓	✓			✓				✓				✓	
	'AUTUMN DAMASK'		✓	✓	✓	✓	✓	✓	✓					✓	✓	✓			✓				✓			✓		
	'BALLERINA'			✓	✓	✓	✓	✓	✓		✓	✓			✓	✓	✓					✓					✓	
	'BARONNE PREVOST'			✓	✓	✓	✓	✓	✓		✓			✓	✓					✓			✓			✓		
	'BELINDA'			✓	✓	✓	✓	✓	✓	✓	✓				✓	✓		✓				✓	✓	✓			✓	
	'BELLE POITEVINE'	✓	✓	✓	✓	✓	✓	✓	✓			✓	✓	✓	✓	✓			✓				✓			✓		✓
	'BELLE STORY'		✓	✓	✓	✓	✓	✓	✓						✓	✓		✓					✓			✓		
	'BETTY PRIOR'		✓	✓	✓	✓	✓	✓	✓		✓			✓	✓	✓	✓					✓	✓					
	'BONICA'		✓	✓	✓	✓	✓	✓	✓			✓	✓	✓					✓				✓					✓
	'BRIDE'S DREAM'			✓	✓	✓	✓	✓	✓						✓	✓			✓				✓				✓	
	'CAREFREE BEAUTY'		✓	✓	✓	✓	✓	✓	✓		✓			✓	✓			✓					✓			✓		
	'CECILE BRUNNER'		✓	✓	✓	✓	✓	✓	✓	✓				✓	✓	✓			✓				✓			✓	✓	
	'CELESTIAL'		✓	✓	✓	✓	✓	✓	✓	✓					✓			✓					✓			✓		
	'CELSIANA'		✓	✓	✓	✓	✓	✓	✓		✓				✓			✓					✓			✓		
	'COMPLICATA'		✓	✓	✓	✓	✓	✓	✓			✓			✓		✓						✓	✓	✓			✓
	'CONSTANCE SPRY'		✓	✓	✓	✓	✓	✓	✓						✓				✓				✓	✓	✓	✓		
	'CRESTED MOSS'		✓	✓	✓	✓	✓	✓	✓		✓				✓					✓			✓			✓		
	'DAINTY BESS'			✓	✓	✓	✓	✓	✓			✓	✓		✓		✓						✓			✓	✓	
	'DUCHESSE DE BRABANT'				✓	✓	✓	✓				✓	✓	✓	✓	✓			✓				✓			✓		
	'FELICITE PARMENTIER'		✓	✓	✓	✓	✓	✓	✓		✓	✓			✓					✓			✓			✓		
	'FRAU DAGMAR HARTOPP'	✓	✓	✓	✓	✓	✓	✓	✓		✓		✓	✓	✓	✓	✓					✓				✓	✓	✓
	'GARTENDIREKTOR OTTO LINNE'		✓	✓	✓	✓	✓	✓	✓		✓				✓	✓			✓				✓		✓	✓		
	'GRUSS AN AACHEN'		✓	✓	✓	✓	✓	✓	✓	✓				✓	✓	✓			✓			✓				✓		
	'HERITAGE'		✓	✓	✓	✓	✓	✓	✓						✓				✓				✓			✓	✓	
	'ISPAHAN'		✓	✓	✓	✓	✓	✓	✓		✓			✓	✓				✓				✓			✓	✓	

Table — Rose selection guide (PINK and RED groups). Header groups: ZONES · TOLERATES · BLOOMING SEASON · BLOOM TYPE · PLANT HABIT · NOTED FOR.

Group	Variety	Zone 3	Zone 4	Zone 5	Zone 6	Zone 7	Zone 8	Zone 9	Zone 10	Partial Shade	Diseases	Heat	Seaside Conditions	Spring	Summer	Fall	Single	Semidouble	Double	Very Double	Miniature	Bush/Shrub <3′	Bush/Shrub 3-6′	Shrub >6′	Climber/Rambler	Fragrance	Cut Flowers	Hips
PINK	'JEANNE LAJOIE'			✔	✔	✔	✔	✔	✔					✔	✔	✔			✔					✔	✔			✔
PINK	'JENS MUNK'	✔	✔	✔	✔	✔	✔	✔	✔			✔	✔	✔	✔	✔			✔				✔			✔		
PINK	'LA MARNE'			✔	✔	✔	✔	✔	✔					✔	✔	✔	✔						✔			✔		
PINK	'LOUISE ODIER'			✔	✔	✔	✔	✔	✔			✔			✔	✔				✔			✔			✔	✔	
PINK	'MADAME ISAAC PEREIRE'			✔	✔	✔	✔	✔	✔						✔	✔				✔			✔			✔	✔	
PINK	'MARCHESA BOCCELLA'			✔	✔	✔	✔	✔	✔					✔	✔	✔				✔			✔			✔		
PINK	'MINNIE PEARL'		✔	✔	✔	✔	✔	✔	✔	✔					✔	✔			✔	✔	✔						✔	
PINK	'MRS. B. R. CANT'				✔	✔	✔	✔	✔			✔		✔	✔	✔				✔		✔	✔			✔	✔	
PINK	'NEW DAWN'			✔	✔	✔	✔	✔	✔	✔	✔				✔			✔						✔	✔	✔		
PINK	'OLD BLUSH'				✔	✔	✔	✔	✔			✔	✔	✔	✔				✔			✔				✔		
PINK	'PENELOPE'			✔	✔	✔	✔	✔	✔	✔	✔				✔	✔		✔					✔			✔		✔
PINK	'QUEEN ELIZABETH'		✔	✔	✔	✔	✔	✔			✔				✔	✔			✔				✔				✔	
PINK	ROSA GLAUCA		✔	✔	✔	✔	✔	✔						✔	✔	✔	✔						✔				✔	✔
PINK	'ROSA MUNDI'		✔	✔	✔	✔	✔	✔	✔			✔			✔			✔					✔				✔	✔
PINK	ROSA PALUSTRIS			✔	✔	✔	✔	✔	✔	✔	✔				✔	✔	✔					✔	✔					✔
PINK	'SOUVENIR DE LA MALMAISON'			✔	✔	✔	✔	✔				✔			✔	✔			✔		✔					✔		
PINK	'THE FAIRY'		✔	✔	✔	✔	✔	✔	✔			✔	✔		✔	✔			✔		✔						✔	
PINK	'TIFFANY'			✔	✔	✔	✔	✔				✔			✔	✔			✔				✔			✔	✔	
PINK	'WILLIAM BAFFIN'	✔	✔	✔	✔	✔	✔	✔				✔			✔	✔		✔					✔	✔	✔			
PINK	'ZEPHIRINE DROUHIN'			✔	✔	✔	✔	✔				✔		✔	✔	✔		✔						✔	✔	✔		
RED	'ALTISSIMO'			✔	✔	✔	✔	✔			✔	✔		✔	✔	✔	✔							✔	✔			
RED	'ARCHDUKE CHARLES'				✔	✔	✔	✔	✔			✔			✔	✔			✔		✔							
RED	'BLAZE'			✔	✔	✔	✔	✔	✔			✔		✔	✔	✔		✔							✔			
RED	'CHAMPLAIN'		✔	✔	✔	✔	✔	✔			✔				✔	✔			✔				✔					
RED	'CHRYSLER IMPERIAL'			✔	✔	✔	✔	✔				✔			✔	✔			✔				✔			✔	✔	
RED	'COUNTRY DANCER'		✔	✔	✔	✔	✔	✔							✔	✔			✔			✔	✔			✔	✔	
RED	'CRIMSON GLORY'			✔	✔	✔	✔	✔				✔			✔	✔			✔				✔			✔		
RED	'DON JUAN'			✔	✔	✔	✔	✔	✔	✔				✔	✔	✔			✔						✔	✔	✔	
RED	'DORTMUND'		✔	✔	✔	✔	✔	✔	✔	✔	✔				✔	✔	✔							✔	✔			✔
RED	'DOUBLE DELIGHT'			✔	✔	✔	✔	✔				✔			✔	✔			✔				✔			✔	✔	
RED	'DREAMGLO'			✔	✔	✔	✔	✔			✔				✔	✔			✔	✔	✔							
RED	'DUBLIN BAY'			✔	✔	✔	✔	✔	✔		✔			✔	✔	✔			✔						✔	✔		

Color	Rose	ZONES Z3	Z4	Z5	Z6	Z7	Z8	Z9	Z10	TOLERATES Partial Shade	Diseases	Heat	Seaside Conditions	BLOOMING SEASON Spring	Summer	Fall	BLOOM TYPE Single	Semidouble	Double	Very Double	PLANT HABIT Miniature	Bush/Shrub <3'	Bush/Shrub 3-6'	Shrub >6'	Climber/Rambler	NOTED FOR Fragrance	Cut Flowers	Hips
RED	'EUROPEANA'		✓	✓	✓	✓	✓	✓	✓	✓					✓	✓			✓				✓				✓	
	'F. J. GROOTENDORST'	✓	✓	✓	✓	✓	✓	✓	✓	✓		✓		✓	✓				✓			✓						
	'FRAGRANT CLOUD'			✓	✓	✓	✓	✓	✓					✓	✓				✓				✓			✓	✓	
	'HANSA'	✓	✓	✓	✓	✓	✓			✓			✓	✓	✓	✓			✓				✓			✓		✓
	'HURDY GURDY'			✓	✓	✓	✓	✓		✓	✓			✓	✓				✓	✓			✓					
	'JOHN CABOT'	✓	✓	✓	✓	✓	✓	✓		✓				✓	✓				✓				✓		✓			
	'JOHN FRANKLIN'			✓	✓	✓	✓	✓	✓	✓	✓			✓	✓	✓		✓					✓			✓		
	'LINDA CAMPBELL'	✓	✓	✓	✓	✓					✓	✓	✓	✓	✓			✓					✓					
	'LOUIS PHILIPPE'				✓	✓	✓	✓		✓				✓	✓				✓				✓			✓		
	'MAGIC CARROUSEL'			✓	✓	✓	✓	✓		✓				✓	✓			✓			✓						✓	
	'MISTER LINCOLN'			✓	✓	✓	✓	✓		✓					✓				✓				✓			✓	✓	
	'OLYMPIAD'			✓	✓	✓	✓	✓						✓	✓				✓				✓				✓	
	'ROGER LAMBELIN'			✓	✓	✓	✓	✓						✓	✓	✓			✓				✓			✓		
	'ROSERAIE DE L'HAY'	✓	✓	✓	✓	✓	✓			✓			✓	✓	✓	✓	✓						✓			✓		
	'SHOWBIZ'		✓	✓	✓	✓	✓	✓	✓	✓				✓	✓				✓		✓						✓	
	'THERESE BUGNET'	✓	✓	✓	✓	✓	✓			✓		✓		✓					✓				✓			✓		
	'UNCLE JOE'			✓	✓	✓	✓	✓						✓	✓					✓			✓			✓	✓	
	'VARIEGATA DI BOLOGNA'		✓	✓	✓	✓	✓								✓					✓			✓		✓	✓	✓	
	'WILL SCARLET'			✓	✓	✓	✓	✓	✓	✓					✓		✓	✓						✓	✓	✓		✓
MAUVE/PURPLE	'ANGEL FACE'		✓	✓	✓	✓	✓							✓	✓			✓				✓			✓	✓	
	'CAMAIEUX'		✓	✓	✓	✓	✓	✓			✓			✓					✓				✓			✓		✓
	'CARDINAL DE RICHELIEU'		✓	✓	✓	✓	✓	✓			✓			✓					✓				✓			✓		
	'CELINA'		✓	✓	✓	✓	✓				✓			✓			✓						✓			✓		
	'DELICATA'	✓	✓	✓	✓	✓	✓	✓	✓	✓		✓		✓	✓		✓					✓				✓		✓
	'ESCAPADE'		✓	✓	✓	✓	✓							✓	✓		✓					✓					✓	
	'LAVENDER LASSIE'			✓	✓	✓	✓	✓	✓	✓	✓			✓	✓				✓				✓	✓	✓	✓		
	'PARADISE'			✓	✓	✓	✓	✓						✓	✓				✓				✓			✓	✓	
	'PLUM DANDY'			✓	✓	✓	✓	✓						✓	✓	✓			✓	✓		✓				✓		
	'REINES DES VIOLETTES'			✓	✓	✓	✓	✓	✓						✓					✓			✓	✓	✓	✓		
	'RUGOSA MAGNIFICA'	✓	✓	✓	✓	✓	✓	✓				✓		✓	✓	✓	✓						✓			✓		✓
	'TUSCANY'		✓	✓	✓	✓	✓	✓				✓			✓			✓					✓			✓		
	'VEILCHENBLAU'			✓	✓	✓	✓	✓		✓				✓				✓						✓	✓	✓		

A Zone Map of the U.S. and Canada

A rose's winter hardiness is critical in deciding whether it is suitable for your garden. The map below divides the United States and Canada into 11 climatic zones based on average minimum temperatures, as compiled by the United States Department of Agriculture. Find your zone and check the zone information in the plant selection guide *(pages 92-96)* or the encyclopedia *(pages 98-149)* to help you choose the roses most likely to flourish in your climate.

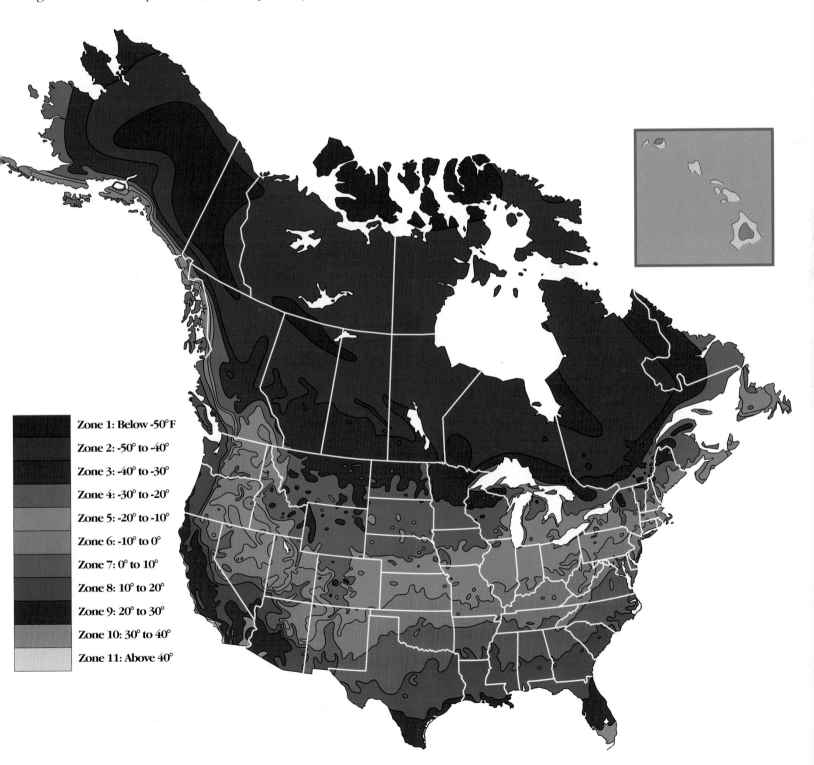

Zone 1: Below -50°F
Zone 2: -50° to -40°
Zone 3: -40° to -30°
Zone 4: -30° to -20°
Zone 5: -20° to -10°
Zone 6: -10° to 0°
Zone 7: 0° to 10°
Zone 8: 10° to 20°
Zone 9: 20° to 30°
Zone 10: 30° to 40°
Zone 11: Above 40°

Encyclopedia of Roses

Presented here is a selection of roses that includes modern and old garden varieties as well as several species. These plants have been chosen from the thousands in existence for their enduring appeal, availability, bloom colors, and landscape uses. They are also representative of their classes. In addition, many are notable for disease resistance, winter-hardiness, or overall low-maintenance requirements—and sometimes all three. The American Rose Society's (ARS) evaluation of overall quality is given for each rose that has received a rating; most of the listed roses are in the excellent (8.0-8.9) or outstanding (9.0-9.9) range. Winners of the coveted All-America Rose Selections (AARS) award are also identified.

Roses generally need plenty of sun and fertile, loamy, well-drained soil to perform at their best. The ability of any to tolerate less than ideal conditions—including partial shade and sandy soil—is mentioned here. Also, ranges are given for most plant heights and flower sizes because these features vary depending on geographical location, local weather conditions, and cultural practices such as fertilizing and pruning.

The information on hardiness refers to the USDA Plant Hardiness Zone Map on page 97. Roses that are grown outside of the recommended zones may do poorly or die. Although a few of the plants on the following pages are reliable in warm climates only, most are winter-hardy, particularly the Dr. Buck and Explorer series roses.

'ALBA SEMI-PLENA'

Classification: *alba*

Bloom period: *summer*

Height: *6 to 8 feet*

Hardiness: *Zones 4-10*

ARS rating: *8.6*

Date introduced: *prior to 1600*

'Alba Semi-plena' is also known as the White Rose of York. Its semidouble white flowers are 2½ inches across with prominent golden stamens, and they produce a powerful old garden fragrance. Borne in clusters, flowers appear in midseason and do not repeat. Elongated orange-red hips appear in late summer and fall. The foliage is gray-green.

With sturdy, arching canes that develop a vase-shaped form, 'Alba Semi-plena' can be grown as a freestanding shrub for a specimen or for use in borders, or it can be trained as a climber on a wall, a trellis, or a fence. Like other alba roses, it tolerates some shade and is quite hardy and disease resistant.

'ALBÉRIC BARBIER'

Classification: *rambler*

Bloom period: *early summer*

Height: *15 to 20 feet*

Hardiness: *Zones 5-10*

ARS rating: *not rated*

Date introduced: *1900*

Clusters of shapely yellow buds of 'Albéric Barbier' open to creamy white flowers with a yellow blush. Semidouble and double blossoms are 2 to 3 inches across and bear a moderate, fruity fragrance. Plants flower heavily in early summer and may repeat, although not reliably, in the fall. Glossy dark leaves are almost evergreen and are carried on purplish canes.

This easy-to-grow rambler requires a lot of space, since canes may grow 20 feet in a single season. It can be trained on fences or pillars, or may be used to cover a building, especially in areas where mildew is not a problem. Tied canes often produce lateral stems that arc downward for a graceful display. This rose can also be used as a ground cover. 'Albéric Barbier' is extremely disease resistant and tolerates light shade and hot, dry climates.

'ALBERTINE'

Classification: *rambler*

Bloom period: *summer*

Height: *15 to 20 feet*

Hardiness: *Zones 5-10*

ARS rating: *not rated*

Date introduced: *1921*

The buds of 'Albertine' open to bright orange-pink double blooms that are golden at the base. Produced in abundant clusters in summer, the cupped, fragrant flowers put on a spectacular show that endures for about 3 weeks. As the blooms age, they fade to a soft blush pink. Leaves are glossy green with coppery red tones. Canes bear numerous hooked prickles.

This vigorous rambler is fast growing and easily trained to a trellis, pergola, or arbor. It can also be grown as a freestanding shrub. It may be prone to mildew after flowering, but it is otherwise disease resistant.

'ALCHYMIST'

Classification: *shrub*

Bloom period: *early summer*

Height: *6 to 12 feet*

Hardiness: *Zones 5-10*

ARS rating: *8.0*

Date introduced: *1956*

Although 'Alchymist' blooms only once each year, the show is long-lasting and glorious. Flowers are large, very double and quartered, and fragrant; the petals are predominantly light to egg yolk yellow, with various shades of orange, pink, and gold infusing the blossoms toward the center. Many early blooms tend to display paler colors. Foliage is rich green-bronze and glossy.

The plant is vigorous and has an upright habit. Its landscaping potential is broad, since it can be grown either as a freestanding shrub, best kept to 6 or 7 feet, in a bed or border, or as a 12-foot climber on a trellis or wall.

'ALOHA'

Classification: *climbing hybrid tea*

Bloom period: *spring to fall*

Height: *6 to 10 feet*

Hardiness: *Zones 5-10*

ARS rating: *7.1*

Date introduced: *1949*

The cup-shaped blossoms of 'Aloha' are double or very double, 3 to 5 inches wide, and very fragrant. They appear in abundance both early in the season and again in the fall, with fairly good production in between. Petals are a clear rose pink on the inside, with a darker pink reverse; centers are shaded a warm orange-pink. Foliage is dark, glossy, and leathery.

Although it's classed as a climber, this rose can be grown as an upright shrub. Or, the nodding habit of its blooms can be shown to advantage growing over a wall, where they can be viewed from below. As a compact climber, it's a good choice for growing on a pillar. Flowers are excellent for cutting.

'ALTISSIMO'

Classification: *large-flowered climber*

Bloom period: *summer to fall*

Height: *6 to 8 feet*

Hardiness: *Zones 5-9*

ARS rating: *9.3*

Date introduced: *1966*

The large, single flowers of 'Altissimo' are 4 to 5 inches across, with seven velvety, deep blood red petals surrounding bright yellow stamens. Blooms occur in small clusters and sometimes singly on both old and new growth, beginning in summer and repeating throughout the season. Although they have only a light scent, the blossoms last a long time without fading, and they make beautiful cut flowers. Leaves are large and dark green.

While generally classed as a climber that is suitable for growing on pillars, fences, and trellises, 'Altissimo' can also be grown as a tall, freestanding shrub with an upright habit. It is vigorous, heat tolerant, and disease resistant.

'AMERICA'

Classification: *large-flowered climber*

Bloom period: *summer to fall*

Height: *8 to 12 feet*

Hardiness: *Zones 5-10*

ARS rating: *8.8*

Date introduced: *1976*

Named to honor the United States bicentennial, 'America' produces 3½- to 5-inch double blossoms in great profusion throughout the season. Flowers are coral colored with high centers and are usually borne in clusters; their fragrance is strong and spicy. Foliage is semiglossy, dark, and leathery.

Plants are upright and bushy, and are suitable for training on pillars, fences, and walls. Flowers, produced on both new and old shoots, can be cut for long-lasting indoor arrangements. 'America' is easy to grow, disease resistant, and hardy. It's an AARS winner.

'AMERICAN PILLAR'

Classification: *rambler*

Bloom period: *summer*

Height: *15 to 20 feet*

Hardiness: *Zones 5-10*

ARS rating: *7.5*

Date introduced: *1902*

The five-petaled single blossoms of 'American Pillar' are carmine-pink with white centers and golden stamens. Erupting once in midsummer, they are produced in large clusters that almost cover the entire plant. Flowers have no scent. Leaves are leathery, large, and dark green; canes are green and prickly.

The plant is very vigorous, growing to 20 feet, and is best used for climbing on a fence or arbor. Like other ramblers, it may be subject to mildew.

'ANGEL FACE'

Classification: *floribunda*

Bloom period: *summer to fall*

Height: *2 to 3 feet*

Hardiness: *Zones 4-9*

ARS rating: *8.1*

Date introduced: *1968*

The pointed buds of 'Angel Face' open to 4-inch double flowers whose ruffled, lavender-mauve petals surround golden stamens. Cup-shaped or flat, the flowers are produced almost continuously throughout the growing season in sprays that include all stages of bloom from bud to fully open. They have a strong, fruity fragrance and are well displayed against lustrous dark green foliage. They are outstanding as cut flowers.

Growing only 2 to 3 feet, 'Angel Face' is dense and compact with a somewhat spreading habit, making it useful as a low hedge or in beds and borders. Although plants are fairly disease resistant, they can be troubled by black spot and mildew in some areas. This rose is an AARS winner.

'APRICOT NECTAR'

Classification: *floribunda*

Bloom period: *summer to fall*

Height: *2 to 3 feet*

Hardiness: *Zones 4-10*

ARS rating: *8.2*

Date introduced: *1965*

The cup-shaped flowers of 'Apricot Nectar' appear in clusters of three or more throughout the growing season. The double 4- to 4½-inch blooms are an exotic blend of apricot and pink with golden centers. Their fruity, apricot-like fragrance is intense. The leaves are dark green, leathery, and glossy.

Plants are very vigorous, bushy, and compact. Their extended flowering display makes them useful in beds or borders, singly or massed. Although resistant to some diseases, they are susceptible to black spot. 'Apricot Nectar' is an AARS winner.

'AQUARIUS'

Classification: *grandiflora*

Bloom period: *spring to fall*

Height: *4 to 5 feet*

Hardiness: *Zones 5-10*

ARS rating: *8.0*

Date introduced: *1971*

Considered by many to be one of the very best grandifloras, 'Aquarius' flowers freely from spring until frost, producing small sprays of up to five double blooms that are lightly fragrant. Buds are dark pink, opening to blended medium-pink-and-white 4-inch flowers with high centers. Foliage is large and leathery.

Plants are urn shaped, upright, and vigorous. They are well suited to beds and borders, and flowers are ideal for cutting. This rose is extremely disease resistant. It is an AARS winner.

'ARCHDUKE CHARLES'

Classification: *China*

Bloom period: *summer to fall*

Height: *2 to 5 feet*

Hardiness: *Zones 6-10*

ARS rating: *7.9*

Date introduced: *1840*

The 3-inch double flowers of 'Archduke Charles' open very slowly, revealing a coloration that varies with the weather from pale pink in cool, overcast conditions to deep pink or crimson under warm, sunny skies. The lightly scented flowers are produced reliably all season. New leaves are red, maturing to a glossy green. Canes are also red, as are the sparse prickles.

This rose is a moderate grower with an erect, bushy, neat form. Its continuous flowers add color to beds and borders, and the plant also makes an attractive hedge. It's moderately disease resistant and tolerates heat, humidity, and slightly alkaline soil.

'AUSBURN'

Classification: *shrub*

Bloom period: *spring*

Height: *3 feet*

Hardiness: *Zones 4-10*

ARS rating: *9.0*

Date introduced: *1986*

'Ausburn' (also known as 'Robbie Burns') is a diminutive modern shrub rose with small, single flowers, each having five petals. Like many of the English roses bred by David Austin, it is reminiscent of older rose types, with a commanding fragrance and an old-fashioned character. The blooms are light pink with a white center, and the small leaves are a medium matte green.

The small size of this rose makes it a useful addition to beds and borders, where it can be used in the foreground. It is very effective planted in groups.

'AUTUMN DAMASK'

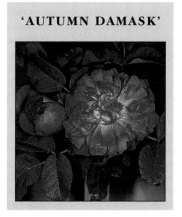

Classification: *damask*

Bloom period: *spring to fall*

Height: *4 to 5 feet*

Hardiness: *Zones 4-10*

ARS rating: *8.0*

Date introduced: *ancient*

This very old rose produces abundant, richly fragrant blossoms in spring followed by scattered blooms throughout summer and fall. Flowers are 3½ inches across, clear pink with deeper centers, and double. It is also known as 'Quatre Saisons' and has been used in breeding both the bourbons and the hybrid perpetuals. Foliage is light gray-green.

Plants are vigorous, of medium height, with a spreading habit. They are quite hardy and tolerate pruning better than most damasks. The long flowering season makes a valuable contribution to beds or borders, and the powerful wine fragrance of the blooms is useful for making potpourri.

'BALLERINA'

'BARONNE PREVOST'

'BELINDA'

'BELLE POITEVINE'

Classification: *hybrid musk*

Bloom period: *summer to fall*

Height: *2 to 4 feet*

Hardiness: *Zones 5-10*

ARS rating: *9.0*

Date introduced: *1937*

Classification: *hybrid perpetual*

Bloom period: *summer to fall*

Height: *4 to 6 feet*

Hardiness: *Zones 5-10*

ARS rating: *8.5*

Date introduced: *1842*

Classification: *hybrid musk*

Bloom period: *summer to fall*

Height: *4 to 8 feet*

Hardiness: *Zones 5-10*

ARS rating: *8.6*

Date introduced: *1936*

Classification: *hybrid rugosa*

Bloom period: *summer to fall*

Height: *3½ to 5 feet*

Hardiness: *Zones 3-10*

ARS rating: *7.8*

Date introduced: *1894*

The small (1-inch) blossoms of 'Ballerina' are soft pink with white centers and are borne in huge clusters of up to 100 blooms each. The flowers are single, each with five petals surrounding bright yellow stamens, and have a light musky scent. Foliage is medium green and dense.

Plants have a low-growing, arching habit that makes them one of the best roses for hedges, either pruned or left to their natural form. They are a good choice for containers or beds, and their flowers are long-lasting both on the plant and when cut for indoor arrangements. Plants are disease resistant and tolerant of light shade.

The elegant 3- to 4-inch blooms of 'Baronne Prévost' are very double, with 100 petals that quarter and fold back on a green button-eyed center. Ranging from pale pink to deep rose pink, the recurring blooms are extremely fragrant. Buds are globular, leaves are medium green, and canes are very prickly.

Best grown as a freestanding shrub, 'Baronne Prévost' grows between 4 and 6 feet high with an approximately equal spread. The plant is vigorous, and it has a less awkward form than do most hybrid perpetuals. Also, the foliage is more attractive and disease resistant than that of most of the class.

'Belinda' produces large erect clusters of semidouble flowers almost continuously throughout the growing season. The soft medium pink blooms are 1 inch or less across, have 12 to 15 petals, and emit a light fragrance. When seen at close range, the blooms show off white centers.

Plants are vigorous, upright, and bushy, and can either be maintained as a dense hedge by pruning or be trained to a pillar. They are quite disease resistant and, like most hybrid musks, adaptable to light shade.

The flowers of 'Belle Poitevine' are fragrant and semidouble, with twirled petals. Their coloring is somewhat dependent on weather, ranging from rose pink to magenta pink, with lighter colors more prevalent under sunny skies. In fall, the plump orange-red hips create a colorful display against the deeply veined, leathery, dark green foliage.

The vigorous plants are nicely shaped, often as broad as they are tall. This rose makes a good choice for a large hedge. Like other hybrid rugosas, it is very hardy, disease resistant, and easy to grow. It also tolerates seaside conditions.

'BELLE STORY'

Classification: *shrub*

Bloom period: *summer to fall*

Height: *4 feet*

Hardiness: *Zones 4-10*

ARS rating: *8.5*

Date introduced: *1984*

The sweetly scented flowers of 'Belle Story' are large and semidouble, resembling peonies. A David Austin rose, this is a heavy bloomer, repeating well through the season. The wide-spreading, soft pink petals curve inward, fashioning a broad cup that accentuates golden yellow stamens. The abundant foliage is light green and semiglossy.

Plants are vigorous and healthy. They grow as broad as they do tall, forming a rounded 4-foot shrub that is well suited to a bed or border. Like many others of David Austin's English roses, this one is very hardy.

'BETTY PRIOR'

Classification: *floribunda*

Bloom period: *summer to fall*

Height: *4 to 5 feet*

Hardiness: *Zones 4-10*

ARS rating: *8.2*

Date introduced: *1935*

The carmine-pink buds of 'Betty Prior' open to 2- to 3-inch cupped single blossoms that flatten with age and bear a light, spicy fragrance. Blossoms occur in large clusters so profuse that they can cover the entire bush. In cool weather, flowers remain carmine-pink, but as temperatures rise they become medium pink. The five petals surround yellow stamens that darken to brown. Foliage is medium green and semiglossy.

Plants are vigorous and bushy with a rounded form. One of the most popular floribundas ever, this rose is effectively used for mass plantings and hedges, in small groups, and singly in a bed. It is also very winter hardy and exceptionally resistant to black spot, but less so to mildew.

'BLANC DOUBLE DE COUBERT'

Classification: *hybrid rugosa*

Bloom period: *spring to fall*

Height: *4 to 6 feet*

Hardiness: *Zones 3-10*

ARS rating: *8.3*

Date introduced: *1892*

This hybrid rugosa blooms heavily early in the season, with scattered blossoms in summer and fall. Flowers are semidouble, 2 to 3 inches wide, and very fragrant. Petals are pure white with a delicate tissue-paper-like texture that contrasts with the crinkled, dark, leathery leaves. Canes are gray, and in fall large orange-red hips are produced.

Plants are typically as broad as they are tall and require a lot of room. Extremely vigorous, they often send out suckers several feet from the plant base. The rose is effective as a hedge, in large beds, and as a specimen. One of the best hybrid rugosas, 'Blanc Double de Coubert' is extremely hardy, resistant to both diseases and insects, and tolerates sandy soil and salt spray, making it a good choice for seaside gardens.

'BLAZE'

Classification: *large-flowered climber*

Bloom period: *spring to fall*

Height: *12 to 15 feet*

Hardiness: *Zones 5-10*

ARS rating: *7.4*

Date introduced: *1932*

Clusters of cup-shaped scarlet blossoms occur on both old and new wood of 'Blaze' throughout the growing season. Flowers are semidouble, 2 to 3 inches across, lightly fragrant, and nonfading, even in hot weather. Early flowers are somewhat larger than those produced later in the season. Dark green leathery foliage contrasts nicely with the continuous show of blooms.

This easy-to-grow rose has a vigorous, upright habit, and its canes are quick to reach their height of 12 to 15 feet, making it a good choice for fences, arbors, pillars, and porches. It is quite hardy but is somewhat susceptible to powdery mildew.

'BONICA'

'BOULE DE NEIGE'

'BRIDE'S DREAM'

'BUFF BEAUTY'

Classification: *shrub*

Bloom period: *summer*

Height: *3 to 5 feet*

Hardiness: *Zones 4-9*

ARS rating: *9.1*

Date introduced: *1981*

Classification: *bourbon*

Bloom period: *summer to fall*

Height: *4 to 5 feet*

Hardiness: *Zones 5-10*

ARS rating: *7.6*

Date introduced: *1867*

Classification: *hybrid tea*

Bloom period: *summer to fall*

Height: *3 to 4 feet*

Hardiness: *Zones 5-10*

ARS rating: *8.0*

Date introduced: *1985*

Classification: *hybrid musk*

Bloom period: *summer to fall*

Height: *5 to 6 feet*

Hardiness: *Zones 5-10*

ARS rating: *8.3*

Date introduced: *1939*

'Bonica' (also called 'Meidomonac') is free flowering and easy to grow. Large, loose clusters of up to 20 flowers appear throughout the summer. Each spiraled bud opens to reveal a 2½- to 3½-inch double blossom with soft pink ruffled petals. The foliage is dark green and glossy. Bright orange hips appear in fall and remain attractive all winter.

The plant has a spreading habit with arching stems spanning 5 to 6 feet. This rose is not fussy about pruning; it can be maintained as a compact hedge or lightly tip pruned for a more informal appearance. 'Bonica' is an excellent choice for beds or borders, for massing, or for use as a hedge along a walk or drive. It is highly disease resistant, exceptionally hardy, and tolerant of harsh climates. This is the first shrub rose to win the AARS award.

The rounded pink buds of 'Boule de Neige' (French for snowball) open to reveal creamy white flowers that are at first tinted with crimson along the petal margins. As they develop, the 2- to 4-inch very double flowers turn pure white with reflexed petals that create a beautifully rounded form. They are intensely fragrant. Foliage is dark green and leathery, providing a perfect foil for the flowers; canes bear few prickles.

Plants, slender and erect in habit, are excellent for combining in beds with lower-growing, bushy plants. This rose is disease resistant.

The large double flowers of 'Bride's Dream' are pale pink, high centered, and lightly fragrant. They usually occur singly on the stem and appear in great abundance throughout the growing season. Foliage is dark green, and stems bear brown prickles.

The plant is a strong grower with a tall, upright habit. It can be situated in beds or borders, and its flowers are excellent for cutting and exhibition. 'Bride's Dream' is judged by some growers to be the best hybrid tea in its color class.

The color of the 3- to 4-inch double flowers of 'Buff Beauty' ranges from buff yellow to deep apricot, depending on weather conditions. Richly fragrant, flattened blossoms are borne in clusters. The abundant foliage emerges bronze-red, turning a glossy dark green as it matures. Canes are smooth and brown.

This rose is a very attractive plant with a graceful, arching habit and is often broader than it is tall. It requires a lot of space but makes a lovely specimen. It can also be trained to a pillar or wall, or can be used as a ground cover on banks.

'CABBAGE ROSE'

Classification: *centifolia*

Bloom period: *summer*

Height: *5 to 6 feet*

Hardiness: *Zones 4-10*

ARS rating: *7.9*

Date introduced: *unknown*

The very double flowers of 'Cabbage Rose' (also called *R. centifolia*) are clear pink and richly fragrant. This is the type of rose, with many-petaled, globular blooms, often depicted in paintings by the old European masters. The 3-inch flowers are supported by long stems and appear singly or in clusters. Though they do not repeat, they produce a stunning summer display. Foliage is gray-green and coarse, and thorns are abundant.

'Cabbage Rose' has a lax, arching habit and is moderately sized, making it useful as a garden shrub. It is extremely hardy.

'CAMAIEUX'

Classification: *gallica*

Bloom period: *summer*

Height: *3 to 5 feet*

Hardiness: *Zones 4-10*

ARS rating: *7.5*

Date introduced: *1830*

Flowers of 'Camaieux' are blush mauve-pink with stripes that change from crimson to pleasing shades of purple and lavender as the blossoms mature. Flowers are double, cup shaped, 3 to 4 inches across, and spicy scented. In fall, the plant produces colorful hips. Foliage is grayish green.

The growth habit of this rose is upright and compact. Arching canes give it a rounded form that is suitable for beds and borders, where its evolving blossom colors can put on a delightful summer show. 'Camaieux' tolerates summer heat and is fairly disease resistant but can be susceptible to mildew in southern climates.

'CANDEUR LYONNAISE'

Classification: *hybrid perpetual*

Bloom period: *early spring to fall*

Height: *4 feet*

Hardiness: *Zones 5-10*

ARS rating: *7.1*

Date introduced: *1914*

'Candeur Lyonnaise' produces a continuous succession of flowers from early spring until the first hard frost. Its buds are long and pointed, opening to very large double flowers that are 5 inches across. Blooms are white, although they sometimes take on a pale yellow tint, and the petals are delicately fringed.

The plants themselves are vigorous, stately, upright, and of moderate height. Their extended flowering season makes this an excellent shrub for nearly any garden and a good source of cut flowers.

'CARDINAL DE RICHELIEU'

Classification: *gallica*

Bloom period: *summer*

Height: *2½ to 5 feet*

Hardiness: *Zones 4-10*

ARS rating: *7.9*

Date introduced: *1840*

The buds of 'Cardinal de Richelieu' are fat, rounded, and mauve pink, opening to become one of the deepest colored of all roses. Flowers are double and 2 to 3 inches across. Petals are a velvety purple-violet with a reverse of silvery rose, and they curve to form a ball-shaped blossom. The fragrance is strong and increases with the flower's age. Leaves are smooth and dark green, and stems are nearly smooth.

The attractive plants are compact, forming arching mounds as wide as they are tall. Unlike some gallicas, this rose responds well to heavy pruning, producing its flowers on new wood. It is extremely hardy and tolerates summer heat and humidity.

'CAREFREE BEAUTY'

Classification: *shrub*

Bloom period: *summer to fall*

Height: *4 to 5 feet*

Hardiness: *Zones 4-10*

ARS rating: *8.5*

Date introduced: *1977*

The long, pointed buds of 'Carefree Beauty' open to semidouble medium pink flowers. Each blossom has 15 to 20 petals and bears a rich, fruity fragrance. Flowers appear in clusters of three to 20 and are produced freely all season. Foliage is a bright apple green.

This rose has a vigorous, bushy, spreading habit. It is easy to grow, as its name implies, and makes an excellent flowering hedge or garden shrub. Space plants 18 inches apart to form a dense hedge. A Dr. Buck rose, it is both disease resistant and very hardy.

'CATHERINE MERMET'

Classification: *tea*

Bloom period: *summer*

Height: *3 to 4 feet*

Hardiness: *Zones 7-10*

ARS rating: *8.1*

Date introduced: *1869*

Flowers of 'Catherine Mermet' open a blush pink with lilac edges and change to soft beige as they mature. Inner petals often display yellow at the base. The double blossoms are 3 inches across and are borne singly or in small clusters on graceful stems. Their fragrance is strong and spicy. Leaves are copper colored when young, maturing to a medium green.

This rose is somewhat delicate, requiring nothing less than a warm, sunny spot and rich, well-drained soil. It is quite tender and is frequently grown in greenhouses. With an upright, arching habit, it is well suited for beds, borders, and specimen plantings. Flowers are excellent for cutting. Pruning should be restricted to removal of dead and weak, spindly canes. It is moderately disease resistant and heat tolerant.

'CECILE BRUNNER'

Classification: *polyantha*

Bloom period: *midspring to frost*

Height: *2 to 4 feet*

Hardiness: *Zones 4-9*

ARS rating: *8.0*

Date introduced: *1881*

Although the flowers of this rose are small—only 1 to 1½ inches across—they are lovely in both form and color, earning it the nickname the sweetheart rose. The dainty spiraled buds are long and pointed. Flowers are sweetly scented and double, with delicate pink petals that become yellow toward their base; they are borne in small clusters and bloom steadily throughout the growing season. Foliage is sparse, glossy, and dark green, and canes bear few thorns.

'Cécile Brunner' is an upright shrub suitable for beds and borders and is an excellent source of cut flowers. A climbing sport that grows 15 to 25 feet was introduced in 1894; its foliage, denser than that of its parent, may hide some of the blooms. Both forms tolerate partial shade and poor soil.

'CELESTIAL'

Classification: *alba*

Bloom period: *summer*

Height: *5 to 6 feet*

Hardiness: *Zones 4-10*

ARS rating: *8.6*

Date introduced: *prior to 1848*

The 3½-inch blooms of 'Celestial' are sweetly fragrant. Borne in clusters, flowers are semidouble and pale blush pink with golden stamens, and they are particularly attractive as the delicate petals unfurl. Flowering occurs in summer with no repeat. The soft blue-gray foliage provides an exquisite contrast to the flowers.

This vigorous rose requires a large space in the garden. Usually as wide as they are tall, the shrubs make outstanding specimens with their complementary flower and foliage tones. Plants are shade tolerant and require only moderate pruning; heavy pruning should be avoided.

'CELINA'

Classification: *moss*

Bloom period: *summer*

Height: *4 feet*

Hardiness: *Zones 4-10*

ARS rating: *8.3*

Date introduced: *1855*

Like others of this classification, the sepals covering the buds of 'Célina' bear a mossy growth that has a firlike scent. The buds open to large semi-double flowers in shades of mauve, pink, crimson, lavender, and purple. When fully open, the blooms reveal golden stamens. Canes are studded with long, sturdy prickles.

Suitable for beds and borders, 'Célina' has a tidy habit and a moderate height. It is a very hardy rose but has a tendency to get mildew late in the season.

'CELINE FORESTIER'

Classification: *noisette*

Bloom period: *summer to fall*

Height: *6 to 10 feet*

Hardiness: *Zones 6-10*

ARS rating: *7.5*

Date introduced: *1842*

The flattened, very double flowers of 'Céline Forestier' are creamy yellow with darker peach or pink tones. Their petals form a quartered pattern and surround a green button eye. The intensely fragrant blooms usually occur in small clusters of three to four and are of very high quality. The plant is almost always in flower throughout the growing season. Foliage is light green.

This rose is not as vigorous or as large as most noisettes, and it takes a while to become established. It performs best in southern climates, growing against a warm wall or trained as a small, free-flowering climber on a pillar or fence. It tolerates summer heat and humidity.

'CELSIANA'

Classification: *damask*

Bloom period: *summer*

Height: *4 to 5 feet*

Hardiness: *Zones 4-10*

ARS rating: *8.8*

Date introduced: *prior to 1750*

The semidouble, gently nodding blooms of 'Celsiana' are 3½ to 4 inches across, cup shaped, and deliciously scented. Borne in clusters, the flowers open a clear pink and fade to a soft blush as they age. Petals are silky textured and surround bright yellow stamens. The flower colors are complemented perfectly by gray-green foliage.

The plant has an upright habit with gracefully arching canes and makes a fine choice for a bed or border, where it can put on a midseason display of color. 'Celsiana' is disease resistant and very hardy.

'CHAMPLAIN'

Classification: *shrub*

Bloom period: *summer to fall*

Height: *3 to 4 feet*

Hardiness: *Zones 4-10*

ARS rating: *8.1*

Date introduced: *1982*

The 2- to 2½-inch double blooms of 'Champlain' are a rich cherry red with darker edges. Blossoms are only slightly fragrant, but once this rose begins flowering in the summer it continues nonstop until a hard frost. Foliage is shiny and dark.

The plant is not a vigorous grower; its compact habit makes it especially well suited to beds. One of the Explorer series roses from Canada, 'Champlain' is a very hardy kordesii shrub. It is also practically immune to both black spot and mildew and appears not to be bothered by aphids.

'CHERISH'

Classification: *floribunda*

Bloom period: *summer to fall*

Height: *3 feet*

Hardiness: *Zones 4-9*

ARS rating: *8.3*

Date introduced: *1980*

The 3- to 4-inch double blossoms of 'Cherish' put out a light cinnamon fragrance and appear over a lengthy season. Borne both singly and in clusters of up to 20, the high-centered flowers are coral-apricot with a creamy white base. The spiraled buds open slowly, and the flowers are extremely long-lasting. New leaves are bronze red, turning very dark green and glossy with age.

The compact, symmetrical habit of the bush is somewhat spreading, making 'Cherish' an appropriate choice for beds and borders. It can also be used as a low hedge. Flowers are exceptional for cutting. Added to the long list of the rose's virtues are good disease resistance and hardiness. It is an AARS winner.

'CHRYSLER IMPERIAL'

Classification: *hybrid tea*

Bloom period: *summer to fall*

Height: *4 to 5 feet*

Hardiness: *Zones 5-10*

ARS rating: *7.8*

Date introduced: *1952*

The deep crimson double flowers of 'Chrysler Imperial' are 4½ to 5 inches across with 45 to 50 petals. Blooming singly on long stems, they have a rich, spicy fragrance and a velvety texture; their color fades to magenta as the blossoms age. The blossoms appear profusely in midsummer and repeat well through fall. Leaves are dark green and semiglossy.

Plants are vigorous with an upright, compact habit and perform best in climates with hot summers. They are somewhat temperamental about their conditions and are subject to mildew. Appropriate for beds and borders, this rose works especially well in a small landscape. The blooms make outstanding cut flowers. The rose is an AARS winner.

'CITY OF YORK'

Classification: *large-flowered climber*

Bloom period: *spring*

Height: *15 feet*

Hardiness: *Zones 5-10*

ARS rating: *8.4*

Date introduced: *1945*

The semidouble cup-shaped blooms of 'City of York' are creamy white with yellow centers and are pleasantly fragrant. They appear once per season over a lengthy period in the spring in large clusters of seven to 15 flowers. Leaves are glossy and leathery.

This vigorous rose is very effective in the spring, when its abundant pale blooms create a dramatic contrast against lush, dark foliage. It is tolerant of partial shade and can be grown on a north wall. It's also a good choice for a trellis.

'COMMUNIS'

Classification: *moss*

Bloom period: *summer*

Height: *4 feet*

Hardiness: *Zones 4-10*

ARS rating: *7.7*

Date introduced: *late 1600s*

Considered by many to be the best moss rose, 'Communis' (also called 'Common Moss') produces mossy growths on its sepals, buds, and stems. Buds are rose pink, opening to pale pink, intensely fragrant double flowers that are 2 to 3 inches wide. Reflexed petals surround a green button eye. The abundant foliage is medium green.

'Communis' plants are moderate growers with an arching habit; they are usually slightly taller than they are broad. The rose is well suited to beds and borders, and is both disease resistant and hardy.

'COMPLICATA'

Classification: *gallica*

Bloom period: *early summer*

Height: *5 to 10 feet*

Hardiness: *Zones 4-10*

ARS rating: *8.4*

Date introduced: *unknown*

Although this rose blooms only in early summer, the display is spectacular. The single flowers are 5 inches across and appear along the entire length of each branch. Blooms are deep pink with a white eye and bright yellow stamens. Leaves are large and light green. Round, bright orange hips are produced in the fall.

Vigorous and easy to grow, this rose requires a good bit of space. It can be maintained as a shrub with a height of 5 feet and a spread of 6 to 8 feet, thanks to its arching canes. 'Complicata' makes an effective hedge and, if allowed, will reach 10 feet in height. It can also be trained as a climber. Poor soils, summer heat and humidity, and winter cold are all tolerated. The plant can become rampant.

'CONSTANCE SPRY'

Classification: *shrub*

Bloom period: *midsummer*

Height: *6 to 15 feet*

Hardiness: *Zones 4-10*

ARS rating: *7.8*

Date introduced: *1961*

The light pink double or very double flowers of 'Constance Spry' resemble peonies. This rose blooms only once each year, but the display is dramatic, producing a wealth of 3½- to 5-inch flowers bearing a rich, myrrhlike fragrance. The flowers appear in clusters, showing up well against abundant dark green foliage. Canes bear lots of bright red prickles.

A very vigorous plant, 'Constance Spry' can either be pruned to maintain a large, rounded shrub or be trained to climb a fence, wall, tripod, or pillar, where it can grow as high as 15 feet.

'COUNTRY DANCER'

Classification: *shrub*

Bloom period: *summer to fall*

Height: *2 to 4 feet*

Hardiness: *Zones 4-10*

ARS rating: *7.5*

Date introduced: *1973*

The high-centered buds of 'Country Dancer', a Dr. Buck rose, open to large, flat, double flowers that are somewhere between deep pink and rosy red in color—and quite fragrant. The petals are slightly yellow toward their base, and they surround golden stamens. Flowers occur in clusters throughout the growing season. Foliage is dark green.

This rose is usually grown as a low, spreading shrub. It can also be used as a hedge. Canes can be trained to a pillar or fence but should be trained horizontally to obtain the best flowering display; canes that grow vertically will produce all of their flowers at the tips. Although it's extremely hardy, 'Country Dancer' is somewhat susceptible to black spot.

'CRESTED MOSS'

Classification: *moss*

Bloom period: *summer*

Height: *4 to 6 feet*

Hardiness: *Zones 4-10*

ARS rating: *7.9*

Date introduced: *1826*

The buds of 'Crested Moss' (also called 'Cristata' and 'Chapeau de Napoleon') are uniquely beautiful, peeking through a set of large, deeply fringed, mossy-edged sepals. Open, the fragrant medium pink blooms are very double and cabbagelike, ranging from 3 to 3½ inches across. The bloom period is lengthy but not recurring. Foliage is abundant and light green.

This rose has a strong, upright form and arching canes, and can be grown as a medium-sized shrub in a bed or border or trained against a support. It is disease resistant and quite hardy.

'CRIMSON GLORY'

Classification: *hybrid tea*

Bloom period: *summer to fall*

Height: *3 to 4 feet*

Hardiness: *Zones 5-10*

ARS rating: *6.8*

Date introduced: *1935*

'Crimson Glory' produces pointed black-red buds and deep crimson velvety flowers with purple shading. Fully opened, the 3- to 4-inch blossoms are double with 30 to 35 petals and splendidly fragrant. Flower necks tend to be weak, allowing the blooms to nod.

The plant has a spreading, asymmetrical habit suitable for a bed or border. A climbing form that grows 10 to 12 feet and has an ARS rating of 7.3 is also available; it produces blooms only on old wood and makes a fine specimen on an arbor or trellis where the nodding habit of its flowers is a viewing asset. Both forms develop leathery dark green leaves and thrive in warm climates, but should be protected from the hottest sun if purple tones are objectionable.

'DAINTY BESS'

Classification: *hybrid tea*

Bloom period: *summer*

Height: *3 to 4 feet*

Hardiness: *Zones 5-10*

ARS rating: *9.0*

Date introduced: *1925*

The silvery pink flowers of 'Dainty Bess' are unusual for a hybrid tea in several respects: They are single, with only five large, wavy petals; the petals surround a center of stamens that are colored deep maroon; and the flowers close at night. Blooms that develop in the shade of the leaves tend to be lighter in color. They are fragrant and long-lasting, both on the stem and when cut.

Plants are sturdy, vigorous, and upright, with abundant dark green leathery foliage. This rose's constant production of flowers makes it a fine choice in a bed or border. Despite its name, it's tough, tolerant of harsh weather, and resistant to disease.

'DELICATA'

Classification: *hybrid rugosa*

Bloom period: *summer to fall*

Height: *3 feet*

Hardiness: *Zones 3-10*

ARS rating: *7.9*

Date introduced: *1898*

The bright pink to mauve flowers of 'Delicata' are semi-double, containing 18 to 24 petals, and open to a width of 3 to 3½ inches. Scented like cloves, the blooms appear in abundance early in the season and repeat until fall. Large orange-red hips follow the blooms and are present at the same time as later flowers—which may create an objectionable color combination for some.

Plants are low growing compared with other hybrid rugosas, and they have a compact, well-branched habit. Rarely over 3 feet in height, they are useful garden shrubs. Like other members of this class, 'Delicata' is extremely hardy, disease resistant, and tolerant of seaside conditions.

'DON JUAN'

Classification: *large-flowered climber*

Bloom period: *late spring to fall*

Height: *8 to 10 feet*

Hardiness: *Zones 5-10*

ARS rating: *8.2*

Date introduced: *1958*

This rose produces extremely large, fragrant flowers, singly or in small clusters, throughout the growing season. The dark red, nearly black buds are oval and open slowly to reveal 4- to 5-inch high-centered or cupped blossoms with a deep velvety color that is among the darkest of all red roses. Flowers are borne on long stems, making them ideal for cutting. Leaves are dark and glossy.

'Don Juan' is a moderate to vigorous grower with an upright habit. Deadheading spent blossoms will encourage rebloom. The plant is very effective on a pillar, fence, wall, or trellis. Although not extremely hardy, its disease resistance is good.

'DORTMUND'

Classification: *shrub*

Bloom period: *summer to fall*

Height: *7 to 15 feet*

Hardiness: *Zones 4-10*

ARS rating: *9.1*

Date introduced: *1955*

The single flowers of 'Dortmund' are 3 to 4 inches across, with a center of yellow stamens, and have a light, spicy scent. Each bloom's brilliant poppy red petals are white at the base. The flowers are set off by glossy, hollylike leaves. With vigorous deadheading, blooming continues throughout the growing season; if spent blooms are allowed to remain, bright orange hips develop.

'Dortmund' is a *Rosa kordesii* hybrid, one of a race of extremely hardy and disease-resistant roses. Versatile as well, it can be grown as a free-standing shrub or a hedge, pegged as a ground cover, or trained as a climber on a pillar, fence, or trellis. It is slow to start in the garden but, once established, is a vigorous and tough plant. It thrives in full sun or partial shade.

'DOUBLE DELIGHT'

Classification: *hybrid tea*

Bloom period: *summer to fall*

Height: *4 feet*

Hardiness: *Zones 5-10*

ARS rating: *8.9*

Date introduced: *1977*

Each blossom of 'Double Delight' is a uniquely colored combination of red and creamy white. The exact coloration depends on light and temperature, but generally the red begins at the petal tips and diffuses to a creamy center. The double flowers are 5½ inches across, borne singly on stems, and have a strong, spicy fragrance. Leaves are a medium matte green.

Its bushy form and free-flowering habit make this rose a fine choice for beds and borders. It is a superb cut flower, prized for its form, color, fragrance, and long vase life. 'Double Delight' is fairly disease resistant but is somewhat tender. It is an AARS winner.

'DREAMGLO'

Classification: *miniature*

Bloom period: *summer to fall*

Height: *18 to 24 inches*

Hardiness: *Zones 5-10*

ARS rating: *8.5*

Date introduced: *1978*

Long and pointed, the buds of 'Dreamglo' open to double flowers. Each bloom bears about 50 white petals that are blended and tipped with red. The blooms are borne singly, appearing abundantly in mid-season and repeating well. They have the classic high-centered hybrid tea form. The 1½-inch-wide blossoms are lightly fragrant and very long lasting; leaves are small, glossy, and dark green.

This vigorous rose has a compact, upright habit and is an excellent choice for the foreground of beds and borders. It is disease resistant.

'DUBLIN BAY'

Classification: *large-flowered climber*

Bloom period: *spring to fall*

Height: *7 to 10 feet*

Hardiness: *Zones 5-10*

ARS rating: *8.5*

Date introduced: *1976*

Produced in clusters, the 4- to 4½-inch blood red flowers of 'Dublin Bay' appear continuously from spring until frost. Blooms are double, cupped, and fragrant. They have a velvety texture and show off well against the rich green foliage.

The plant is somewhat slow growing. It can perform as a shrub during its first few seasons and then become a fine climber with an upright, well branched habit, perfect for a low fence, pillar, stone wall, or trellis. 'Dublin Bay' is disease resistant.

'DUCHESSE DE BRABANT'	'ELINA'	'ERFURT'	'ESCAPADE'

Classification: *tea*

Bloom period: *early spring to fall*

Height: *3 to 5 feet*

Hardiness: *Zones 7-10*

ARS rating: *8.2*

Date introduced: *1857*

The 2- to 3-inch double flowers of 'Duchesse de Brabant' occur freely all throughout the growing season. Rounded and cupped blossoms open from tulip-shaped buds and range in color from soft, clear pink to bright rosy pink. They are extremely fragrant. The abundant foliage is medium green, and the canes are well supplied with prickles.

This rose has a bushy, spreading habit—it is nearly as broad as it is tall—and is suitable for a bed or border. It is vigorous, disease resistant, and heat tolerant but tender. A white sport of 'Duchesse de Brabant', 'Madame Joseph Schwartz', was introduced in 1880.

Classification: *hybrid tea*

Bloom period: *summer to fall*

Height: *3 to 4 feet*

Hardiness: *Zones 5-10*

ARS rating: *8.6*

Date introduced: *1985*

The large double blooms of 'Elina' (also known as 'Peaudouce') are a delicate pale yellow to ivory. Beautifully formed flowers appear continuously throughout the season, each bearing around 35 petals and producing a light fragrance. Leaves are large, glossy, and dark green, providing a dramatic foil for the flowers.

The plants are vigorous and upright. Blossoms are produced in abundance on long, straight stems, making this rose an excellent source for cut roses. It is hardy and resistant to black spot but somewhat susceptible to mildew.

Classification: *hybrid musk*

Bloom period: *summer to fall*

Height: *5 to 6 feet*

Hardiness: *Zones 5-10*

ARS rating: *8.4*

Date introduced: *1939*

Buds of 'Erfurt' are rosy red, long, and pointed, opening to deep cerise-pink semidouble flowers with white centers and bright golden yellow stamens. Once plants begin to bloom, they continue nonstop until frost. The flowers exude a pleasing musky fragrance. Foliage is leathery and wrinkled with a coppery green tone that enhances the brightly colored flowers. Stems are brown with hooked prickles.

The plants are vigorous and bushy, with arching canes that may spread outward to 6 feet. The long show of blooms and abundance of attractive foliage make 'Erfurt' an outstanding garden shrub for beds or borders. Like other hybrid musks, this rose is disease resistant and tolerates some shade and poor soil.

Classification: *floribunda*

Bloom period: *summer to fall*

Height: *2½ to 3 feet*

Hardiness: *Zones 4-10*

ARS rating: *8.8*

Date introduced: *1967*

The 3-inch semidouble flowers of 'Escapade' are light mauve-pink or lilac to rosy violet with creamy white centers. They are borne in both large and small clusters, and each bloom has about 12 petals that surround amber stamens. Blooms commence in midseason, repeating consistently until a hard frost. The blooms are lightly fragrant. Leaves are light green and glossy.

'Escapade' plants have an upright, bushy habit and are vigorous growers. They are useful in beds and borders and can also be planted as a low hedge. The flowers are excellent for cutting.

'EUROPEANA'

Classification: *floribunda*

Bloom period: *summer to fall*

Height: *2 to 3 feet*

Hardiness: *Zones 4-10*

ARS rating: *9.0*

Date introduced: *1968*

Borne in large clusters, the double blooms of 'Europeana' are 3 inches across and cup shaped. Petals are deep crimson and have a velvety texture. Beginning in midseason, flowering continues prolifically until the fall. Leaves emerge bronze red, maturing to deep, glossy green with reddish tints.

This bush is quite robust. Its enormous flower clusters can cause the stems to bend under their weight, so it should be grouped with plants that will provide support for the flower-laden stems. Because it has a bushy, spreading habit, 'Europeana' is suitable for beds, borders, and low hedges. Flowers are good for cutting, and the plants are disease resistant and very hardy. This rose is an AARS winner.

'FAIR BIANCA'

Classification: *shrub*

Bloom period: *summer to fall*

Height: *3 feet*

Hardiness: *Zones 4-10*

ARS rating: *8.2*

Date introduced: *1983*

The very double, medium-sized blossoms of 'Fair Bianca', a David Austin rose, are shallowly cupped and bear a strong myrrh fragrance. Their small pure white petals are tightly arranged around a green button eye. As they mature, petals reflex at the edges. Blooms appear almost continuously throughout the season. Foliage is light green and semiglossy.

The plants are vigorous and compact, growing as broad as they are tall. Their neat habit and outstanding flowers make them ideally suited for beds or patio plantings. They can also be effectively used for a low hedge.

'FANTIN-LATOUR'

Classification: *centifolia*

Bloom period: *late spring*

Height: *4 to 6 feet*

Hardiness: *Zones 4-10*

ARS rating: *8.2*

Date introduced: *unknown*

Although 'Fantin-Latour' has a relatively short bloom period and does not repeat, the quality of the blossoms makes up for their short season. Each 2- to 3-inch very double flower is composed of 200 petals, giving it the full appearance typical of centifolia roses. When it first opens, the pale blush pink bloom is cupped; it then flattens as it matures. The blossoms emit a delicate fragrance. Leaves are dark green, and canes are nearly smooth.

'Fantin-Latour' plants produce arching canes that usually reach 5 feet in height and a little less in spread. They perform well in a bed or border where their late-spring flower display is breathtaking. This is a very hardy rose, but its disease resistance is only moderate.

'FELICITE PARMENTIER'

Classification: *alba*

Bloom period: *early summer*

Height: *4 to 5 feet*

Hardiness: *Zones 4-10*

ARS rating: *8.6*

Date introduced: *1834*

The pale blush pink, very double blooms of 'Félicité Parmentier' open flat, then reflex to form a ball. As the 2- to 2½-inch flowers age, the tightly quartered petals fade to creamy white at their outer edges. Flowers are borne in clusters in profusion in early summer, but they do not repeat. Their fragrance is heady. Leaves are gray-green, and the abundant prickles are dark.

This rose has a bushy, compact habit, reaching 4 to 5 feet in height and 4 feet in width, and is less upright than most albas. The tidy form requires little pruning. It tolerates poor soil, partial shade, and climatic extremes, and is resistant to disease.

'FERDINAND PICHARD'

Classification: *hybrid perpetual*

Bloom period: *summer to fall*

Height: *4 to 6 feet*

Hardiness: *Zones 5-10*

ARS rating: *7.4*

Date introduced: *1921*

The cupped double blooms of 'Ferdinand Pichard' are fragrant and colorful. Ranging from 2½ to 4 inches across, each flower bears pink petals splashed with white or crimson stripes, and as the blossom ages its pink fades to white and the crimson to purple. Flower clusters appear in abundance in early summer and again in the fall with sporadic blooms in between. Foliage is yellowish green, and canes are nearly thornless.

This rose has an upright, compact habit and is ideally suited to beds. It does especially well with regular fertilizing and copious watering and should be pruned heavily in winter. While fairly resistant to mildew, it is susceptible to black spot.

'FIRST EDITION'

Classification: *floribunda*

Bloom period: *summer to fall*

Height: *3½ feet*

Hardiness: *Zones 4-10*

ARS rating: *8.6*

Date introduced: *1976*

The pointed coral-orange buds of 'First Edition' open to luminous coral-rose blossoms with orange tints. The petals surround yellow anthers. Flowers are double, 2 to 2½ inches across, and lightly fragrant, and they are borne in flat-topped clusters. Their color deepens in cool weather. Foliage is glossy and medium green.

The bushes are vigorous and upright. They are suited to many uses, including beds and borders, low hedges, and containers. Flowers are excellent for cutting and exhibition, and the plants have good disease resistance. 'First Edition' is an AARS winner.

'FIRST PRIZE'

Classification: *hybrid tea*

Bloom period: *summer to fall*

Height: *5 to 8 feet*

Hardiness: *Zones 5-10*

ARS rating: *8.9*

Date introduced: *1970*

Gorgeous large pointed buds open to high-centered rosy pink flowers with ivory centers. Each 5- to 6-inch double blossom has 25 to 35 petals. These are borne singly or in small clusters on strong stems and are mildly fragrant. Leaves are dark and leathery.

'First Prize' has an upright habit and can be very effective in a bed or border, where it will produce abundant flowers all summer. The classical form of its huge buds and open blossoms and its long vase life make it an ideal selection for cut flowers and exhibitions. It is tender and fairly resistant to black spot. This rose is an AARS winner.

'F. J. GROOTENDORST'

Classification: *hybrid rugosa*

Bloom period: *summer to fall*

Height: *5 feet*

Hardiness: *Zones 3-10*

ARS rating: *7.7*

Date introduced: *1918*

'F. J. Grootendorst' produces clusters of up to 20 small, scentless, crimson flowers throughout the growing season. Individual blooms are double and have a carnation-like appearance with fringed petals. The abundant foliage is somewhat coarse, leathery, and dark green. This rose has given rise to several sports, including 'Pink Grootendorst', which has soft pink flowers; 'White Grootendorst', whose white blooms are borne on a considerably smaller plant; and 'Grootendorst Supreme', whose blossoms are lightly scented and a deeper red than those of its parent.

This rugosa hybrid is a vigorous grower with a bushy, upright habit. It is easy to grow, tolerant of seaside conditions, and disease resistant.

'FOLKLORE'	'FRAGRANT CLOUD'	'FRAU DAGMAR HARTOPP'	'FRAU KARL DRUSCHKI'

Classification: *hybrid tea*

Bloom period: *summer to fall*

Height: *4 to 5 feet*

Hardiness: *Zones 5-10*

ARS rating: *8.5*

Date introduced: *1977*

Beautiful double blossoms of 'Folklore' appear in midseason and repeat in strong flushes until fall. The long, pointed buds open slowly to reveal 4- to 5-inch high-centered flowers that are a blend of orange tones with a yellow reverse. Blooms appear singly or in clusters and are very fragrant and long lasting. The foliage is medium green and glossy.

Plants are vigorous and easy to grow. They have a tall, upright, and bushy habit, and make attractive additions to beds and borders, as well as being useful as screens and hedges. Flowers are excellent for cutting or exhibition. The foliage is disease resistant.

Classification: *hybrid tea*

Bloom period: *summer to fall*

Height: *4 to 5 feet*

Hardiness: *Zones 5-10*

ARS rating: *8.3*

Date introduced: *1963*

'Fragrant Cloud' is named for its scent, which is among the most powerful of all roses and is both sweet and spicy. The double flowers are 4 to 5 inches across and coral red, deepening to a purplish red as they age. Blooms are composed of 25 to 30 petals and are produced in great numbers throughout the summer. The leaves are large, dark, and semiglossy.

The plant is vigorous and upright; its freely branching habit makes it well suited to a border or bed. The rose is highly valued as a cut flower both for its appearance and for its perfume. Leaves are subject to mildew.

Classification: *hybrid rugosa*

Bloom period: *spring to fall*

Height: *2½ to 3 feet*

Hardiness: *Zones 3-10*

ARS rating: *8.5*

Date introduced: *1914*

'Frau Dagmar Hartopp' flowers in spring and continues nonstop until freezing weather calls a halt to the show. The blossoms are deliciously fragrant and single, with five silvery pink petals surrounding creamy stamens. Foliage is crinkled and deep green. In fall the leaves turn deep maroon and golden yellow with coppery tones, and the plant sets beautiful large hips that are colored deep red. Stems are exceedingly prickly.

This hybrid rugosa is compact, low growing, and wider than it is tall. Requiring little pruning, it is a neat, well-behaved shrub ideally suited to smaller gardens and is also perfect for a low hedge or for massing. The flowers last well and are wonderful for cutting. This rose is exceptionally hardy and disease resistant, and it tolerates sandy soil and salt spray.

Classification: *hybrid perpetual*

Bloom period: *early summer and fall*

Height: *4 to 7 feet*

Hardiness: *Zones 5-10*

ARS rating: *7.8*

Date introduced: *1901*

This rose produces a great abundance of double blossoms from high-centered buds in early summer and repeats the show in fall. The elegant white flower is 4 to 4½ inches across with 30 to 35 rolled petals that display a touch of lemon yellow at their base. Canes are nearly smooth, supporting leathery, coarse, light green foliage.

The plant is vigorous and erect, with stout branches and long, strong stems. The color and form of its flower makes it useful in combination with other roses, both in beds and in indoor arrangements. Buds are reluctant to open in damp weather, and leaves are susceptible to mildew.

'FRENCH LACE'

Classification: *floribunda*

Bloom period: *summer to fall*

Height: *3½ feet*

Hardiness: *Zones 4-9*

ARS rating: *8.2*

Date introduced: *1981*

Flowers of 'French Lace' are borne singly or in clusters of up to 12 and bloom continuously from early summer to frost. Buds are pointed, opening to flat, 3- to 4-inch double blossoms that are ivory with apricot tones and emit a light tea fragrance. The thorny canes produce small, dark green hollylike leaves.

Plants are well branched, bushy, and upright. Their attractive form and abundant flowering potential recommend them for use as a low hedge or in a bed or border. Flowers are long-lasting and beautiful in indoor arrangements. To top off its list of virtues, 'French Lace' is highly resistant to disease. It is an AARS winner.

'GABRIELLE PRIVAT'

Classification: *polyantha*

Bloom period: *spring to fall*

Height: *2 to 4 feet*

Hardiness: *Zones 5-10*

ARS rating: *8.5*

Date introduced: *1931*

Large pyramidal clusters of 30 to 50 semidouble blooms are produced on the neat, low-growing plants of 'Gabrielle Privat'. Flowering begins in spring and continues in great profusion through fall. Individual blooms are carmine-pink and 1¼ inches across. They are attractively displayed against lush bright green foliage.

The bush has a full, mounding habit and requires little pruning except to thin and remove dead growth. Plants of 'Gabrielle Privat' are rugged and tolerate a wide range of soils. A good choice for small gardens or for massing, they are also pretty in containers.

'GARDEN PARTY'

Classification: *hybrid tea*

Bloom period: *summer to fall*

Height: *2½ to 4 feet*

Hardiness: *Zones 5-10*

ARS rating: *8.2*

Date introduced: *1959*

The lightly fragrant blooms of 'Garden Party' are pale yellow fading to white, with light pink petal tips. Each flower is cup shaped and double, with petals flaring 4 to 5 inches across. Their color deepens somewhat in fall. They bloom profusely in midseason, with a good repeat. Leaves are semiglossy and dark green with reddish undersides.

The vigorous, bushy plants are valuable in the garden, where they are especially dramatic when planted in large groups. The flowers are excellent for cutting. 'Garden Party' is somewhat susceptible to mildew and may develop black spot in damp weather. This rose is an AARS winner.

'GARTENDIREKTOR OTTO LINNE'

Classification: *shrub*

Bloom period: *summer to fall*

Height: *5 feet*

Hardiness: *Zones 4-10*

ARS rating: *8.9*

Date introduced: *1934*

The ruffled blossoms of 'Gartendirektor Otto Linne' are borne on long stems in slightly pendulous clusters of up to 30 blooms. Individual flowers are double and have a moderate, carnation-like fragrance. The carmine-pink petals are edged with a darker pink and are yellow-white at the base. Foliage is leathery and bright apple green.

This rose is vigorous and bushy. It can be used to create an elegant hedge and in mild climates can be trained as a climber. Disease resistance is very good.

'GENE BOERNER'

Classification: *floribunda*

Bloom period: *summer to fall*

Height: *3½ to 5 feet*

Hardiness: *Zones 4-10*

ARS rating: *8.5*

Date introduced: *1968*

The blooms of 'Gene Boerner' are double, high centered, and 2½ to 3½ inches across. Petals are deep pink, and they reflex back to form points. The lightly fragrant blossoms occur singly or in clusters from midseason to autumn. Foliage is light green and glossy.

This vigorous rose is medium-sized with an upright habit. Its flowers are borne profusely and are well displayed on the plant, making it very attractive in beds, borders, and hedges. Blooms are good for cutting and exhibition. The plant is disease resistant. 'Gene Boerner' is an AARS winner.

'GOLDEN SHOWERS'

Classification: *large-flowered climber*

Bloom period: *summer to fall*

Height: *6 to 10 feet*

Hardiness: *Zones 5-9*

ARS rating: *7.1*

Date introduced: *1956*

'Golden Showers' produces a profusion of lemon-scented, bright yellow flowers throughout summer and fall. These open quickly from long, pointed buds to 3½- to 4-inch double flowers with red anthers. Flowers are borne both singly and in loose clusters on strong stems and are well distributed throughout the plant. Leaves are dark and glossy.

The plants are excellent for training on pillars, trellises, walls, and fences. The sturdy stems require little support; with pruning, this rose can even be grown as a freestanding shrub. The flowers are suitable for cutting. 'Golden Showers' tolerates light shade and is somewhat disease resistant. It is an AARS winner.

'GOLDEN WINGS'

Classification: *shrub*

Bloom period: *spring to fall*

Height: *4 to 5 feet*

Hardiness: *Zones 4-10*

ARS rating: *7.9*

Date introduced: *1956*

The sulfur yellow blooms of 'Golden Wings' are sweetly fragrant and appear abundantly throughout the season. Long, pointed buds open to single 4- to 5-inch saucer-shaped blossoms. Flowers can have as many as 10 petals, though most have five, surrounding dark amber stamens. Flowers are borne singly or in clusters. Orange hips are very showy. Leaves are intensely yellow-green.

The vigorous shrubs are about equal in height and spread. Their compact habit can be encouraged by pruning the canes back by one-third in spring. The plants are attractive in beds and borders, and the blossoms make beautiful cut flowers. 'Golden Wings' is hardy and disease resistant.

'GOLD MEDAL'

Classification: *grandiflora*

Bloom period: *summer to fall*

Height: *4 to 5½ feet*

Hardiness: *Zones 5-10*

ARS rating: *8.8*

Date introduced: *1982*

The deep yellow flowers of 'Gold Medal' are flushed and edged with orange-red. High-centered double blossoms appear singly or in clusters on long stems and are 3½ to 4 inches across; they bear a fruity fragrance. Blooming in abundance throughout the season, this is one of the last roses to quit in the fall. Leaves are dark and glossy, and canes have few thorns.

Plants are tall, bushy, and upright. They take well to pruning but prefer to be pruned high. The bush is suitable for beds and borders, and its flowers are excellent for cutting and exhibition. Plants are disease resistant.

'GRAHAM THOMAS'

Classification: *shrub*

Bloom period: *summer to fall*

Height: *4 to 12 feet*

Hardiness: *Zones 4-10*

ARS rating: *7.9*

Date introduced: *1983*

The apricot-pink buds of 'Graham Thomas', one of the best known of David Austin's English roses, open to medium-sized double flowers. The recurrent blooms are loosely petaled and cup shaped, and their color is an unusual rich butter yellow that deepens toward the center. They bear a strong tea rose fragrance. Leaves are small, bright green, smooth, and glossy.

This rose is usually grown as a 4- to 6-foot shrub but in warmer climates can also be grown as a 10- to 12-foot climber. Plants are vigorous and bushy, with a graceful, slightly arching form. As a shrub it is almost as wide as it is tall.

'GRANADA'

Classification: *hybrid tea*

Bloom period: *summer to fall*

Height: *5 feet*

Hardiness: *Zones 5-10*

ARS rating: *8.3*

Date introduced: *1963*

The 4- to 5-inch blooms of 'Granada' are extremely colorful, including shades of yellow, pink, and orange-red. Buds are spiraled, opening to high-centered double flowers that flatten with age and emit a rich, spicy fragrance. Blossoms are borne singly or in clusters continuously throughout the season. Leaves are leathery, crinkled, dark green, and distinctly serrated.

Plants are upright, vigorous, and bushy. They can be grown in beds or borders and provide a constant source of spectacularly colored flowers for indoor arrangements. While resistant to black spot, plants are prone to mildew. 'Granada' is an AARS winner.

'GREAT MAIDEN'S BLUSH'

Classification: *alba*

Bloom period: *early summer*

Height: *5 to 6 feet*

Hardiness: *Zones 4-10*

ARS rating: *8.5*

Date introduced: *prior to 1600*

The 2- to 3-inch double flowers of 'Great Maiden's Blush' are white with a delicate pink blush. As a blossom matures, its outer petals reflex and fade to a pale cream, while the center remains blush pink. Borne in clusters in early summer, blooms do not repeat. They have an exceptionally sweet fragrance. Foliage is lush and blue-gray, providing a lovely foil for the softly colored flowers.

This rose is a vigorous grower, well branched and arching. It makes a fine garden shrub for large beds and an attractive informal hedge. It is very hardy.

'GRUSS AN AACHEN'

Classification: *floribunda*

Bloom period: *spring to fall*

Height: *2 to 3 feet*

Hardiness: *Zones 4-10*

ARS rating: *8.3*

Date introduced: *1909*

Buds of 'Gruss an Aachen' are tinted with red-orange and yellow but open to reveal pale apricot-pink blooms that fade to creamy white. The flowers, reminiscent of old garden roses, are 3 inches across, double, and cup shaped, with a rich fragrance. They are borne in clusters throughout the season. Leaves are rich green and leathery.

This rose has a low growing, bushy habit and is very free blooming, even in partial shade. It is a good choice for a bed or low hedge. The plants are quite hardy and disease resistant.

'HANDEL'

Classification: *large-flowered climber*

Bloom period: *summer to fall*

Height: *12 to 14 feet*

Hardiness: *Zones 5-9*

ARS rating: *8.2*

Date introduced: *1965*

The cream-colored double flowers of 'Handel' are edged with rosy pink. They open from shapely spiraled buds to high-centered or cupped 3½-inch blooms that produce a light fragrance. Blooms appear in abundance in early summer and repeat well through fall. Hot weather increases the pink flower color in both area and intensity. Foliage is olive green and glossy.

'Handel' grows upright and is a popular climber for pillars, walls, fences, and small structures because of its prolific flowering ability and the unusual coloring of its blooms. It tolerates light shade but is prone to black spot.

'HANNAH GORDON'

Classification: *floribunda*

Bloom period: *spring to fall*

Height: *3 feet*

Hardiness: *Zones 4-10*

ARS rating: *8.2*

Date introduced: *1983*

The large double flowers of 'Hannah Gordon' are white with bold cerise-pink markings and petal edges. Each bloom has about 35 petals and a light fragrance. Flowers appear continuously throughout the season. The foliage is large, medium green, and semiglossy.

Plants are upright, compact, and bushy. They are useful in beds and borders, can be very effective when massed, and also do nicely when used as a low hedge.

'HANSA'

Classification: *hybrid rugosa*

Bloom period: *spring to fall*

Height: *4 to 5 feet*

Hardiness: *Zones 3-8*

ARS rating: *8.3*

Date introduced: *1905*

'Hansa' produces short-stemmed clusters of rich crimson blooms prolifically throughout the growing season. Flowers are double, cup shaped, and 3 to 3½ inches across; they bear a strong clovelike fragrance. Foliage is dark green and crinkled, and canes are gray and thorny. Large red-orange hips provide a stunning fall display.

This rose is upright and vigorous. It makes an attractive barrier hedge, providing landscape interest from spring to late fall with its succession of spicy-scented flowers followed by showy fruit. Like other hybrid rugosas, 'Hansa' tolerates sandy soil and salt spray, is extremely hardy, and resists diseases and insects.

'HENRY HUDSON'

Classification: *hybrid rugosa*

Bloom period: *spring to fall*

Height: *3 to 4 feet*

Hardiness: *Zones 3-10*

ARS rating: *9.1*

Date introduced: *1976*

The pink-tipped buds of 'Henry Hudson' open to semi-double white blooms that are scented like cloves. Flowers consist of about 25 petals that surround bright yellow stamens. They appear continuously throughout the season and are beautifully set off by copious deep green foliage.

This rugosa hybrid, one of the Explorer series, has an extremely dense, low-growing habit, making it an excellent choice for a bed or ground cover. It produces suckers, so should be either contained or placed where its spreading tendency can be used to advantage. Remove spent flowers for best effect. The plant tolerates sandy soil and salt spray and is extremely hardy and disease resistant.

'HERITAGE'	'HONORINE DE BRABANT'	'HURDY GURDY'	'ICEBERG'

Classification: *shrub*

Bloom period: *summer*

Height: *4 to 5 feet*

Hardiness: *Zones 4-10*

ARS rating: *8.7*

Date introduced: *1984*

The blush pink double flowers of this David Austin rose are colored a bit deeper toward their centers. Their form is exquisite, with the outer petals forming a deep cup around precisely arranged and folded inner petals. Profusely borne in clusters throughout the summer, they create a cloud of rich scent that is a blend of myrrh and lemon. Foliage is dark green and semiglossy. The canes have few thorns.

The plant is a robust grower with a bushy, upright habit. It is a fine addition to beds or borders, makes a wonderful hedge, and provides a long season of cut flowers. Plants are fairly disease resistant but may be susceptible to rust.

Classification: *bourbon*

Bloom period: *summer to fall*

Height: *5 to 6 feet*

Hardiness: *Zones 5-10*

ARS rating: *7.6*

Date introduced: *unknown*

The 3½- to 4-inch soft pink blooms of 'Honorine de Brabant' are striped and spotted with darker shades of violet, crimson, and mauve. Its main crop of flowers appears in midsummer, but it repeats well, and fall flowers are less prone to bleaching by the hot sun. Blossoms are double, loosely cupped, and quartered, with a raspberry scent. Foliage is light green, large, and leathery. Canes are green and bear a few large prickles.

Plants are vigorous, large, and bushy. As a shrub, it grows nearly as broad as it is tall. It can also be trained as a climber. It is more compact and blooms more continuously than most bourbons.

Classification: *miniature*

Bloom period: *spring to summer*

Height: *12 to 24 inches*

Hardiness: *Zones 5-10*

ARS rating: *8.0*

Date introduced: *1986*

The blossoms of 'Hurdy Gurdy' are dark red with white stripes. Each small double bloom has 26 to 40 petals and a light fragrance. Medium green glossy leaves are also small.

This miniature has an upright habit and is a good choice for an edging. It is effective when placed in the foreground of a rose bed or incorporated into a perennial border. It can also be grown in containers or in a patio planting. Deadheading the spent blooms will encourage its flowers to repeat through the summer. It is heat tolerant and disease resistant.

Classification: *floribunda*

Bloom period: *summer to fall*

Height: *3 to 4½ feet*

Hardiness: *Zones 4-9*

ARS rating: *8.7*

Date introduced: *1958*

Throughout summer, 'Iceberg' produces large clusters with up to a dozen pure white blossoms that stand out beautifully against small, light green, glossy foliage. Buds are long and pointed with high centers. Each double flower is 2 to 4 inches across, somewhat flat, and sweetly scented.

'Iceberg' is an all-purpose rose in that the vigorous plant can be grown as a hedge or a border or as a container specimen, trained as a tree rose, or used for cutting flowers for indoor arrangements. It is bushy and well branched and is easily trained. A climbing version is also available, rated 8.8 by the ARS. Both forms are disease resistant.

'IMMENSEE'

Classification: *shrub*

Bloom period: *spring to fall*

Height: *1½ to 3 feet*

Hardiness: *Zones 4-10*

ARS rating: *9.0*

Date introduced: *1982*

The small flowers of 'Immensee' are pale pink to almost white, single, and quite fragrant. The blooms appear in profusion in the spring and repeat well throughout the season. The leaves are small in proportion to the flowers and are dark green and glossy.

This rose has a low-growing, spreading habit; canes may spread as wide as 13 feet. It is useful as a flowering ground cover. This rose, bred by Kordes of Germany using *R. wichuraiana,* is very hardy and resistant to disease.

'IRRESISTIBLE'

Classification: *miniature*

Bloom period: *spring to fall*

Height: *18 to 24 inches*

Hardiness: *Zones 5-10*

ARS rating: *8.0*

Date introduced: *1989*

The perfectly formed double flowers of 'Irresistible' are white with a pale pink center and are produced on long stems. Borne singly and in clusters, the high-centered blooms have more than 40 petals each and put off a moderate, spicy fragrance. Hips are green to yellow brown, and leaves are medium green and semiglossy.

Plants are upright and larger than most miniatures. They are well suited to growing in beds, borders, and containers. Their abundant production of long-stemmed hybrid-tea-type blooms makes them ideal for flower cutting and exhibiting.

'ISPAHAN'

Classification: *damask*

Bloom period: *spring to summer*

Height: *4 to 6 feet*

Hardiness: *Zones 4-10*

ARS rating: *8.7*

Date introduced: *prior to 1832*

The very fragrant, double blooms of 'Ispahan' (also called 'Pompon des Princes') appear in profusion over a 2-month period in early and midseason, but they do not repeat. Borne in clusters, the bright clear pink flowers are 2½ to 3 inches across, cup shaped, and loosely reflexing. They are long-lasting, holding both their shape and their color well. Foliage is small with a blue-green cast.

This rose is bushy and upright. With a flowering season that is remarkably long for a damask, it is valued both as a garden shrub and for cut flowers. The plant is vigorous, disease resistant, and quite hardy.

'JEAN KENNEALLY'

Classification: *miniature*

Bloom period: *summer to fall*

Height: *22 to 30 inches*

Hardiness: *Zones 5-10*

ARS rating: *9.7*

Date introduced: *1984*

The dainty 1½-inch double blossoms of 'Jean Kenneally' are pale to medium apricot blended with yellow and pink. They appear singly or in clusters and have a hybrid tea form with high centers and petals folding back to form points. Leaves are medium green and semiglossy.

This rose is upright, well branched, and taller than most miniatures. It can be grown in beds and borders or used as an edging, and it makes a good container specimen for outside or indoors near a sunny window. It is disease resistant.

'JEANNE LAJOIE'

Classification: *climbing miniature*

Bloom period: *spring to fall*

Height: *8 feet*

Hardiness: *Zones 5-10*

ARS rating: *9.2*

Date introduced: *1975*

'Jeanne Lajoie' produces long, pointed buds that open to miniature two-toned pink flowers. Usually borne in clusters, the flowers are most abundant during cool weather. The high-centered blooms have 20 to 25 pointed petals and are lightly fragrant. In fall, this rose produces small orange hips. Foliage is lush, glossy, and dark.

A very vigorous grower, 'Jeanne Lajoie' is upright and bushy. It can be trained as a climber, or used as a freestanding shrub or hedge rose. Deadheading after its first flush of blooms will significantly increase later flowering. Plants are disease resistant and hardy.

'JENS MUNK'

Classification: *hybrid rugosa*

Bloom period: *spring to fall*

Height: *4 to 5 feet*

Hardiness: *Zones 3-10*

ARS rating: *8.4*

Date introduced: *1974*

The lavender-pink double flowers of 'Jens Munk' are 2 to 3 inches across and appear continuously throughout the growing season. Their 25 petals surround attractive yellow stamens. Blooms are clustered and bear a strong, spicy fragrance.

This Explorer series rose is upright, bushy, and very vigorous. In the landscape it is effective both as a large garden shrub and as a dense hedge. It is very resistant to most diseases but susceptible to stem borer, and it's extremely hardy and tolerant of sandy soil and salt spray.

'JOHN CABOT'

Classification: *shrub*

Bloom period: *summer to fall*

Height: *4 to 10 feet*

Hardiness: *Zones 3-10*

ARS rating: *8.2*

Date introduced: *1978*

The rose pink to cherry red blooms of 'John Cabot' are produced in abundance over a 6-week period in the summer and then sporadically into the fall. Each 2½-inch double flower has 30 to 35 petals arranged in a loose cup around yellow stamens. Blossoms are borne in clusters and show up well against medium green foliage.

'John Cabot', a kordesii shrub in the Explorer series, can be grown as a shrub or a climber. As a shrub it can be maintained at a height of 4 to 5 feet but needs considerable room to spread. The plant is very vigorous, with an upright habit and long, arching canes. If grown as a climber, it takes about four seasons to reach its ultimate height of 8 to 10 feet. Foliage is disease resistant. This is an exceptionally hardy rose.

'JOHN FRANKLIN'

Classification: *shrub*

Bloom period: *spring to fall*

Height: *3 to 4 feet*

Hardiness: *Zones 5-10*

ARS rating: *not rated*

Date introduced: *1980*

Clusters of up to 30 medium red flowers are produced continuously on this rose. The semidouble blooms are 2½ inches across, and each has approximately 25 petals. Flowers are fragrant. Leaves are round, and canes bear yellow-green prickles tinted with purple.

The upright, bushy plants are easy to use in the landscape. Their extended bloom period make them an asset in beds and borders. An Explorer series rose, 'John Franklin' tolerates both heat and cold and is disease resistant.

'JOSEPH'S COAT'

Classification: *large-flowered climber*

Bloom period: *summer to fall*

Height: *8 to 10 feet*

Hardiness: *Zones 6-9*

ARS rating: *7.6*

Date introduced: *1964*

The clusters of double blossoms of 'Joseph's Coat' create an amazing riot of color, with yellows, pinks, oranges, and reds all present at the same time. The red and orange tones become more prominent in autumn. Buds are urn shaped, and unlike those of many climbers they occur on new wood. Flowers are 3-inch cups that are lightly fragrant, leaves are dark green and glossy, and canes are prickly.

The plant is tall and upright. It can be trained as a climber on a pillar, fence, or trellis or, because it is not very robust, can be allowed to grow as a loose, freestanding shrub. It is somewhat tender and prone to powdery mildew.

'JUST JOEY'

Classification: *hybrid tea*

Bloom period: *summer*

Height: *3 feet*

Hardiness: *Zones 5-10*

ARS rating: *7.7*

Date introduced: *1972*

Blossoms of 'Just Joey' are 4 to 6 inches across, composed of 30 exceptionally large petals with interestingly frilly edges. Buds are large, elegantly pointed, and brandy colored, opening to double apricot blooms that lighten as they mature. Flowers bear a deep fruity scent. Both the flowers and their fragrance are longlasting. Leaves are large and glossy, and stems are prickly.

Plants are rather squat and spreading, with a moderate growth rate. They are fairly disease resistant. The flowers are particularly outstanding for indoor arrangements because of their large size and long vase life.

'KEEPSAKE'

Classification: *hybrid tea*

Bloom period: *summer to fall*

Height: *5 to 6 feet*

Hardiness: *Zones 5-10*

ARS rating: *8.4*

Date introduced: *1981*

Borne singly or in small clusters, the oval buds of 'Keepsake' open to 5-inch double blooms. The flowers are high centered and deep pink with lighter pink shades, and are fragrant. Foliage is dark green, large, and glossy, and canes are armed with stout prickles.

Plants are upright and bushy. They are effective in beds or borders, and the flowers are excellent for cutting and exhibition. Though somewhat tender, this rose is very disease resistant. It performs best in climates with cool summers.

'KINGIG'

Classification: *miniature*

Bloom period: *spring to fall*

Height: *18 to 24 inches*

Hardiness: *Zones 5-10*

ARS rating: *9.0*

Date introduced: *1987*

This popular miniature produces medium-sized high-centered flowers singly or in sprays of three to five. Each double blossom has about 18 petals that are light pink with a light or dark pink reverse. As they mature, flowers fade to creamy pink. The matte leaves are medium in color and size, and canes bear slightly crooked white prickles. Hips are oval and green.

Upright 'Kingig' bushes can be combined attractively with other plants in borders and beds, or can be used as edgings or grown as container specimens.

'KONIGIN VON DANEMARK'

Classification: *alba*

Bloom period: *summer*

Height: *5 to 6 feet*

Hardiness: *Zones 4-9*

ARS rating: *8.3*

Date introduced: *1826*

The very double blooms of 'Königin von Dänemark' (or 'Queen of Denmark') appear in midseason and do not repeat. Short, deep pink buds open to 2½- to 3½-inch light pink flowers that are more deeply colored toward the center, where the quartered petals surround a button eye. The flowers are borne singly or in small clusters of three to five and are intensely fragrant. Foliage is an attractive blue-green.

'Königin von Dänemark' has a graceful, open habit and canes that are wide spreading. To encourage a more compact habit, shorten the canes to 2 feet in spring. Use this rose in beds or borders or train it to a trellis, wall, fence, or pillar. Flowers are good for cutting. This rose is extremely hardy and virtually immune to black spot and mildew.

'KORICOLE'

Classification: *floribunda*

Bloom period: *spring to fall*

Height: *3 feet*

Hardiness: *Zones 4-9*

ARS rating: *9.0*

Date introduced: *1985*

Borne in clusters, the blooms of 'Koricole' are large and lightly fragrant. Each double blossom has about 35 white petals with pink edges. Flowers bloom on short stems throughout the growing season. Leaves are large, dark green, and semiglossy.

The bushy, upright plants are easy to grow and are excellent for beds and borders. Their long-lasting and prolific flower display and their low-growing habit make them ideal for placement in front of taller, leggy roses.

'KRISTIN'

Classification: *miniature*

Bloom period: *spring to fall*

Height: *20 to 24 inches*

Hardiness: *Zones 5-10*

ARS rating: *not rated*

Date introduced: *1993*

The pointed, urn-shaped buds of 'Kristin' open to display high-centered double flowers with a classic hybrid tea form. The petals are a blend of red and white. Blooms are borne singly or in small sprays on long stems; they are outstanding when halfway open and may not open further, but last for a remarkably long time at this stage. Leaves are deep green and glossy.

This vigorous miniature is exceptionally attractive as an edging in a rose garden or perennial border, and it also makes a fine container specimen. Flowers are excellent for cutting and exhibition. Plants are quite disease resistant.

'LAFTER'

Classification: *hybrid tea*

Bloom period: *summer to fall*

Height: *4 to 5 feet*

Hardiness: *Zones 5-10*

ARS rating: *not rated*

Date introduced: *1948*

This rose produces semidouble flowers that are a blend of bright, warm colors; the salmon pink petals are yellow at the base and have an apricot reverse. Each large, fragrant flower is loosely cup shaped; petals surround visible yellow stamens. Leaves are light green and leathery, and canes have red prickles. Bloom begins late in the season and continues in waves.

The plants are vigorous and bushy, with graceful, arching canes. They can be planted in beds and borders or used as a colorful hedge. 'Lafter' is probably the most disease resistant hybrid tea, and it's also hardier than most.

'LA MARNE'

Classification: *polyantha*

Bloom period: *spring to fall*

Height: *2 to 4 feet*

Hardiness: *Zones 5-10*

ARS rating: *8.3*

Date introduced: *1915*

The delicately fragrant, cup-shaped blooms of 'La Marne' appear continuously throughout the season; it is one of the most profusely blooming roses grown. Semidouble flowers are borne in loose clusters and are blush white with a vivid pink edge; their color deepens in cool weather. Foliage is dense and glossy.

This bushy, vigorous rose is tall for a polyantha. It is happiest in sunny, open locations. The luxuriant foliage and non-stop blooming ability make it a superb choice for a hedge or garden shrub, and it is a fine container specimen as well.

'LAMARQUE'

Classification: *noisette*

Bloom period: *summer to fall*

Height: *15 feet*

Hardiness: *Zones 7-10*

ARS rating: *8.6*

Date introduced: *1830*

The medium-sized, very double flowers of 'Lamarque' are deliciously fragrant. The petals quarter and are colored white with a touch of lemon yellow at their base; the flowers are nodding, borne on long stems. They are well displayed against abundant light green foliage. Canes bear few prickles.

This vigorous noisette can be maintained as a large free-standing shrub or trained as a voluptuous climber. It's a good choice for warm climates, where it performs best against a sunny wall or similarly sheltered location; neither summer heat nor humidity bothers it. Flowers are perfect for cutting.

'LA REINE VICTORIA'

Classification: *bourbon*

Bloom period: *summer to fall*

Height: *4½ to 6 feet*

Hardiness: *Zones 6-10*

ARS rating: *7.8*

Date introduced: *1872*

The double blossoms of 'La Reine Victoria' are lilac-pink to deep rose; their color is deeper in bright sun. The flowers have a silky texture and a delicate appearance; they are cupped and rounded, with overlapping, shell-shaped petals. Fragrance is strong and fruity. Flowers are held well above the lush soft green foliage. 'Madame Pierre Oger' is a color sport that bears creamy, flesh-colored blooms but is similar in all other respects.

The plants are slender, upright, and graceful. They make attractive specimens and can be used in beds or borders. Flowers are excellent for cutting. Both 'La Reine Victoria' and its sport are susceptible to black spot.

'LAVENDER LASSIE'

Classification: *hybrid musk*

Bloom period: *summer to fall*

Height: *5 to 16 feet*

Hardiness: *Zones 6-10*

ARS rating: *7.5*

Date introduced: *1960*

The double flowers of 'Lavender Lassie' range from lilac-pink to pale lavender. They bloom in large clusters throughout the summer and repeat into the fall. Flowers are 3 inches across and are very fragrant. Leaves are dark and glossy.

This hybrid musk is more upright than most others in the class. It produces gracefully arching branches that bow under the weight of the abundant flower clusters. Maintain it at about 5 feet as a specimen shrub, plant several and prune them as an informal hedge, or train it as a climber. 'Lavender Lassie' is very vigorous, disease resistant, and tolerant of partial shade.

'LEANDER'	'LEDA'	'LINDA CAMPBELL'	'LINVILLE'

Classification: *shrub*

Bloom period: *spring to summer*

Height: *6 to 8 feet*

Hardiness: *Zones 4-10*

ARS rating: *8.3*

Date introduced: *1982*

'Leander', a David Austin rose, produces a dizzying profusion of deep-apricot-colored flowers in spring and early summer. Borne in clusters, the blooms are small and very double, and have a fruity fragrance. Although the rose is not considered a repeat bloomer, flowers may reappear later in the season. Semiglossy leaves are medium in both size and color.

This rose has a full habit, growing nearly as wide as it is tall, and makes a fine large garden shrub. It is among the most disease resistant of the English roses.

Classification: *damask*

Bloom period: *summer*

Height: *3 feet*

Hardiness: *Zones 4-10*

ARS rating: *7.6*

Date introduced: *before 1827*

Flowers of 'Léda' (also called 'Painted Damask') are double, 2½ to 4 inches across, and very fragrant. The buds are reddish brown, opening to reveal milky white to blush pink petals with crimson markings on their edges. The petals reflex to form a ball-shaped bloom. A pink sport of 'Léda' is also available. Leaves of both roses are round, downy, and gray-green.

This is a compact, rounded shrub. It has a neat habit, making it useful in beds and borders. A hardy plant, it prefers cooler climates and languishes where summers are very hot.

Classification: *hybrid rugosa*

Bloom period: *summer to fall*

Height: *5 feet*

Hardiness: *Zones 3-8*

ARS rating: *7.4*

Date introduced: *1990*

This hybrid rugosa produces pointed buds that open to brilliant crimson blooms, an unusual color for this class. The semidouble flowers are slightly lighter in reverse and are borne in clusters of five to 15 blooms. They have no fragrance. Flowers repeat well with as many as six or seven flushes each season. Leaves are large, medium green, and semiglossy. Canes bear fewer prickles than most shrub roses.

Plants are full and bushy with a moderate growth rate; they may reach a height of 5 feet and a width of 8 feet. 'Linda Campbell' is suitable for beds and borders. This rose tolerates heat and seaside conditions and is extremely hardy.

Classification: *miniature*

Bloom period: *spring to fall*

Height: *18 to 24 inches*

Hardiness: *Zones 5-10*

ARS rating: *7.8*

Date introduced: *1989*

The pointed buds of 'Linville' open to double white flowers that have a touch of pink in them. As the blooms age, they become pure white, though in cool weather they tend to retain their pink tones. High-centered flowers are usually borne singly on long stems and produce a light, fruity fragrance. The leaves are medium green and semiglossy; stems bear straight, pink prickles.

Plants are upright and tall for a miniature, with a medium growth rate. They are useful as edgings, in beds or borders, and as container specimens in a large pot. Flowers are good for cutting and exhibiting.

'LOUISE ODIER'

Classification: *bourbon*

Bloom period: *summer to fall*

Height: *4½ to 6 feet*

Hardiness: *Zones 5-9*

ARS rating: *8.3*

Date introduced: *1851*

The bright rose pink flowers of 'Louise Odier' are softly shaded with a hint of lilac. They appear abundantly in midseason and repeat well into fall. Blooms are very double and cup shaped, resembling camellias; petals are quartered. Their scent is deliciously rich. Borne in clusters, the heavy flowers may weigh down the branches, creating a graceful, arching effect.

Plants are vigorous and upright with slender canes. A favorite choice in Victorian gardens, 'Louise Odier' makes an elegant shrub, and it can be trained to climb a pillar or post. This rose is hardy and disease resistant.

'LOUIS PHILIPPE'

Classification: *China*

Bloom period: *spring to fall*

Height: *4 to 5 feet*

Hardiness: *Zones 7-10*

ARS rating: *8.5*

Date introduced: *1834*

The repeating flowers of 'Louis Philippe' are deep crimson to purple with lighter-colored petal edges. Blooms are double, cup shaped, quartered, and pleasantly fragrant. The somewhat sparse foliage is distinctly rounded, and canes bear few prickles.

This rose has a compact, arching form. Rich soil is required for best performance. Its continuous flowering habit makes it a good choice for a container or patio. A tender plant, 'Louis Philippe' tolerates summer heat and humidity well and is disease resistant.

'LOVING TOUCH'

Classification: *miniature*

Bloom period: *spring to fall*

Height: *22 to 30 inches*

Hardiness: *Zones 5-10*

ARS rating: *8.6*

Date introduced: *1982*

The apricot blooms of 'Loving Touch' are large for a miniature, especially in cool weather. Flowers are double with about 25 petals each and are produced in abundance, mostly one per stem. Each bloom is high centered with a light fragrance. Leaves are medium green and semiglossy. The rose produces pretty, globular hips.

Plants are bushy and spreading, well suited to beds and borders and for use as edgings. They also are beautiful as patio and container plants. Flowers are excellent for cutting and exhibition.

'MADAME ALFRED CARRIERE'

Classification: *noisette*

Bloom period: *summer to fall*

Height: *8 to 16 feet*

Hardiness: *Zones 6-9*

ARS rating: *8.3*

Date introduced: *1879*

The 3- to 4-inch gardenia-like double blooms of 'Madame Alfred Carrière' are creamy blush white. Produced in clusters on upright stems, flowers are full, loosely formed, and globular, appearing in midseason and repeating well into fall. They are very fragrant. Leaves are large and light green, and canes are thorny.

Like most noisettes, this rose is a climber, and a vigorous one. The nodding habit of the blossoms makes it a good choice for viewing from below, as on a pergola, arch, or wall. It can also be trained as a shrub for a bed or border. Tolerant of partial shade, summer heat, and humidity, it's also fairly disease resistant.

'MADAME HARDY'

Classification: *damask*

Bloom period: *late spring to early summer*

Height: *4 to 6 feet*

Hardiness: *Zones 4-9*

ARS rating: *9.2*

Date introduced: *1832*

The 2½- to 3½-inch, remarkably fragrant flowers of 'Madame Hardy' are very double and appear in large clusters. Each pale pink bud opens to a cup-shaped ivory blossom that gradually flattens, revealing some 200 intricately folded petals surrounding a green button center. Lime green leaves grow densely along the prickly canes.

The vigorous plant has a bushy, upright habit, but the weight of the flowers often causes the canes to droop. This tendency can be used to advantage by massing three or more bushes to create a billowy mound. Canes can also be tied together or staked for support. The flowers are beautiful in indoor arrangements; gather them before they have fully matured. Plants are very hardy and disease resistant.

'MADAME ISAAC PEREIRE'

Classification: *bourbon*

Bloom period: *summer to fall*

Height: *5 to 7 feet*

Hardiness: *Zones 5-9*

ARS rating: *8.0*

Date introduced: *1881*

Although the magenta flowers of 'Madame Isaac Pereire' appear throughout summer, they do not reach their peak until fall. Each double bloom is anywhere from 3 to 6 inches across, depending on climate, with quartering petals that are rolled at their edges. The fruity-scented blossoms are possibly the most fragrant of all roses; they may be dried for potpourris. The abundant foliage is large, dark green, and semiglossy.

Plants are bushy with a somewhat spreading habit. They can be grown as free-standing shrubs or pegged; a climbing version that grows to 12 feet can be trained on a trellis or fence. Flowers are superb for cutting. Plants are vigorous, tough, and hardy, and will tolerate poor soil. A color sport of this rose, 'Madame Ernest Calvat', produces pale lavender-pink flowers.

'MADAME LEGRAS DE ST. GERMAIN'

Classification: *alba*

Bloom period: *early summer*

Height: *6 to 15 feet*

Hardiness: *Zones 4-9*

ARS rating: *8.6*

Date introduced: *1846*

The very double, 3½-inch blooms of 'Madame Legras de St. Germain' are white with a rich, creamy center and bursting with 200 petals. The plants flower once per season and remain in bloom for several weeks, although the blooms don't stand up well to wet weather. Their sweet fragrance is very strong. Soft gray-green foliage provides a lovely foil for the flowers. Canes are nearly smooth.

This rose is a vigorous grower and can be maintained as a 6- to 7-foot shrub or trained on a support, in which case it can reach 12 to 15 feet. Its habit is upright and arching. The plant is well suited to beds, where it combines nicely with perennials. Flowers are good for cutting. It tolerates partial shade and is disease resistant.

'MADAME PLANTIER'

Classification: *alba*

Bloom period: *summer*

Height: *5 to 6 feet*

Hardiness: *Zones 4-10*

ARS rating: *8.1*

Date introduced: *1835*

The very double blooms of 'Madame Plantier' are creamy white, with a green button eye. Borne in large clusters, the 2½- to 3-inch flowers completely cover the plant in early to midseason; they do not recur. Blooms are somewhat flattened, and they are extremely fragrant. Leaves and stems are a light gray-green.

A vigorous grower, this rose has a spreading, lax, bushy habit suitable for large gardens. As a shrub it can easily spread to 6 feet wide, and it can also be trained to climb a pillar or trellis. 'Madame Plantier' is very hardy as well as disease and shade tolerant.

'MAGIC CARROUSEL'

Classification: *miniature*

Bloom period: *summer to fall*

Height: *18 to 24 inches*

Hardiness: *Zones 5-10*

ARS rating: *9.0*

Date introduced: *1972*

The semidouble flowers of 'Magic Carrousel' are creamy white and brightly tinged with red. This bold and attractive color combination and the fact that the rose blooms profusely have made it one of the most popular miniatures grown. Each flower is 1¾ to 2 inches across and bears a light scent. Leaves are small, leathery, and glossy.

'Magic Carrousel' has a spreading habit and should be pinched back to avoid legginess. It is useful in beds and borders, as an edging, and in containers. Plants are easy to grow and disease resistant. The flowers are frequently used by florists for boutonnieres.

'MAMAN COCHET'

Classification: *tea*

Bloom period: *summer to fall*

Height: *3 to 4 feet*

Hardiness: *Zones 6-10*

ARS rating: *7.2*

Date introduced: *1893*

The pointed, globe-shaped buds of 'Madam Cochet' open to 4-inch high-centered blossoms. Each double flower consists of 35 to 45 petals that are colored light pink with a lemon yellow base; the flower color deepens in bright sun. Blooms are very fragrant and are nicely set off against leathery deep green foliage. Canes bear few thorns.

This old garden rose is a vigorous grower with an upright, bushy habit. Its attractive foliage and steady production of flowers make it a good choice for beds and borders. It tolerates summer heat and humidity and is disease resistant.

'MARCHESA BOCCELLA'

Classification: *hybrid perpetual*

Bloom period: *spring to fall*

Height: *4 to 5 feet*

Hardiness: *Zones 5-10*

ARS rating: *8.9*

Date introduced: *1842*

'Marchesa Boccella' (also known as 'Jacques Cartier') produces large, full flowers in repeat flushes throughout the growing season. Each very double bloom is delicate pink with blush edges. Borne in tight clusters on short, stiff stems, they are very fragrant. The petals are more numerous but smaller than those of most hybrid perpetuals. Foliage is dense and bright green.

One of the finest of the class, this rose is a robust grower with a medium to tall erect form and is somewhat spreading. Its recurring flowering habit and lush foliage are suited to large beds and borders.

'MARCHIONESS OF LONDONDERRY'

Classification: *hybrid perpetual*

Bloom period: *spring and fall*

Height: *5 to 8 feet*

Hardiness: *Zones 5-9*

ARS rating: *7.0*

Date introduced: *1893*

The huge, fragrant flowers of 'Marchioness of Londonderry' are ivory white with a pale pink to rose pink blush. They open from high-centered buds to cup-shaped, cabbagy double blossoms 4 to 5 inches across. Though not continuous bloomers, the plants produce a fine floral display in spring and fall. Foliage is leathery; canes are nearly thornless.

This hybrid perpetual is a very vigorous grower. The plants have a sturdy, upright habit and are suitable for use in large beds and borders. They can also be trained to a fence or trellis.

'MARGO KOSTER'

Classification: *polyantha*

Bloom period: *summer to fall*

Height: *1 to 2 feet*

Hardiness: *Zones 5-9*

ARS rating: *8.3*

Date introduced: *1931*

The double blooms of 'Margo Koster' are globular and 1 to 1½ inches across. Borne in sprays, they are somewhat variable in color, ranging from salmon pink to orange. They have little fragrance. Plants commence blooming late in the season and repeat well through fall. A climbing sport is available. Leaves are gray-green and semiglossy. Canes bear few prickles.

This rose is bushy and compact, and is often grown as a container plant for both indoors and outside. It is disease resistant.

'MARIE LOUISE'

Classification: *damask*

Bloom period: *late spring*

Height: *4 feet*

Hardiness: *Zones 4-10*

ARS rating: *8.0*

Date introduced: *before 1813*

The huge, very double blossoms of 'Marie Louise' are so heavy they weigh down the ends of the branches. Flowers are a brilliant mauve-pink with reflexed petals that quarter around a green button eye, and their rich scent hints of lemon. When fully opened, the blooms are somewhat flattened. Foliage is dense, and canes have few prickles.

Plants are bushy and compact, making this a useful shrub for beds, borders, and small gardens. It has a graceful, arching form. Like other damasks, it is quite hardy.

'MARIE PAVIE'

Classification: *polyantha*

Bloom period: *spring to fall*

Height: *2 to 3 feet*

Hardiness: *Zones 4-9*

ARS rating: *8.1*

Date introduced: *1888*

The long, pointed pink buds of 'Marie Pavié' open to creamy white double flowers. Borne in small clusters, blossoms are 2 inches across and deliciously fragrant. Flowering is profuse throughout the season. Leaves are large and dark green. Canes have no prickles.

'Marie Pavié' is vigorous, upright, and bushy, and is adaptable to many landscape uses: It makes a fine border plant, specimen shrub, low hedge, or container plant. This rose is hardy.

'MAX GRAF'

Classification: *hybrid rugosa*

Bloom period: *late spring*

Height: *2 feet*

Hardiness: *Zones 3-10*

ARS rating: *7.2*

Date introduced: *1919*

The single blossoms of 'Max Graf' are bright pink with white centers, surrounding prominent yellow stamens. They are borne prolifically in late spring and last for several weeks but do not recur. Blooms are sweetly scented, and leaves are rich green, glossy, and leathery.

The value of this hybrid rugosa is in its vigorous, low-growing, spreading habit. It makes an outstanding flowering ground cover that chokes out weeds; its stems root where they come in contact with the ground to spread even further. It is ideal for sunny banks, for cascading over walls, and in front of taller shrubs. It can also be trained to grow along a low fence. 'Max Graf' is extremely hardy.

'MINNIE PEARL'

Classification: *miniature*

Bloom period: *summer to fall*

Height: *18 to 24 inches*

Hardiness: *Zones 5-10*

ARS rating: *9.4*

Date introduced: *1982*

The double flowers of 'Minnie Pearl' are creamy pink with a light yellow base and a deeper pink reverse. High-centered blossoms are held singly at the end of long stems, making them ideal as cut flowers; their long vase life further recommends them for this use. Leaves are small, semiglossy, and medium green.

Its small size makes this rose a good choice for edgings or foregrounds of beds and borders, and for containers. It's vigorous and disease resistant.

'MISTER LINCOLN'

Classification: *hybrid tea*

Bloom period: *summer*

Height: *4 to 6 feet*

Hardiness: *Zones 5-10*

ARS rating: *8.8*

Date introduced: *1964*

'Mister Lincoln' produces 4½- to 6-inch deeply fragrant, cherry red flowers in abundance. Buds are red-black, high centered, and pointed. The flowers have a velvety texture and are very long lasting and nonfading, usually appearing singly on long, sturdy stems. Foliage is medium green and leathery.

This is a robust hybrid tea with an upright, vase-shaped habit. It is at home in beds or borders. The form and keeping quality of its flowers make this an excellent rose for cutting and exhibition. It has greater disease resistance than most red hybrid teas, and performs best when days are warm and nights cool. It's an AARS winner.

'MONSIEUR TILLIER'

Classification: *tea*

Bloom period: *spring to fall*

Height: *3½ to 4 feet*

Hardiness: *Zones 7-10*

ARS rating: *9.0*

Date introduced: *1891*

The double flowers of 'Monsieur Tillier' are light red to rose pink, shaded and marked with violet-purple and salmon. Petals are intricately arranged to give the bloom a loosely full, ruffled appearance. Flowers are produced freely from early spring through late fall; they bear little fragrance. The foliage is very lush.

Plants are vigorous. Because their stems are thin, they develop a lax, wide-spreading growth habit. With their long flowering season, they add months of color to beds and borders in mild climates. They tolerate slightly alkaline soil and summer heat and humidity, and are fairly hardy for a tea rose.

'MRS. B. R. CANT'

Classification: *tea*

Bloom period: *spring to fall*

Height: *4 to 8 feet*

Hardiness: *Zones 7-10*

ARS rating: *8.2*

Date introduced: *1901*

The cabbagelike flowers of 'Mrs. B. R. Cant' (also called 'Reine Marie Henriette') are a beautifully colored silvery rose with a deep rose reverse. The blooms are very double, cupped, and richly scented, and appear nonstop throughout the season. They are especially lovely in fall, when cooler weather brings out deep red tones at the edges of the petals. Leaves are more rounded than those of most of this class.

This rose is vigorous with a wide-spreading habit; unless it's pruned it will require a large space. It makes an attractive garden shrub or specimen, and its flowers are excellent for cutting. Summer heat and humidity don't bother it.

'MRS. DUDLEY CROSS'	'MUTABILIS'	'NASTARANA'	'NEARLY WILD'

Classification: *tea*

Bloom period: *spring to fall*

Height: *4 to 6 feet*

Hardiness: *Zones 7-10*

ARS rating: *8.7*

Date introduced: *1907*

Classification: *China*

Bloom period: *summer to fall*

Height: *3 to 8 feet*

Hardiness: *Zones 7-10*

ARS rating: *8.2*

Date introduced: *prior to 1894*

Classification: *noisette*

Bloom period: *summer to fall*

Height: *3 to 4 feet*

Hardiness: *Zones 6-10*

ARS rating: *8.3*

Date introduced: *1879*

Classification: *floribunda*

Bloom period: *spring to summer*

Height: *2 to 4 feet*

Hardiness: *Zones 4-10*

ARS rating: *7.6*

Date introduced: *1941*

The large pointed buds of 'Mrs. Dudley Cross' open to pale yellow flowers with a pink blush. Appearing in small clusters, the flattened, pleasantly fragrant blooms are 2 to 3 inches across. In fall they often display a crimson tint. Leaves are medium green, and canes have no prickles.

'Mrs. Dudley Cross' is a vigorous grower and is best suited to drier climates. Compact and bushy, the plants are attractive in beds, borders, and hedges. The flowers, which are long-lasting, are excellent for cutting. Plants are tender but disease resistant.

The pointed orange buds of 'Mutabilis' open to single blooms that start out sulfur yellow, change to coppery pink, and then deepen to crimson. All three colors can be present on a bush at the same time. Irregularly shaped flowers resemble butterflies, earning the plant the nickname butterfly rose. The flowers are very fragrant. Leaves emerge in an attractive shade of bronze.

If grown beneath the protection of a wall, these vigorous, robust plants are capable of reaching 8 feet in height with a 6 foot spread. In a more open site, plants usually reach only 3 feet. They benefit from regular feeding and abundant watering. 'Mutabilis' tolerates slightly alkaline soil and summer heat and humidity but is fairly tender.

The semidouble blooms of 'Nastarana' are white tinged with pink and appear in large clusters on new wood. Each flower is about 2 inches across and bears a pleasant tea rose fragrance. Flowering repeats well throughout the season. Leaves are smooth, oval, and medium green.

Plants are very vigorous, with an upright habit. They prefer an open, sunny site but are tolerant of partial shade. They also tolerate poor soils, summer heat, and humidity, but may require winter protection. They may be susceptible to mildew and black spot.

The small, tapered buds of 'Nearly Wild' open to rose pink blooms that have five petals and are very fragrant. The flowers occur prolifically along the length of each stem. The main flowering season is spring, but some blooms appear through summer.

Plants are compact and bushy, and are often wider than tall. This rose makes an excellent ground cover for sunny banks; space plants 2½ to 3 feet apart. It can also be planted to cascade down a wall or trained to climb a low fence. Placed in front of taller shrubs, it provides good foreground color, and it makes a fine container specimen. 'Nearly Wild' tolerates slightly alkaline soil and is very hardy.

'NEW DAWN'

Classification: *large-flowered climber*
Bloom period: *summer*
Height: *12 to 20 feet*
Hardiness: *Zones 5-9*
ARS rating: *7.9*
Date introduced: *1930*

'New Dawn' is a sport of an older climbing rose, 'Dr. W. Van Fleet,' but unlike its parent, it blooms throughout the summer. Plants produce an abundance of 3- to 4-inch semidouble flowers that are shaded a blush pink with a slightly darker center and have bright yellow stamens. They are sweetly scented and are usually borne in large clusters. Leaves are dark green and glossy on prickly canes.

This robust plant is upright and spreading. It is somewhat slow growing, but once established it produces a breathtaking display on pillars, fences, walls, and trellises that is well worth the wait. It can also be grown as a freestanding shrub. 'New Dawn' adapts to partial shade, albeit with fewer flowers, and it is extremely disease resistant.

'NOZOMI'

Classification: *climbing miniature*
Bloom period: *summer*
Height: *12 to 18 inches*
Hardiness: *Zones 5-10*
ARS rating: *7.9*
Date introduced: *1968*

'Nozomi' produces a bounty of flat, star-shaped, pearly pink to white flowers. The small blossoms occur in clusters and are lightly fragrant. During their single bloom period in midsummer, they cover the entire plant. Leaves are small, glossy, and dense, and canes bear numerous hooked prickles.

This very versatile rose has a trailing habit, rarely exceeding a foot in height but spreading 3 to 5 feet. Planted 2½ feet apart, it can be used as a dense ground cover on a bank or in front of taller shrubs. It also makes a nice addition to a rock garden, can be situated to cascade down a wall, and is lovely when grown in a container. Finally, it can be trained as a climber, or even a weeping standard.

'OLD BLUSH'

Classification: *China*
Bloom period: *summer to fall*
Height: *3 to 5 feet*
Hardiness: *Zones 6-10*
ARS rating: *8.3*
Date introduced: *1752*

'Old Blush' produces clusters of dainty blush pink flowers. Each is double, cup shaped, and loosely formed with 24 to 30 petals that deepen in color with age. Their scent is reminiscent of sweet peas. Foliage is a soft green, growing on nearly smooth canes. A climbing form, rated 8.1 by the ARS, grows to 20 feet.

Its bushy, mounding habit makes this rose an attractive addition to beds or borders. It can also be used effectively as a flowering hedge, and it makes an outstanding container specimen. 'Old Blush' requires little pruning and tolerates summer heat and humidity and a range of soils. It is disease resistant as well, but tender.

'OLYMPIAD'

Classification: *hybrid tea*
Bloom period: *summer to fall*
Height: *3 to 5 feet*
Hardiness: *Zones 5-10*
ARS rating: *9.1*
Date introduced: *1984*

The abundant 4- to 5-inch scarlet blossoms of 'Olympiad' are borne singly or in small clusters on long, sturdy stems. Buds are high centered, opening to velvety-textured double flowers with 30 to 35 petals. They are extremely long-lasting, and their bright color does not fade with age. The flowers have little fragrance. Foliage is distinctively gray-green and semiglossy; canes are prickly.

Plants are vigorous; their compact, bushy, upright habit makes them well suited to beds and borders. The flowers are outstanding for cutting and exhibition. This is an AARS winner.

'PAPER DOLL'

Classification: *miniature*

Bloom period: *spring to fall*

Height: *18 to 24 inches*

Hardiness: *Zones 5-10*

ARS rating: *not rated*

Date introduced: *1992*

The light apricot flowers of 'Paper Doll' have a pale pink blush that fades first to light amber and then to white. Each semidouble bloom has 15 to 25 petals and is 1¾ to 2¾ inches across. Occurring in small clusters of three to five, blooms are plentiful throughout the growing season. They have no fragrance. Leaves are small, dark green, and glossy.

Plants are low growing but upright. They can be incorporated into a perennial border, placed in the foreground of a rose bed, or used as an edging or container plant. Their disease resistance is good.

'PARADISE'

Classification: *hybrid tea*

Bloom period: *summer to fall*

Height: *4 feet*

Hardiness: *Zones 5-10*

ARS rating: *8.3*

Date introduced: *1978*

The long, pointed buds of 'Paradise' open to 3½- to 4½-inch silvery lavender blossoms whose petals are edged with ruby red. Flowers are double and beautifully formed, with 25 to 30 petals curling to create a bull's-eye center. Their fragrance is fruity. Leaves are glossy and dark green.

Plants are medium height and have an upright, well-branched habit. They can be used in beds or borders, where they provide a continuous display of blooms. The flowers are excellent for cutting. 'Paradise' is hardy but may be prone to mildew. It's an AARS winner.

'PARTY GIRL'

Classification: *miniature*

Bloom period: *summer to fall*

Height: *12 to 15 inches*

Hardiness: *Zones 5-10*

ARS rating: *9.0*

Date introduced: *1979*

'Party Girl' produces long, pointed buds that open into soft apricot-yellow high-centered blooms. Borne singly or in clusters, each flower is 1 to 1½ inches across and bears a pleasant, spicy fragrance. Leaves are dark green and glossy.

This miniature is bushy and compact—and very versatile. It makes a lovely potted plant, indoors or out, and it's well suited for mixing into perennial borders or for edging a rose or shrub garden. The flowers are outstanding for cutting and exhibition. Plants are hardy and disease resistant.

'PAULII ROSEA'

Classification: *shrub*

Bloom period: *summer*

Height: *3 feet*

Hardiness: *Zones 4-10*

ARS rating: *8.3*

Date introduced: *prior to 1912*

The flowers of 'Paulii Rosea' are single and a clear pink. Their silky-textured petals are deeply notched, pleated, and white at the base, surrounding bright yellow stamens. Flowers, which are lightly fragrant, appear in summer only and do not repeat. Foliage is medium green; young wood is lime colored.

'Paulii Rosea' is low and sprawling, rarely exceeding 3 feet in height but spreading up to 10 or 12 feet. It is useful as a ground cover on sunny slopes or can be trained as a climber on fences and trellises. It prefers an open, sunny site and rich soil, and is susceptible to mildew.

'PAUL NEYRON'

Classification: *hybrid perpetual*

Bloom period: *spring and fall*

Height: *3 to 6 feet*

Hardiness: *Zones 5-10*

ARS rating: *8.1*

Date introduced: *1869*

The huge, very double blossoms of 'Paul Neyron' are the size of small plates, measuring 4½ to 7 inches across. They are colored pink to rose pink with lilac shading, and the petals are intricately swirled. Flowers are very fragrant and appear in spring and repeat in fall. Foliage is large and matte green, and canes are nearly smooth.

This hybrid perpetual is a strong, vigorous grower with an upright habit. It's a nice choice for beds or borders, and its spectacular blooms are exceptional in indoor arrangements. 'Paul Neyron' is significantly more disease resistant than other roses in this class.

'PEACE'

Classification: *hybrid tea*

Bloom period: *summer to fall*

Height: *4 to 6 feet*

Hardiness: *Zones 5-10*

ARS rating: *8.6*

Date introduced: *1945*

No two flowers of 'Peace' are exactly alike. Each blossom's color ranges from pale to golden yellow with a pink edging or blush. In cool weather, the pink may be missing entirely. Flowers are double, high centered, 5 to 6 inches across, and mildly fragrant. They are borne singly or in clusters. Leaves are large, glossy, and dark green. Canes are prickly.

The upright, bushy plant is extremely vigorous. It puts on an outstanding show in beds or borders, where its flower color varies pleasantly with temperature and light conditions. Strong stems keep the large flowers from drooping in indoor arrangements. 'Peace' tends to be more disease resistant than other yellow hybrid teas. It is an AARS winner.

'PENELOPE'

Classification: *hybrid musk*

Bloom period: *summer to fall*

Height: *5 to 6 feet*

Hardiness: *Zones 5-10*

ARS rating: *8.5*

Date introduced: *1924*

The salmon-colored buds of 'Penelope' open to shell pink blooms that fade to white as they age. Borne in huge clusters, the semidouble flowers display bright yellow stamens at their centers. Fragrance is rich and musky. In fall, small coral hips decorate the canes for several weeks. Leaves are glossy, ribbed, and dark green.

Plants are vigorous and dense, and they grow equally tall and wide. This rose is a good choice for a flowering hedge or for combining with other flowering shrubs or perennials in beds. It can tolerate partial shade and is fairly disease resistant, but may be prone to mildew.

'PERLE D'OR'

Classification: *polyantha*

Bloom period: *spring to fall*

Height: *3 to 4 feet*

Hardiness: *Zones 4-9*

ARS rating: *8.0*

Date introduced: *1884*

'Perle d'Or' produces clusters of small, perfectly formed creamy yellow-orange buds that open to very double salmon to golden pink blossoms. The flowers are fragrant and bloom over a lengthy season. Leaves are a soft, rich green, and canes bear few prickles.

Plants are vigorous, with an upright habit. They are densely leaved and often twice as tall as they are wide. This rose is seldom out of bloom during the growing season. Beautiful in beds and borders, it also makes a fine container specimen. 'Perle d'Or' is hardy.

'PETITE DE HOLLANDE'

Classification: *centifolia*

Bloom period: *summer*

Height: *3 to 4 feet*

Hardiness: *Zones 4-10*

ARS rating: *7.7*

Date introduced: *1800*

The rose pink double blooms of 'Petite de Hollande' are borne in clusters. Flowers are 1½ inches across and cupped until fully open, when their darker centers become visible. They are sweetly fragrant. In keeping with the dainty scale of the flowers, the leaves are also small; they are glossy and coarsely toothed.

Plants are moderate growers. Bushy and compact, they are ideal for smaller gardens and containers, and are also excellent for training as a standard. This rose is hardy and disease resistant.

'PIERRINE'

Classification: *miniature*

Bloom period: *spring to fall*

Height: *15 to 18 inches*

Hardiness: *Zones 5-10*

ARS rating: *9.4*

Date introduced: *1988*

The high-centered double flowers of 'Pierrine' are colored medium salmon pink with a lighter reverse. Blossoms are borne singly, and each has about 40 petals. Their fragrance is reminiscent of damask roses. Leaves are medium green and semiglossy, with serrated edges; stems bear light green curved prickles. Hips are round, and range in color from green to orange-yellow.

This plant is a moderate grower with an upright habit. Its diminutive size makes it most useful as an edging or container specimen.

'PINKIE'

Classification: *polyantha*

Bloom period: *spring and fall*

Height: *1½ to 3 feet*

Hardiness: *Zones 5-10*

ARS rating: *7.9*

Date introduced: *1947*

Flowers of 'Pinkie' have 14 to 16 petals that are rose pink with a salmon blush. These form a cup-shaped 1½- to 2½-inch semidouble blossom. The flowers occur in large clusters in spring and repeat in fall; they are heavily fragrant. Leaves are soft green and glossy.

'Pinkie' is small and bushy, with a width often equal to its height. Useful in the foreground of a bed or border, it also makes a fine container plant. This rose is tolerant of partial shade. A climbing sport, which grows 6 to 12 feet tall, has thornless canes that are easily trained on fences and trellises, although it can also be grown without support as a graceful shrub or hedge with cascading blooms. 'Pinkie' is an AARS winner.

'PLAYBOY'

Classification: *floribunda*

Bloom period: *spring to fall*

Height: *3 feet*

Hardiness: *Zones 4-10*

ARS rating: *8.1*

Date introduced: *1976*

The burgundy-bronze buds of 'Playboy' open to display large flowers that are a vivid blend of orange, yellow, and scarlet. Each 3½-inch bloom has seven to 10 petals and a yellow eye. Borne in clusters, the flowers are delightfully fragrant and appear all season. In fall, spent blooms produce attractive hips. Foliage is dark and glossy.

'Playboy' is aggressive and easy to grow. The bushes are useful in beds and borders, and the long-stemmed flower sprays are long-lasting both in the garden and when cut for indoor arrangements. This rose is disease resistant and tolerates partial shade.

'PLUM DANDY'

Classification: *miniature*

Bloom period: *spring to fall*

Height: *24 inches*

Hardiness: *Zones 5-10*

ARS rating: *9.0*

Date introduced: *1991*

The plump, pointed buds of 'Plum Dandy' open to cup-shaped medium lavender flowers that are a lighter shade toward the base of the petals; flowers fade to light lavender with age. Each very double bloom is 1½ to 2 inches across and bears a fruity fragrance. Foliage is medium green and semiglossy.

Plants are moderate growers. They are compact and bushy, with a somewhat spreading habit, and are useful for tucking into small places to add color to a shrub bed or perennial border. They are excellent for containers.

'PRISTINE'

Classification: *hybrid tea*

Bloom period: *summer*

Height: *4 to 5 feet*

Hardiness: *Zones 5-10*

ARS rating: *9.2*

Date introduced: *1978*

Gardenia-like 'Pristine' blooms are lightly scented and colored a delicate ivory with a fragile pink blush. The long, spiraled buds open to 4- to 6-inch high-centered double flowers, each with 25 to 35 large petals. Flowers usually appear singly on stems but may be clustered; they bloom in midseason and repeat sparsely. Leaves are also large and are attractively colored a glossy reddish green.

Despite their daintily colored flowers, 'Pristine' plants are extremely vigorous, requiring greater space and more rigorous pruning than most other hybrid teas. They are well placed in a bed or border. For cutting, the flowers should be harvested when they are barely open to lengthen their vase life. Plants are tender and very disease resistant.

'PROSPERITY'

Classification: *hybrid musk*

Bloom period: *summer to fall*

Height: *5 to 6 feet*

Hardiness: *Zones 6-10*

ARS rating: *8.5*

Date introduced: *1919*

The buds of 'Prosperity' are pale pink and open to reveal 1½-inch double ivory flowers that often display a pink blush. The blossoms are fragrant, appear all season in large, heavy clusters, and show off well against the abundant dark, glossy foliage.

This rose is a vigorous grower with an upright habit; its erect canes arch gracefully from the weight of the flowers. The bush can be as wide as it is tall and requires a large space in the garden. It makes a fine flowering hedge and tolerates partial shade.

'PROSPERO'

Classification: *shrub*

Bloom period: *spring to fall*

Height: *2 to 2½ feet*

Hardiness: *Zones 4-9*

ARS rating: *8.2*

Date introduced: *1983*

The double gallica-like blooms of 'Prospero' open crimson with mauve shadings and mature to a rich purple. Flowers are flat, with small petals perfectly arranged in symmetrical rosettes, and exceptionally fragrant. They begin blooming in spring and repeat well throughout the season. Foliage is a dark matte green. This is a David Austin rose.

'Prospero' has an upright, bushy habit. Its compact size makes it appropriate for small gardens and containers, and the blooms are glorious in arrangements. A somewhat finicky plant, it requires exceptionally good soil for satisfactory growth.

'QUEEN ELIZABETH'

Classification: *grandiflora*

Bloom period: *summer to fall*

Height: *4 to 7 feet*

Hardiness: *Zones 4-9*

ARS rating: *9.0*

Date introduced: *1954*

The 3½- to 4-inch double flowers of 'Queen Elizabeth' appear in a variety of soft pink shades in great abundance from summer to fall. They are borne singly or in clusters on extremely long stems, opening from pointed buds to lightly scented, cupped flowers. This was the first grandiflora rose introduced, and many consider it to be still the finest. Leaves are leathery, dark green, and glossy; stems are purplish brown and nearly thornless.

The tall, upright, vigorous plant is easy to grow and should not be overpruned. It can be effective planted either alone or in groups in beds or borders, or it may be used as a tall flowering hedge. The long-stemmed flowers are ideal for cutting and exhibition. Plants are disease resistant. This rose is an AARS winner.

'RAINBOW'S END'

Classification: *miniature*

Bloom period: *summer to fall*

Height: *10 to 18 inches*

Hardiness: *Zones 5-10*

ARS rating: *9.0*

Date introduced: *1984*

'Rainbow's End' produces 1½-inch double flowers that are deep yellow with red petal edges. As the blooms age, they turn completely red. The flowers have the classic hybrid tea form and are nearly scentless. Leaves are small, dark, and glossy.

This miniature rose is upright and well branched, making it an excellent choice for edging a bed or walkway. It can also be incorporated into perennial borders and makes a fine container specimen, indoors or outside. Plants are hardy and disease resistant.

'RED CASCADE'

Classification: *climbing miniature*

Bloom period: *spring to fall*

Height: *3 to 12 feet*

Hardiness: *Zones 5-10*

ARS rating: *7.2*

Date introduced: *1976*

This miniature climber produces a profusion of 1-inch blossoms that cover the entire length of the plant throughout the growing season. The flowers are double and deep red; petals are white at their base. Leaves are small and leathery, and canes have lots of prickles.

'Red Cascade' is vigorous and versatile. Unsupported, it makes an attractive spreading ground cover, and is very pretty cascading over a wall. Or it can be trained to climb on supports and will reach 12 feet in height in warm climates. This rose is also an excellent container plant, shown to its best advantage when spilling out of a hanging basket or when trained as a standard. It tolerates partial shade.

'REINE DES VIOLETTES'

Classification: *hybrid perpetual*

Bloom period: *summer*

Height: *5 to 8 feet*

Hardiness: *Zones 5-10*

ARS rating: *8.0*

Date introduced: *1860*

The 3-inch flowers of this hybrid perpetual are very double, opening rosy purple and fading to violet. The undersides of the petals are lighter and silkier than the velvety upper surfaces. Petals are quartered and surround a button eye. The blossoms are borne singly or in small clusters and bear a strong, complex fragrance. Flowers fade quickly after they have fully matured. Foliage is sparse and silvery green; canes are nearly smooth.

This bushy plant grows tall and spreads wide; hard pruning is necessary to maintain a compact habit. The long, flexible canes can be trained to climb. The rose is particularly attractive grown on walls. It requires rich soil to perform at its best.

'REVE D'OR'

Classification: *noisette*

Bloom period: *spring to fall*

Height: *8 to 12 feet*

Hardiness: *Zones 6-10*

ARS rating: *8.1*

Date introduced: *1869*

The pendulous, globe-shaped flowers of 'Rêve d'Or' are buff yellow with a hint of salmon. Flowers become lighter as they age; stamens are dark yellow. The blooms are loosely double and fragrant. Flowering begins in the spring and recurs intermittently throughout the season. In some areas, flowering is best in fall. Leaves are coppery when young, maturing to a glossy, rich green. Canes bear few prickles.

This rose is a vigorous grower, suitable for a warm, sunny spot in the garden. It has a climbing habit and is a good choice for training on a wall or pillar. It tolerates summer heat and humidity.

'RISE 'N' SHINE'

Classification: *miniature*

Bloom period: *summer to fall*

Height: *12 to 16 inches*

Hardiness: *Zones 5-10*

ARS rating: *9.1*

Date introduced: *1977*

The 1½- to 2-inch blossoms of 'Rise 'n' Shine' are a bright, clear yellow, providing a dramatic contrast with foliage that is dark and glossy. The buds are long and pointed and open to high-centered flowers with 35 petals. Blossoms are borne singly or in clusters continuously throughout the summer, with a good repeat. They bear little fragrance.

Plants are upright and well branched, forming a short, rounded bush. They are perfect for edgings and containers and can easily be incorporated into beds or borders. They are easy to grow and disease resistant.

'ROBUSTA'

Classification: *shrub*

Bloom period: *spring to fall*

Height: *5 to 6 feet*

Hardiness: *Zones 6-10*

ARS rating: *8.9*

Date introduced: *1979*

The 2½-inch single scarlet flowers of 'Robusta' are borne prolifically throughout the season on this aptly named plant. The blooms are pleasantly scented. Foliage is dense and very handsome, though somewhat coarse. The dark green, leathery, glossy leaves provide a rich foil for the blooms. Thick canes are armed with nail-like prickles.

This vigorous rose has a full, bushy habit. It is ideal for use as an impenetrable hedge when plants are spaced 4 feet apart, and it's a good choice for a specimen shrub or for planting along a fence.

'ROGER LAMBELIN'

Classification: *hybrid perpetual*

Bloom period: *summer to fall*

Height: *4 feet*

Hardiness: *Zones 5-10*

ARS rating: *7.2*

Date introduced: *1890*

The value of 'Roger Lambelin' is in the unique color pattern of its repeating double flowers: Petals are bright crimson edged and streaked with white, so that blooms appear to be wearing petticoats. As they age, the blooms fade to maroon. Each flower has about 30 fringed, velvety-textured petals. They are extremely fragrant.

This vigorous hybrid perpetual has a full, bushy habit. It is finicky, though, requiring very good soil, and is susceptible to both black spot and mildew. 'Baron Girod de l'Ain', a similar rose in this class, has flowers that are a little less richly colored but is a more reliable performer.

ROSA BANKSIAE BANKSIAE

Classification: *species*

Bloom period: *spring to early summer*

Height: *12 to 25 feet*

Hardiness: *Zones 8-10*

ARS rating: *8.6*

Date introduced: *1807*

The double white flowers of *R. banksiae banksiae* appear in profusion in spring and continue for up to 6 weeks. The flowers cover the plant during this period. Each blossom is less than 1 inch across, pure white, and extremely fragrant with the scent of violets. Leaves are long, light green, and shiny, and the canes are nearly thornless.

Where it is hardy, this rose is a fast, vigorous grower and is quite long-lived. It grows well on a tree, wall, or trellis but may become rampant where the growth is not controlled. The related variety *R. banksiae lutea* bears pale to deep yellow double flowers and is slightly hardier and less fragrant; its ARS rating is 8.8. Both varieties are known as the Lady Banks' Rose.

ROSA EGLANTERIA

Classification: *species*

Bloom period: *late spring*

Height: *8 to 14 feet*

Hardiness: *Zones 5-10*

ARS rating: *8.6*

Date introduced: *prior to 1551*

R. eglanteria is commonly called the sweetbrier or eglantine rose. Its single blush pink flowers are 2 inches across, with petals surrounding golden stamens. They appear singly or in small clusters in late spring. Bright red hips follow the flowers. The leaves are tough and dark green and are distinctly apple scented, while flowers are sweetly fragrant. Canes bear abundant prickles.

This is a large, vigorous rose with a rambling habit. It has become naturalized in North America and can be found growing in pastures. In the garden, plants should be heavily pruned to contain them and to encourage new growth, which is especially fragrant.

ROSA FOETIDA BICOLOR

Classification: *species*

Bloom period: *late spring*

Height: *4 to 8 feet*

Hardiness: *Zones 5-9*

ARS rating: *8.1*

Date introduced: *prior to 1590*

This wild rose also goes by the name 'Austrian Copper'. It is a sport of the yellow species *R. foetida*. Its 2- to 3-inch flowers are orange to coppery red on the upper surface with a yellow reverse. Occasionally a branch spontaneously reverts to the species, resulting in both yellow and copper-colored flowers on the same bush. Foliage is small, neat, and light green; the prickly canes are chestnut brown.

Plants typically grow 4 to 5 feet with arching canes but can sometimes reach 8 feet. They usually require little pruning to maintain their attractive form. The plants are effective in beds or borders for a colorful spring flower display but should be kept apart from soft, pastel flowers, which do not blend well with the bold tones of this variety. This rose is hardy but susceptible to black spot.

ROSA GLAUCA

Classification: *species*

Bloom period: *late spring to early summer*

Height: *6 to 7 feet*

Hardiness: *Zones 4-9*

ARS rating: *8.9*

Date introduced: *prior to 1830*

R. glauca (sometimes listed as *R. rubrifolia*) is grown as much for its attractive foliage as for its flowers. The blooms are single with five medium pink petals with white bases surrounding bright yellow stamens. Leaves are gray-green with distinctive coppery and reddish overtones. Small scarlet hips follow the flowers. Canes are nearly thornless and purple-red.

This rose has a relaxed, rounded, arching habit and provides landscape interest over a very long season. It is useful in a shrub border and makes a fine hedge. Also, cuttings in flower arrangements provide foliage color contrast.

'ROSA MUNDI'

Classification: *gallica*

Bloom period: *summer*

Height: *3 to 4 feet*

Hardiness: *Zones 4-10*

ARS rating: *8.6*

Date introduced: *prior to 1581*

'Rosa Mundi' (*R. gallica versicolor*) is a sport of 'Apothecary's Rose' (*R. gallica officinalis*). Its 2- to 3-inch semidouble flowers are spectacularly striped crimson, pink, and deep pink over blush white. Borne singly or in small sprays, the very fragrant flowers open to wide and flattened cups. An occasional branch will revert to the deep-pink-colored flowers of its parent. Red hips appear in late summer. Leaves are a dark matte green, and stems are nearly smooth.

This upright, bushy rose is very hardy and tolerates summer heat and humidity. It is useful in beds or borders, and its flowers can be used for indoor arrangements and potpourri. This rose is somewhat prone to mildew.

ROSA PALUSTRIS

Classification: *species*

Bloom period: *summer*

Height: *4 to 8 feet*

Hardiness: *Zones 5-10*

ARS rating: *not rated*

Date introduced: *1726*

Also known as the swamp rose, *R. palustris* produces its single dark pink blooms intermittently throughout the summer, providing a longer flowering season than most species roses. Flowers are 2 inches across and are followed by oval hips. Foliage is medium to dark green; stems are reddish.

This rose has an erect, sparse form. Though typically about 4 feet tall, it may reach 8 feet in some areas. It prefers damp, swampy soil but also grows and flowers in poor, dry, sandy soil. It is tolerant of summer heat and humidity and can adapt to partial shade.

ROSA RUGOSA ALBA

Classification: *species*

Bloom period: *summer*

Height: *4 to 6 feet*

Hardiness: *Zones 3-8*

ARS rating: *9.0*

Date introduced: *1870*

A color sport of *R. rugosa*, *R. rugosa alba* produces large single white flowers throughout the summer. Usually borne in clusters, each bloom is 2½ to 4 inches across and bears a strong clovelike fragrance. The flowers are followed by huge orange-red hips that stand out beautifully against the foliage, which turns from bright green to yellow in the fall. Another rugosa sport, *R. rugosa rubra*, bears magenta-purple flowers and red hips.

This vigorous and spreading rose may outgrow its space unless controlled. It is useful in shrub borders, as a hedge, or as a specimen shrub. An easy-to-grow rose, it thrives in sandy soil, is an excellent choice for seaside gardens, and is extremely hardy and resistant to diseases and insects.

'ROSE DE MEAUX'

Classification: *centifolia*

Bloom period: *summer*

Height: *18 to 24 inches*

Hardiness: *Zones 3-9*

ARS rating: *7.0*

Date introduced: *1789*

This diminutive rose bears medium pink to light rose pompom-type double blooms in summer, with no repeat. The 1½-inch flowers have frilly petals and are very fragrant. Leaves are also small, in keeping with the overall size of the plant. Canes bear abundant straight prickles.

The plants have an upright, bushy, compact habit. They are useful for small gardens or for tucking into a small space, and are also a good choice for containers. 'Rose de Meaux' requires very good soil and can be somewhat temperamental; it is prone to black spot.

'ROSE DE RESCHT'

Classification: *damask*

Bloom period: *summer to fall*

Height: *2 to 3 feet*

Hardiness: *Zones 4-10*

ARS rating: *8.6*

Date introduced: *unknown*

The bright fuchsia-red blooms of 'Rose du Rescht' display lilac and purple tints and age to magenta-pink. Appearing abundantly in midseason and repeating well, each flower is 2 to 2½ inches across and very double, with about 100 petals. Blooms are borne in small, upright clusters and are intensely fragrant. The abundant medium green leaves have red margins when young.

This rose is short, with a compact and bushy habit. It provides a long season of color in beds or borders, but hard pruning of older plants is necessary to keep the flowers repeating. Plants are quite vigorous and tolerate heat well.

'ROSE DU ROI'

Classification: *portland*

Bloom period: *summer to fall*

Height: *3 to 4 feet*

Hardiness: *Zones 5-10*

ARS rating: *7.6*

Date introduced: *1815*

The double flowers of 'Rose du Roi' are bright red mottled with violet and purple. Each loosely arranged bloom is 2½ inches across and is rich in fragrance. Flowers appear abundantly in midseason and repeat well. Foliage is pointed, small, and dark green.

Plants are short and spreading with a somewhat straggly form. They provide a long season of heavily perfumed blooms in beds and borders, and are particularly well suited to smaller gardens. 'Rose du Roi' is disease resistant and winter-hardy.

'ROSERAIE DE L'HAY'

Classification: *hybrid rugosa*

Bloom period: *spring to fall*

Height: *4 to 6 feet*

Hardiness: *Zones 3-8*

ARS rating: *8.1*

Date introduced: *1901*

The long, pointed, scrolled buds of 'Roseraie de l'Hay' open to deep crimson blossoms with cream-colored stamens and age to a magenta pink. Flowers are 4½ to 5 inches across and semidouble, with loosely arranged, folded petals. The blooms are very fragrant. Few hips are produced. Foliage is dense and apple green, with vibrant color in the fall.

Like other hybrid rugosas, this vigorous rose is a tough plant with good disease resistance, and it tolerates a wide range of soils and seaside conditions. Its repeating blooms and attractive foliage make it an excellent choice for mixed-shrub plantings or hedges.

'RUGOSA MAGNIFICA'

Classification: *hybrid rugosa*

Bloom period: *spring to fall*

Height: *4 to 6 feet*

Hardiness: *Zones 3-9*

ARS rating: *8.3*

Date introduced: *1905*

The deep red-purple to lavender petals of repeat-blooming 'Rugosa Magnifica' surround golden yellow stamens. The fragrant blooms are double and are followed by abundant large orange-red hips. Foliage is dense.

This shrub is a very vigorous grower with a wide-spreading habit. It is good in mixed-shrub plantings, as a specimen, or as a hedge. Like other hybrid rugosas, it is extremely hardy and disease resistant, adapts to a wide range of soils, and tolerates seaside conditions.

'SALLY HOLMES'

Classification: *shrub*

Bloom period: *early summer to fall*

Height: *4 to 12 feet*

Hardiness: *Zones 5-9*

ARS rating: *8.9*

Date introduced: *1976*

The single blossoms of 'Sally Holmes' are borne in profusion in large, compact clusters. Buds are apricot, opening to creamy white 3½-inch blooms that turn pure white as they mature. Petals surround bright golden stamens. The flowers are delicately fragrant. Foliage is leathery, dark green, and shiny.

This robust rose can be grown as a large mounding shrub with a height of 4 to 6 feet and an equal spread. It makes a dramatic specimen or can be used in a large border. 'Sally Holmes' can also be trained as a climber, in which case it can reach 12 feet. Plants are disease resistant and tolerant of heat and partial shade. The flowers are exceptionally long-lasting in indoor arrangements.

'SEA FOAM'

Classification: *shrub*

Bloom period: *summer to fall*

Height: *2½ to 3 feet*

Hardiness: *Zones 4-9*

ARS rating: *8.0*

Date introduced: *1964*

The creamy white flowers of 'Sea Foam' are 2 to 3 inches across and are borne in large clusters throughout the growing season. Buds are rounded, and open to cupped or flat blossoms with short petals that stand out well against the small, dark, glossy leaves. It has a slight fragrance.

The plant is exceptionally versatile, with a vigorous, semiprostrate or trailing habit that, unless supported, generally does not exceed 2½ or 3 feet in height. Its long, arching canes, however, may spread 8 to 12 feet. 'Sea Foam' can be used in the landscape as a ground cover, a mounded shrub, or as a climber on pillars or walls. Its flowers are delightful for cutting. Plants are easy to grow and quite disease resistant.

'SEXY REXY'

Classification: *floribunda*

Bloom period: *spring to fall*

Height: *3 feet*

Hardiness: *Zones 4-10*

ARS rating: *9.0*

Date introduced: *1984*

The 2½- to 3½-inch double flowers of 'Sexy Rexy' are carried in large clusters throughout the season. Each mildly fragrant blossom is composed of 40 or more medium to light pink petals. Flowers flatten as they mature. The abundant small leaves are light green and glossy.

This free-flowering rose is vigorous and bushy. It is effective in beds with perennials or in front of taller roses, where it can cover leggy stems. It also makes an attractive low hedge. Plants are very disease resistant.

'SHOWBIZ'

Classification: *floribunda*

Bloom period: *summer to fall*

Height: *2½ to 3 feet*

Hardiness: *Zones 4-10*

ARS rating: *8.6*

Date introduced: *1981*

The short, pointed buds of 'Showbiz' open to 2½- to 3-inch scarlet flowers. Blooming in large sprays, they are double and loosely cupped, with ruffled petals and bright yellow stamens, and have a slight fragrance. The abundant leaves are dark green and glossy.

This rose is bushy, low, and compact. A fine contribution to beds and borders with its boldly colored blooms and rich foliage, it also can be planted in numbers as an attractive low hedge or mass planting. The flowers are good for cutting, and plants are disease resistant. 'Showbiz' is an AARS winner.

'SILVER MOON'

Classification: *large-flowered climber*

Bloom period: *summer*

Height: *15 to 20 feet*

Hardiness: *Zones 5-10*

ARS rating: *7.3*

Date introduced: *1910*

The long, pointed yellow buds of 'Silver Moon' open to large creamy white single or semidouble flowers. Borne singly or in clusters, the flowers are 4½ inches across with up to 20 petals that surround golden amber stamens. Blooms do not repeat. Their fragrance is fruity. Foliage is large, dark, leathery, and glossy.

'Silver Moon' is a very vigorous and strong climber, and may reach beyond 20 feet. Effective on a trellis or other support, it is also an ideal rose for training into a tree. Though somewhat shy about flowering, the blooms it does produce are outstanding.

'SIMPLICITY'

Classification: *floribunda*

Bloom period: *summer to fall*

Height: *3 to 6 feet*

Hardiness: *Zones 4-10*

ARS rating: *8.1*

Date introduced: *1979*

The 3- to 4-inch semidouble flowers of 'Simplicity' are borne in clusters. Each blossom is cupped or flattened, with 18 medium pink petals surrounding yellow stamens that darken with age. Flowers bear little fragrance. Foliage is a fresh light to medium green and is semiglossy.

Bushy and dense with graceful, arching canes, 'Simplicity' is an excellent choice for a hedge; when first introduced it was even marketed as a "living fence." It also works well in beds and borders, and the flowers are good for cutting. Plants are disease resistant.

'SNOW BRIDE'

Classification: *miniature*

Bloom period: *summer to fall*

Height: *15 to 18 inches*

Hardiness: *Zones 5-10*

ARS rating: *9.3*

Date introduced: *1982*

'Snow Bride' is a prolific bloomer with long, pointed, hybrid-tea-type buds opening to 1½-inch double flowers with high centers. Petals are white with just a hint of yellow, and they surround yellow stamens. Leaves are semiglossy and dark green.

This vigorous miniature is easy to grow. Compact and well branched, it may be used as an edging or incorporated with other plants into a bed or border. 'Snow Bride' is also a perfect container plant. The flowers are excellent for cutting and exhibition.

'SOMBREUIL'

Classification: *climbing tea*

Bloom period: *summer to fall*

Height: *8 to 12 feet*

Hardiness: *Zones 6-10*

ARS rating: *8.8*

Date introduced: *1850*

The exquisite very double blooms of this rose are creamy white with pale blush tones, and they are deliciously fragrant. Borne in clusters on nodding stems, the flowers are quartered, 3½ to 4 inches across, and saucer shaped. Unlike many old roses, 'Sombreuil' blooms throughout the growing season. Its leaves are light green and semiglossy, and its canes are thorny.

The plant is a moderately vigorous climber, with pliable canes that are easily trained on a trellis, fence, or wall. Its blooms, often pendulous, occur along the entire length of the cane, making it a good choice for an arbor where it can be viewed from below. Flowers are good for cutting. 'Sombreuil' likes to be fed frequently; it tolerates partial shade and hot summers.

'SOUVENIR DE LA MALMAISON'

Classification: *bourbon*

Bloom period: *summer to fall*

Height: *3 feet*

Hardiness: *Zones 5-9*

ARS rating: *8.4*

Date introduced: *1843*

The delicate blush pink blossoms of 'Souvenir de la Malmaison' are slightly darker toward the center. They are cupped when they first open but gradually flatten into flowers that are 4 or 5 inches across. As the blooms age they fade slightly to almost white. Flowers are double and quartered, with a rich, spicy fragrance. Foliage is medium green and glossy.

This rose is a bit of a challenge to grow. It thrives in hot, dry weather but does poorly during wet periods, when buds may refuse to open. Dwarf, bushy, and rounded, it is lovely in beds and borders. A climbing form, rated 8.2 by the ARS, reaches 6 to 8 feet and is well suited to growing up a pillar.

'STARINA'

Classification: *miniature*

Bloom period: *summer to fall*

Height: *12 to 15 inches*

Hardiness: *Zones 6-10*

ARS rating: *9.0*

Date introduced: *1965*

The lightly fragrant, bright orange-scarlet flowers of 'Starina' are touched with yellow at their base. They are double with a classic hybrid tea form; each is 1½ inches across and has about 35 petals. Blooms appear continuously during the season. Foliage is small and glossy.

Plants are upright, bushy, and compact, usually about a foot tall and wide. Exceptional as a uniform edging, they are also attractive in beds and borders with perennials and shrubs, and grow well as container plants.

'SUN FLARE'

Classification: *floribunda*

Bloom period: *summer to fall*

Height: *2 to 3 feet*

Hardiness: *Zones 4-10*

ARS rating: *8.1*

Date introduced: *1983*

The small, pointed buds of 'Sun Flare' open to 3-inch flat, double blossoms. Colored bright lemon yellow, the flowers have 25 to 30 petals and a licorice fragrance. They are borne freely, mostly in large clusters but sometimes singly. The leaves are very glossy and deep green, providing a dramatic foil for the blooms.

Plants are vigorous, with a round, somewhat spreading habit. Attractive landscape plants, they are well suited to many purposes, including beds, borders, and hedges. Flowers are good for cutting. 'Sun Flare' is highly disease resistant, a rare trait in a yellow rose. It's an AARS winner.

'SUNSPRITE'

Classification: *floribunda*

Bloom period: *spring to fall*

Height: *2½ to 3 feet*

Hardiness: *Zones 5-10*

ARS rating: *8.7*

Date introduced: *1977*

The high-centered oval buds of 'Sunsprite' open to deep yellow flowers. Appearing in clusters of five or more, the blossoms are double, each with about 28 petals, and are richly scented. Flowers are borne continuously throughout the season. Foliage is light green and glossy.

This rose has a compact, upright habit. It is suitable for use in beds and borders, where its low growth neatly covers the base of taller, leggier plants. Its flowers are excellent for cutting and exhibition. It is disease resistant.

'TAUSENDSCHON'	'THE FAIRY'	'THERESE BUGNET'	'TIFFANY'

Classification: *rambler*

Bloom period: *summer*

Height: *8 to 12 feet*

Hardiness: *Zones 5-10*

ARS rating: *8.5*

Date introduced: *1906*

Classification: *polyantha*

Bloom period: *summer to fall*

Height: *1½ to 3 feet*

Hardiness: *Zones 4-9*

ARS rating: *8.7*

Date introduced: *1932*

Classification: *hybrid rugosa*

Bloom period: *summer*

Height: *5 to 6 feet*

Hardiness: *Zones 3-9*

ARS rating: *8.2*

Date introduced: *1950*

Classification: *hybrid tea*

Bloom period: *summer to fall*

Height: *4½ feet*

Hardiness: *Zones 5-10*

ARS rating: *8.3*

Date introduced: *1954*

Produced in enormous loose clusters, the double flowers of 'Tausendschön' have wavy petals that are colored a deep rose pink with a white base. As they age, blooms fade to soft pink, lavender, blush, and white, and all colors may be present on the same cluster. Plants bloom once in the summer, and flowers are lightly fragrant. Leaves are light green and glossy; canes are smooth.

Although 'Tausendschön' grows tall, it is not as rampant as some ramblers. Its long, pliable canes are easily trained to a pillar or fence, but supports that don't allow plenty of air circulation—such as a wall—should be avoided because the rose is prone to mildew. Prune sparingly immediately after it flowers.

'The Fairy' produces large clusters of small buds that open to ruffled light pink blooms. The cupped, double flowers fade to almost white under the summer sun. They have no scent but are produced in abundance. Foliage is bright green and glossy.

This easy-to-grow, vigorous rose has a compact, spreading habit. Usually wider than it is tall, it is useful as a ground cover or in beds or borders in front of taller shrubs. Also, its nonstop bloom makes it a good choice for a low flowering hedge, and its small size is suitable for containers. Flowers are long-lasting when cut. The plant is extremely disease resistant and tolerates both heat and humidity. A climbing sport of this rose grows 8 to 12 feet high.

The long, lilac buds of 'Thérèse Bugnet' open to rose red flowers that fade to pale pink with age. Blooms are 4 inches across and double, with 35 petals, and have a moderately spicy scent. Foliage is gray-green with a quilted appearance; the leaves provide a particularly attractive foil for the richly colored flowers.

This vigorous hybrid rugosa is large and shrubby—usually equal in height and width—and perfect for use as a tall, flowering hedge. It is disease resistant, hardy, and tolerant of seaside conditions.

Long and pointed, the buds of 'Tiffany' have a beautiful, classic form; they open to 4- to 5-inch double blossoms whose soft rose pink petals blend to yellow at their base. Flowers are produced singly and in clusters over a long season; they are high centered and bear a strong, sweet, fruity fragrance. The foliage is dark green and glossy.

'Tiffany' is vigorous and easy to grow. Tall and upright in habit, it is effective in beds and borders and makes an exceptional, long-lasting cut flower. Performing best in warm climates, it is more disease resistant than most hybrid teas. This is an AARS winner.

'TOUCH OF CLASS'

Classification: *hybrid tea*

Bloom period: *summer to fall*

Height: *4 feet*

Hardiness: *Zones 5-10*

ARS rating: *9.5*

Date introduced: *1984*

'Touch of Class' produces spiraled orange buds whose color takes on coral and cream shading as they open and eventually evolves to pink. Flowers are 4½ to 5½ inches across and double. They have little or no fragrance. Usually borne singly on long stems, the blooms are attractively set off against dark green, semiglossy foliage.

This rose has a tall, upright, bushy habit. It is well suited to beds and borders, where it produces its flowers over a lengthy season. The long-stemmed blooms are long-lasting in indoor arrangements. Foliage is prone to mildew. 'Touch of Class' is an AARS winner.

'TOURNAMENT OF ROSES'

Classification: *grandiflora*

Bloom period: *spring to fall*

Height: *4 to 6 feet*

Hardiness: *Zones 5-10*

ARS rating: *8.0*

Date introduced: *1989*

Flowers of 'Tournament of Roses' are shades of pink and beige with a darker pink reverse that fades to coral pink with age. The double blooms are high centered, 4 inches across, and lightly fragrant. They usually appear in small sprays of three to six flowers. Leaves are large, glossy, and dark green, and canes bear large prickles.

This rose is moderately vigorous and has an upright habit. It performs best maintained as a 5-foot shrub, although it will grow taller if allowed, and is suitable for beds and borders. Flowers are borne freely and are long-lasting, but may not be ideal for cutting because stems can be short or weak. It is highly disease resistant. This is an AARS winner.

'TROPICANA'

Classification: *hybrid tea*

Bloom period: *summer to fall*

Height: *4 to 5 feet*

Hardiness: *Zones 5-10*

ARS rating: *7.9*

Date introduced: *1960*

The 4- to 5-inch double flowers of 'Tropicana' are bright orange-red and fruity with fragrance. Buds are very large and pointed. Borne singly, the blooms are high centered, becoming cup shaped as they mature. They appear over a lengthy season, and their color holds up well even in hot weather. Foliage is glossy and dark green.

Plants are vigorous, upright, and bushy. The vibrant color of its flowers can be stunning in beds and borders but is difficult to blend with soft pastel shades. The blooms are excellent for cutting. Plants are prone to mildew. 'Tropicana' is an AARS winner.

'TUSCANY'

Classification: *gallica*

Bloom period: *spring*

Height: *3 to 4 feet*

Hardiness: *Zones 4-10*

ARS rating: *7.7*

Date introduced: *prior to 1820*

The large semidouble flowers of 'Tuscany' are dark crimson to deep purple with a velvety texture. Petals are flat and are arranged around prominent yellow stamens, creating a dramatic contrast. Although very fragrant, the flowers are not as heavily scented as some gallicas. They appear in abundance in spring and do not repeat. Leaves are small and dark green.

The vigorous plants have a tidy, rounded form and are well suited to small gardens. The intense colors of the flowers make them spectacular in bloom. They are winter-hardy and tolerant of summer heat and humidity.

'UNCLE JOE'

Classification: *hybrid tea*

Bloom period: *summer to fall*

Height: *5 feet*

Hardiness: *Zones 5-10*

ARS rating: *7.7*

Date introduced: *1971*

'Uncle Joe' (sometimes listed as 'Toro') bears its 6-inch double blooms singly on long stems. The buds open slowly to become high-centered medium to dark red flowers with a strong fragrance. The large, leathery leaves are a glossy dark green.

Plants are vigorous growers with a tall, upright habit. Their stems are quite strong and amply able to hold up the huge blossoms. This rose is suitable for beds and borders and is excellent for cutting. Cool, damp weather may stunt the production of flowers.

'VARIEGATA DI BOLOGNA'

Classification: *bourbon*

Bloom period: *summer*

Height: *5 to 8 feet*

Hardiness: *Zones 5-9*

ARS rating: *7.6*

Date introduced: *1909*

No two flowers of 'Variegata di Bologna' are exactly alike in coloration: Petals are white and individually striped with various shades of crimson and purple. The very double blooms are 3 to 4 inches across and globular, flattening and quartering with age. Borne in clusters of three to five, the blossoms bear a strong and long-lasting fragrance. They appear in abundance in midseason but repeat sparsely, if at all. Leaves are narrow and glossy; canes are nearly smooth.

The bushes are vigorous, upright, and slender, and are versatile in the landscape. Their long, flexible canes are easily trained to climb a fence, trellis, or pillar, or can be pegged. Heavy pruning will produce a more compact, 4- to 5-foot shrub suitable for borders. Flowers are good for cutting.

'VEILCHENBLAU'

Classification: *rambler*

Bloom period: *late spring*

Height: *10 to 15 feet*

Hardiness: *Zones 5-9*

ARS rating: *7.9*

Date introduced: *1909*

'Veilchenblau' produces large clusters of cupped semidouble flowers whose violet color is about as close to blue as any rose has come; in fact it is sometimes referred to as the blue rose. Petals are streaked with white, especially near the center, where golden stamens are prominent. As they age, the blooms fade to blue-gray. Their fragrance is long-lasting and fruity. In some areas flowers repeat in summer. Foliage is light green and glossy. Canes bear very few prickles.

This vigorous plant can be trained to climb a pillar, fence, or trellis for an outstanding display. It can also be pruned to maintain a loose, open shrub. It is drought resistant and tolerates partial shade. In partially shaded sites the flower color remains intense without fading.

'WHITE MEIDILAND'

Classification: *shrub*

Bloom period: *summer to fall*

Height: *2 to 2½ feet*

Hardiness: *Zones 4-9*

ARS rating: *8.3*

Date introduced: *1986*

Clusters of small, double, pure white flowers cover the plant of 'White Meidiland' from early summer through fall. They are enhanced by a background of dark green, glossy leaves; canes are not visible through the dense foliage.

This rose is vigorous and very easy to grow. It has a low, spreading habit and is often twice as wide as it is tall, making it useful as a ground cover, especially on sunny banks. If used for this purpose, plants should be spaced 4 feet apart. 'White Meidiland' is hardy and pest and disease resistant, and requires little pruning.

'WHITE PET'

Classification: *polyantha*

Bloom period: *spring to fall*

Height: *2 feet*

Hardiness: *Zones 5-9*

ARS rating: *7.2*

Date introduced: *1879*

'White Pet' is a profuse bloomer with small, creamy white buds touched with carmine that open to rosette-type double flowers. Appearing in large clusters, the flowers are borne continuously throughout the season and are well displayed against abundant dark green foliage.

Plants are small and round, up to 2 feet with an equal spread. Their neat form and free-flowering nature make them good candidates for edging or for incorporating into beds or borders. 'White Pet' is also perfectly suited to growing in containers and is a good source of flowers for cutting.

'WILLIAM BAFFIN'

Classification: *shrub*

Bloom period: *summer to fall*

Height: *5 to 10 feet*

Hardiness: *Zones 3-9*

ARS rating: *9.4*

Date introduced: *1983*

This kordesii shrub, one of the Explorer series, produces clusters of up to 30 deep pink blooms over a lengthy season. Each loosely arranged, semidouble blossom is 2 to 3 inches across. Blooms have little or no fragrance. Foliage is medium green and glossy.

'William Baffin' is robust and upright, with arching canes. Versatile in the landscape, it can be grown as a climber with a spread equal to its height or as a stunning large hedge, or it can be pruned as a border shrub. The canes can also be trained to sprawl on the ground for use as a ground cover. One of the hardiest roses available, it is disease resistant as well.

'WILL SCARLET'

Classification: *hybrid musk*

Bloom period: *spring and fall*

Height: *6 to 12 feet*

Hardiness: *Zones 5-10*

ARS rating: *8.2*

Date introduced: *1947*

The bright red buds of 'Will Scarlet' open to vivid rose red semidouble flowers that lighten in color toward the flower center. Hot weather tends to induce shades of lilac at the center, which makes an especially pleasing contrast with the flowers' numerous yellow stamens. The flowers are delicately scented. Plants bloom profusely in spring and again in fall. The blooms are followed by clusters of round orange hips.

This rose can be grown as a large shrub, best maintained at 6 to 7 feet with a nearly equal spread. It is also a fine climber, reaching up to 12 feet on a trellis or pillar. It has a graceful, arching form, and it tolerates partial shade.

'ZEPHIRINE DROUHIN'

Classification: *bourbon*

Bloom period: *spring to fall*

Height: *8 to 20 feet*

Hardiness: *Zones 5-10*

ARS rating: *7.9*

Date introduced: *1868*

The semidouble cerise-pink flowers of 'Zéphirine Drouhin' are 3½ to 4 inches across and are loosely formed. Borne in profusion in spring, they continue to appear intermittently until fall, when the plant once again flowers heavily. Blooms are very sweetly scented. Young leaves are a coppery purple, maturing to dark green, and the canes are smooth.

'Zéphirine Drouhin' is a vigorous grower with an upright, semiclimbing habit. It can be pruned as a shrub placed in a large border or displayed as a specimen, and it makes a fine formal hedge. Or, train it as a climber on a trellis, fence, or porch, where it may grow as high as 20 feet. The lack of prickles makes it a good choice for planting near walkways or play areas.

Acknowledgments and Picture Credits

The editors wish to thank the following for their valuable assistance in the preparation of this volume:

Philip J. Hamman, Department of Entymology, Texas A&M University, College Station; H. Brent Pemberton, Texas Agricultural Experiment Station, Texas A&M University, Overton; Craig Regelbrugge, Director of Regulatory Affairs and Grower Services, American Association of Nurserymen, Washington, D.C.; Holly Shimizu, United States Botanic Garden, Washington, D.C.; Betty Spar, United States Botanic Garden, Washington, D.C.

The sources for the illustrations in the book are listed below. Credits from left to right are separated by semicolons; credits from top to bottom are separated by dashes.

Cover: Roger Foley/designed by Karen Burroughs and Gary Hayre, Ashton, Md. Back cover insets: © Alan L. Detrick—art by Nicholas Fasciano and Yin Yi—Leonard G. Phillips/designed by Joe Saury, courtesy Patricia Alliger. End papers: © Charles Mann. 2, 3: Virginia R. Weiler. 4: Courtesy Peter Haring; © Charles Mann. 6, 7: Jerry Pavia/designed by Mary Matthews. 8, 9: Art by Lorraine Moseley Epstein and Yin Yi (4)—art by Sharron O'Neil (5). 10, 11: © John Marshall; © Alan L. Detrick. 12-14: © Alan L. Detrick. 15: Lauren Springer. 16, 17: © John Marshall. 18, 19: © Karen Bussolini; © Alan L. Detrick. 20: Renée Comet. 21: © Alan L. Detrick. 22: © Karen Bussolini. 24: Art by Lorraine Moseley Epstein and Yin Yi. 25: © Karen Bussolini. 26, 27: Leonard G. Phillips/courtesy Wayne Stokes Goodall, Charlottesville, Va. 28: Ken Druse/

The Natural Garden. 29: Bernard Fallon/designed by Sandy Kennedy. 30: © Cynthia Woodyard. 31: Lauren Springer—© Cynthia Woodyard. 32: © Karen Bussolini—© Alan L. Detrick. 33: Jerry Pavia/courtesy Diane and Jon Spieler, garden designed by Johnathan Plant, Los Angeles. 34, 35: © Charles Mann; art by Stephen R. Wagner. 36: Bernard Fallon/designed by Sandy Kennedy. 37: © Charles Mann. 38: Art by Stephen R. Wagner—© Saxon Holt. 39: Leonard G. Phillips/courtesy Lillian B. Salley Martin, Charlottesville, Va. 40: © Carole Ottesen. 41: © Charles Mann. 42, 43: Michael Bates/designed by Michael Bates. 44, 45: © Dency Kane/design, The Penick Garden at Reedy Mill, Ruther Glen, Va. 46, 47: Dency Kane/courtesy Martha Stewart, East Hampton, N.Y. 48, 49: Leonard G. Phillips/designed by Joe Saury, courtesy Patricia Alliger. 50, 51: Mike Shoup. 52, 53: Leonard G. Phillips/courtesy Kreis and Sandy Beall, Point Clear, Ala. 54, 55: © Saxon Holt/designed by Michael Bates. 56: © Dency Kane/design, The Penick Garden at Reedy Mill, Ruther Glen, Va. (2)—Dency Kane/courtesy Martha Stewart, East Hampton, N.Y. (2). 57: Leonard G. Phillips/designed by Joe Saury, courtesy Patricia Alliger (2). 58: Mike Shoup (2)—Leonard G. Phillips/courtesy Kreis and Sandy Beall, Point Clear, Ala. (2). 59: © Saxon Holt/designed by Michael Bates (2). 60, 61: © Charles Mann. 62: Art by Sharron O'Neil. 63: © Michael S. Thompson. 64: Art by Sharron O'Neil. 65: © Charles Mann. 67, 68: Art by Nicholas Fasciano and Yin Yi. 70: © Alan L. Detrick. 71: Art by Nicholas Fasciano and Yin Yi. 72: © Alan L. Detrick. 73: Art by Nicholas Fasciano and Yin Yi. 74: Art by Mike Wanke—art by

Nicholas Fasciano and Yin Yi (3). 75, 76: Art by Mike Wanke. 77: Art by Nicholas Fasciano and Yin Yi. 78: Art by Mike Wanke. 79: Jerry Pavia/courtesy Wing Haven, Charlotte, N.C. 80, 81: Art by Mike Wanke; Leonard G. Phillips/designed by Jan Daggett, Charlottesville, Va. 86: Art by Lorraine Moseley Epstein. 87: Art by Sharron O'Neil—art by Lorraine Moseley Epstein (2)—art by Sharron O'Neil. 88, 89: Art by Lorraine Moseley Epstein. 90: Art by Lorraine Moseley Epstein (2)—art by Sharron O'Neil (2). 91: Art by Lorraine Moseley Epstein. 97: Map by John Drummond, Time-Life Books. 98: Peter Haring; Mike Shoup. 99: Mike Shoup; Peter Haring; © Alan L. Detrick; Peter Haring. 100: Peter Haring; Jerry Pavia (2); Michael M. Smith. 101: © Cheryl R. Richter; Peter Haring (3). 102: Peter Haring; Jerry Pavia; Peter Haring; © Alan L. Detrick. 103: Peter Haring; Jerry Pavia; Peter Haring; Jerry Pavia. 104: Jerry Pavia; Peter Haring; Jerry Pavia (2). 105: © Priscilla Connell/Photo/Nats Inc.; Peter Haring; Roses of Yesterday and Today; Mike Shoup. 106: Peter Haring. 107: Peter Haring (2); Jerry Pavia; © Alan L. Detrick. 108: Jerry Pavia; Mike Shoup; © Alan L. Detrick; Peter Haring. 109: Peter Haring; Jerry Pavia (2); Peter Haring. 110: Peter Haring; © Alan L. Detrick; Peter Haring (2). 111: Peter Haring; Jerry Pavia; Peter Haring (2). 112: Peter Haring (3); Jerry Pavia. 113: Joanne Pavia; Peter Haring (3). 114: Peter Haring; Jerry Pavia; Peter Haring; © Alan L. Detrick. 115: Peter Haring; © Cheryl R. Richter; Peter Haring; Jerry Pavia. 116: Joanne Pavia; Mike Shoup; Michael M. Smith; Peter Haring. 117: Jerry Pavia; © Alan L. Detrick (2); Peter Haring. 118: © Alan L. Detrick; Peter Haring (2); Jerry Pavia. 119: Peter Haring; Jerry

Pavia; Mike Shoup; © Alan L. Detrick. 120: Jerry Pavia; Peter Haring (2); Jerry Pavia. 121: Photos Horticultural, Ipswich, Suffolk, U.K.; Peter Haring; Jerry Pavia; Peter Haring. 122: Jerry Pavia; Peter Haring (2); Mike Shoup. 123: Jerry Pavia (2); Peter Haring (2). 124: © Alan L. Detrick; Peter Haring (2); Mike Shoup. 125: Jerry Pavia; Peter Haring; © Alan L. Detrick; Peter Haring. 126: Jerry Pavia; Peter Haring (3). 127: © Alan L. Detrick; Peter Haring (3). 128: Peter Haring. 129: © Alan L. Detrick; Mike Shoup; Jerry Pavia; Peter Haring. 130: Peter Haring; © Alan L. Detrick (2); Mike Shoup. 131: Peter Haring; © Cheryl R. Richter; Peter Haring (2). 132: Peter Haring (2); Jerry Pavia (2). 133: Peter Haring; Photos Horticultural, Ipswich, Suffolk, U.K.; © Alan L. Detrick; © Cheryl R. Richter. 134: © Carole Ottesen; © Cheryl R. Richter; Peter Haring; John Glover, Churt, Surrey, U.K. 135: Jerry Pavia; © Alan L. Detrick; Peter Haring; Mike Shoup. 136: © Alan L. Detrick; Peter Haring (2); Jerry Pavia. 137: Jackson & Perkins (photographer: Goodman); Peter Haring (3). 138: Jerry Pavia; Peter Haring (2); © Alan L. Detrick. 139: Peter Haring; Jerry Pavia; Photos Horticultural, Ipswich, Suffolk, U.K.; Peter Haring. 140: Peter Haring (2); © Alan L. Detrick (2). 141: Jerry Pavia; Mike Shoup (2); Peter Haring. 142: Peter Haring (2); Photos Horticultural, Ipswich, Suffolk, U.K.; Peter Haring. 143: Peter Haring (2); Jerry Pavia (2). 144: Peter Haring; Jerry Pavia; Peter Haring (2). 145: Jerry Pavia; Peter Haring (3). 146: © Alan L. Detrick (2); Peter Haring (2). 147: Jerry Pavia; Peter Haring; © Alan L. Detrick; Peter Haring. 148: Jerry Pavia (2); Mike Shoup; Peter Haring. 149: Peter Haring; Mike Shoup (2); Peter Haring.

BOOKS:

All about Roses. San Ramon, Calif.: Ortho Books, 1990.

Austin, David. *David Austin's English Roses.* Boston: Little, Brown, 1993.

Bales, Suzanne Frutig. *Roses* (Burpee American Gardening series). New York: Prentice Hall Gardening, 1994.

Barash, Cathy Wilkinson. *Roses.* Secaucus, N.J.: Chartwell Books, 1991.

Beales, Peter. *Classic Roses.* New York: Holt, Rinehart and Winston, 1985.

Boisset, Caroline. *Vertical Gardening.* New York: Weidenfeld & Nicolson, 1988.

Cairns, Thomas (Ed.). *Modern Roses 10.* Shreveport, La.: American Rose Society, 1993.

Christopher, Thomas. *In Search of Lost Roses.* New York: Avon Books, 1989.

Clarke, Ethne. *Making a Rose Garden.* New York: Grove Weidenfeld, 1992.

Clausen, Ruth Rogers, and Nicolas H. Ekstrom. *Perennials for American Gardens.* New York: Random House, 1989.

Coats, Alice M. *Garden Shrubs and Their Histories.* New York: Simon and Schuster, 1992.

Cresson, Charles. *Charles Cresson on the American Flower Garden* (Burpee Expert Gardener series). New York: Prentice Hall Gardening, 1993.

Dirr, Michael A. *Manual of Woody Landscape Plants* (4th ed.). Champaign, Ill.: Stipes Publishing, 1990.

Druitt, Liz, and G. Michael Shoup. *Landscaping with Antique Roses.* Newtown, Conn.: Taunton Press, 1992.

Enjoying Roses. San Ramon, Calif.: Ortho Books, 1992.

Fearnley-Whittingstall, Jane. *Rose Gardens: Their History and Design.* New York: Henry Holt, 1989.

Foster, Steven, and James A. Duke. *A Field Guide to Medicinal Plants: Eastern and Central North America* (Peterson Field Guide series). Boston: Houghton Mifflin, 1990.

Greenlee, John. *The Encyclopedia of Ornamental Grasses.* Emmaus, Pa.: Rodale Press, 1992.

Hansen, Michael, and the Editors of Consumer Reports Books. *Pest Control for Home and Garden.* Yonkers, N.Y.: Consumer Reports Books, 1993.

Hessayon, D. G. *The Rose Expert.* London: Transworld Publishers, 1993.

Hobhouse, Penelope: *Flower Gardens.* Boston: Little, Brown, 1991. *Plants in Garden History.* London: Pavilion, 1992.

Horst, R. Kenneth (Comp.). *Compendium of Rose Diseases.* St. Paul: American Phytopathological Society, 1986.

Jekyll, Gertrude, and Edward Mawley. *Roses.* Salem, N.H.: Ayer, 1983.

Johnson, Warren T., and Howard H. Lyon. *Insects That Feed on Trees and Shrubs* (2d ed., rev.). Ithaca, N.Y.: Cornell University Press, 1991.

Lawson, Andrew. *Performance Plants.* New York: Penguin Books, 1992.

Le Rougetel, Hazel. *A Hermitage of Roses.* Owings Mills, Md.: Stemmer House, 1988.

Liberty Hyde Bailey Hortorium. *Hortus Third.* New York: Macmillan, 1976.

Miller, Amy Bess. *Shaker Herbs.* New York: Clarkson N. Potter, 1976.

Ogden, Scott. *Gardening Success with Difficult Soils.* Dallas: Taylor Publishing, 1992.

Osborne, Robert. *Hardy Roses* (Garden Way Publishing). Pownal, Vt.: Storey Communications, 1991.

Oster, Maggie. *The Rose Book.* Emmaus, Pa.: Rodale Press, 1994.

Phillips, Roger, and Martyn Rix. *The Quest for the Rose.* New York: Random House, 1993.

Pirone, Pascal P. *Diseases and Pests of Ornamental Plants* (5th ed.). New York: John Wiley, 1978.

Reddell, Rayford Clayton. *The Rose Bible.* New York: Harmony Books, 1994.

Sammis, Kathy. *Rose Gardening* (American Garden Guides). New York: Pantheon Books, 1995.

Scanniello, Stephen, and Tania Bayard: *Climbing Roses.* New York: Prentice Hall, 1994. *Roses of America: The Brooklyn Botanic Garden's Guide to Our National Flower.* New York: Henry Holt, 1990.

Sinclair, Wayne A., Howard H. Lyon, and Warren T. Johnson. *Diseases of Trees and Shrubs.* Ithaca, N.Y.: Cornell University Press, 1987.

Springer, Lauren. *The Undaunted Garden: Planting for Weather-Resilient Beauty.* Golden, Colo.: Fulcrum Publishing, 1994.

Strong, Roy. *Creating Formal Gardens.* Boston: Little, Brown, 1989.

Successful Rose Gardening (Better Homes and Gardens). Des Moines: Meredith® Books, 1993.

Swanson, Faith H., and Virginia B. Rady. *Herb Garden Design.* Hanover, N.H.: University Press of New England, 1984.

Taylor, Jane. *Climbing Plants* (Kew Gardening Guides). Portland, Ore.: Timber Press, 1987.

Taylor's Guide to Roses. Boston: Houghton Mifflin, 1961.

Thomas, Graham Stuart: *The Art of Gardening with Roses.* New York: Henry Holt, 1991. *The Graham Stuart Thomas Rose Book* (rev.). Portland, Ore.: Timber Press, 1994.

Walheim, Lance. *The Natural Rose Gardener.* Tucson, Ariz.: Ironwood Press, 1994.

Wasowski, Sally, with Andy Wasowski. *Gardening with Native Plants of the South.* Dallas: Taylor Publishing, 1994.

Welch, William C. *Antique Roses for the South.* Dallas: Taylor Publishing, 1990.

PERIODICALS:

"Antique Roses: Try These Proven Winners." *Texas Gardener,* November/December 1994.

Dardick, Karen. "Shrub Rose Revolution." *National Gardening,* July/August 1995.

Dean, Molly. "Luscious Pink Roses." *Flower & Garden,* March 1993.

Fenyvesi, Charles. "America's Rose Duds: Going, Going, Gone?" *U.S. News & World Report,* January 9, 1995.

Fish, Gary. "Straight Facts on Pesticide Use." *Horticulture,* May 1995.

"The Hip Harvest." *Avant Gardener,* August 1995.

Reddell, Rayford Clayton. "Pruning Roses." *Horticulture,* March 1995.

Rogers, Marilyn. "Easy Roses for Busy Gardeners." *Garden Gate,* Vol. 1, no. 3, n.d.

"Roll out the Red Carpet." *Avant Gardener,* April 1995.

Welch, William C. "Choosing the Right Rose." *Neil Sperry's Gardens,* April 1994.

Yronwode, Catherine. "Growing Roses Organically." *Organic Flower Gardening,* Spring 1994.

OTHER SOURCES:

"American Standard for Nursery Stock." ANSI Z60.1-1990. Washington, D.C.: American Association of Nurserymen,

1990.
"Facts about Roses." Information sheet. New York: Armstrong's News Bureau, n.d.
"Flower Carpet Roses USA Info Sheet." Brooklyn, N.Y.: Ferguson Caras Public Relations,

1995.
"1995 Handbook for Selecting Roses." Shreveport, La.: American Rose Society, 1994.
"Pests of Landscape Trees and Shrubs." Publication no. 3359. Oakland: ANR Publica-

tions (University of California), 1994.
"Roses." Handbook no. 92. Brooklyn, N.Y.: Brooklyn Botanic Garden, 1990.
"Roses in Cosmetics and Medicine." Information sheet. New

York: Armstrong's News Bureau, n.d.
Scanniello, Stephen (Ed.). "Easy-Care Roses." Handbook no. 142. Brooklyn, N.Y.: Brooklyn Botanic Garden, 1995.

Index

TIME®
LIFE
BOOKS

Other Publications:
VOICES OF THE CIVIL WAR
THE NEW HOME REPAIR AND IMPROVEMENT
JOURNEY THROUGH THE MIND AND BODY
WEIGHT WATCHERS® SMART CHOICE RECIPE COLLECTION
TRUE CRIME
THE AMERICAN INDIANS
THE ART OF WOODWORKING
LOST CIVILIZATIONS
ECHOES OF GLORY
THE NEW FACE OF WAR
HOW THINGS WORK
WINGS OF WAR
CREATIVE EVERYDAY COOKING
COLLECTOR'S LIBRARY OF THE UNKNOWN
CLASSICS OF WORLD WAR II
TIME-LIFE LIBRARY OF CURIOUS AND UNUSUAL FACTS
AMERICAN COUNTRY
VOYAGE THROUGH THE UNIVERSE
THE THIRD REICH
MYSTERIES OF THE UNKNOWN
TIME FRAME
FIX IT YOURSELF
FITNESS, HEALTH & NUTRITION
SUCCESSFUL PARENTING
HEALTHY HOME COOKING
UNDERSTANDING COMPUTERS
LIBRARY OF NATIONS
THE ENCHANTED WORLD
THE KODAK LIBRARY OF CREATIVE PHOTOGRAPHY
GREAT MEALS IN MINUTES
THE CIVIL WAR
PLANET EARTH
COLLECTOR'S LIBRARY OF THE CIVIL WAR
THE EPIC OF FLIGHT
THE GOOD COOK
WORLD WAR II
THE OLD WEST

*For information on and a full description of any of the
Time-Life Books series listed above, please call
1-800-621-7026 or write:*
Reader Information
Time-Life Customer Service
P.O. Box C-32068
Richmond, Virginia 23261-2068